CW01072878

How t Choose a Pet

Clare Chandler

Acknowledgements

Photos
ZEFA, cover main image. Oxford Scientific Films/Max Gibbs, cover top left,
page 4 top left, page 6. FLPA/J Bastable, page 5 top right. Sally Anne
Thompson, page 4 middle right, page 11 bottom, page 15 bottom, page 19
top right. Thompson/Willbie Animal Photography, page 18 bottom left.
Willbie Animal Photography, page 19 bottom left. Telegraph Colour
Library/Carola Bayer, page 20 bottom. Planet Earth Pictures/Doug Perrine,
page 21 bottom. Photomax, goldfish equipment, page 22 bottom.
All other photographs, Trevor Clifford.

Illustrations
All illustrations by Oxford illustrators

**We recommend that you consult a specific book on each animal before
choosing or buying any pet.**

Heinemann Educational Publishers
Halley Court, Jordan Hill, Oxford OX2 8EJ
a division of Reed Educational & Professional Publishing Ltd

OXFORD   MELBOURNE   AUCKLAND
JOHANNESBURG   BLANTYRE   GABORONE
IBADAN   PORTSMOUTH (NH) USA   CHICAGO

© Reed Educational & Professional Publishing Ltd 1997

First published 1997

02 01 00 99 98

10 9 8 7 6 5 4

British Library Cataloguing in Publication Data
A catalogue record for this book is available from the British Library.

ISBN 0 435 09520 X   *How to Choose a Pet* individual copy pack:
                                    6 copies of 1 title

ISBN 0 435 09415 7   Stage E pack: 1 each of 7 titles

All rights reserved. No part of this publication may be reproduced or
transmitted in any form by any means, electronic or mechanical, including
photocopy, recording or any information storage and retrieval system
without permission in writing from the publishers.

Colour reproduction by Reacta Graphics.

Printed and bound in Great Britain by Scotprint.

Contents

Choosing your pet

It is very exciting to get a pet. It is a new
friend to play with and it will need looking
after.

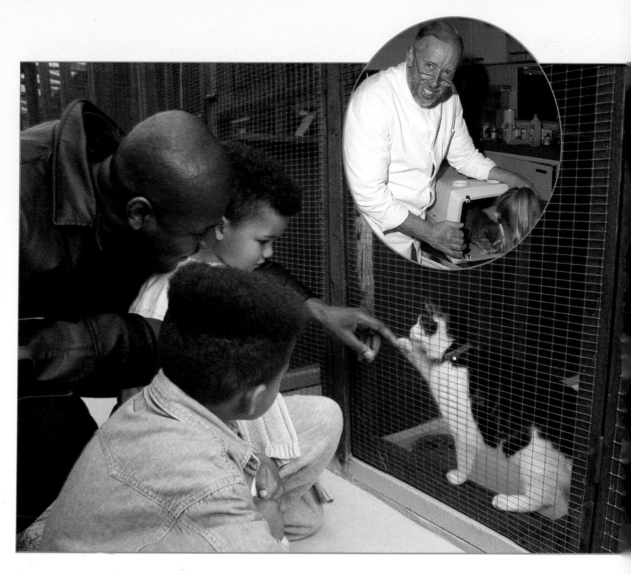

A vet may know of an animal that needs a home.
You can also get a pet from an animal shelter.
You can buy a pet from a pet shop or from private
owners or breeders.

This book gives you information about six
different animals. It will help you to decide
which pet you could best look after.

Goldfish

A goldfish is easy to look after.

Home

A goldfish needs

- to live in a tank with clean, fresh water
- places to hide, like rocks and plants
- to live with other goldfish

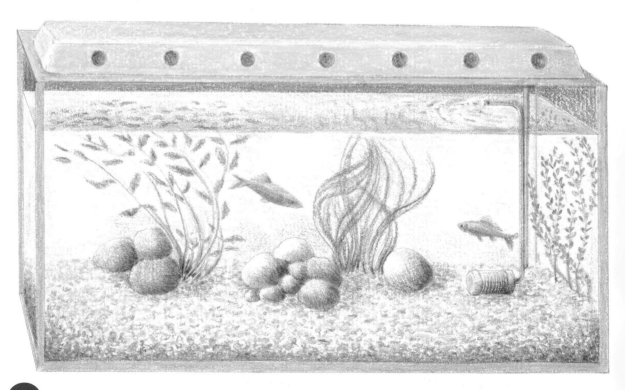

Food

A goldfish needs

- fish flakes, every day

- frozen worms or water fleas, once a week

Care

Remember to

- change some of the water in the tank once every two weeks

- use a net, not your hands, to take out your goldfish

Hamster

A hamster is fun to watch while it plays.

Home

A hamster needs

- to live alone in a large cage
- hay for bedding
- places to exercise, like ladders and wheels

Food

Every day, a hamster needs

- fresh fruit and vegetables
- a mixture of seeds, grains and nuts
- clean, fresh water

Care

Remember to

- clean out the cage once a week
- be careful when you pick up your hamster or it may bite you

Guinea pig

A guinea pig is furry and friendly.

Home

A guinea pig needs

- a hutch that can be put inside when it is cold
- to live with other guinea pigs or rabbits
- to play in a safe, grassy place every day

Food

Every day, a guinea pig needs

- a mixture of grains, fresh fruit and vegetables
- hay and leaves
- clean, fresh water

Care

Remember to

- clean out the hutch one or two times a week
- let your guinea pig have lots of exercise
- handle your guinea pig gently

Rabbit

Rabbits come in all shapes and sizes.

Home

A rabbit needs

 a large, warm hutch

to live with other rabbits or guinea pigs

to play in a safe, grassy place every day

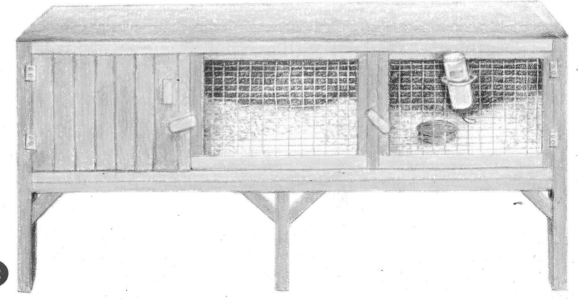

Food

Every day, a rabbit needs

- a mixture of oats, wheat and rabbit pellets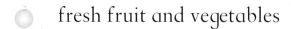

- fresh fruit and vegetables

- hay

- clean, fresh water

Care

Remember to

- clean out the hutch two or three times a week

- brush your rabbit if it has long hair

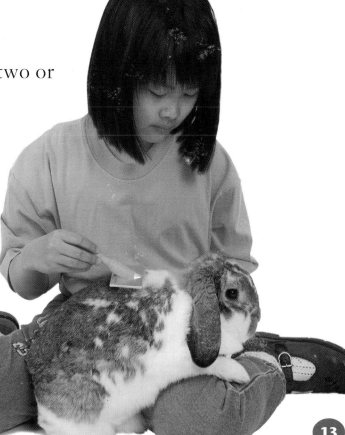

Cat

A cat likes to play and also likes time to itself.

Home

A cat needs

- a warm, cosy place to sleep

- somewhere to sharpen its claws

- lots of space to run around

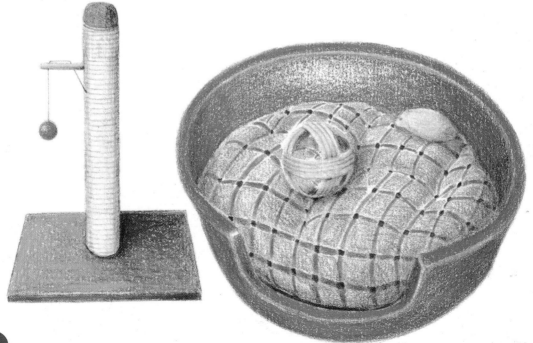

Food

Every day, a cat needs

- tinned and dry cat food
- clean, fresh water

Care

Remember to

- toilet train your cat
- take your cat to the vet for regular injections

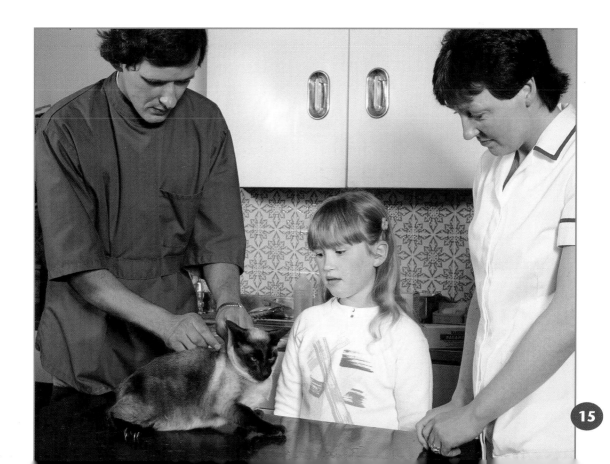

Dog

A dog can be a very good friend.

Home

A dog needs

- a warm bed with a blanket
- not to be left on its own for too long
- lots of space to run around
- toys and things to chew

Food

Every day, a dog needs

- tinned and dry dog food

- clean, fresh water

Care

Remember to

- walk your dog every day for exercise

- clean up after your dog

- take your dog to the vet for regular injections

- train your dog to be well-behaved

What care will your pet need?

Before you choose a pet, think about how much care it will need. These are some questions you should think about.

Will your pet need a garden for exercise?

✔	✘

Will its home sometimes need to be outdoors?

Will you need to clean out its home often?

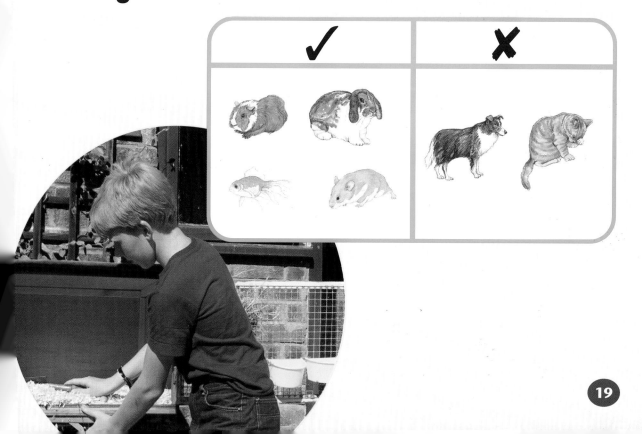

Will you need to groom your pet?

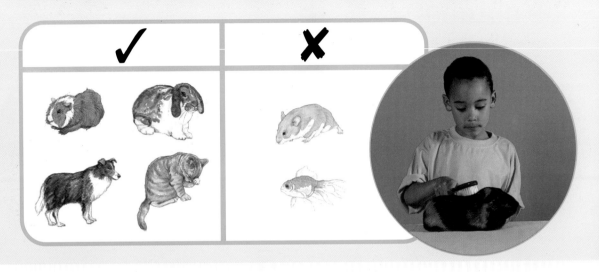

Will you need to play with your pet often?

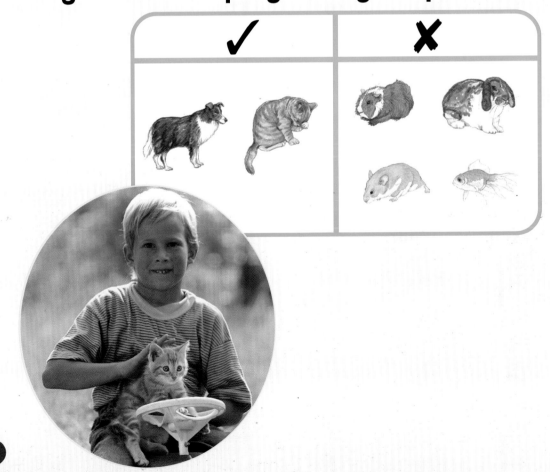

All pets need care and love. Some pets need more attention than others. Some are more expensive to keep. Which pet could you look after well?

If you cannot have a pet in your home, you could

- adopt an animal in a zoo

- help a wild animal in danger by sponsoring a seal, a gorilla or even a whale!

Getting ready for your pet

When you have chosen your pet, try to have things ready for it when it arrives.

Buy or borrow a book about your pet. Find out the address of a vet near you. Your pet may need injections.

Make a list of all the things your pet will need. Make sure you have everything ready.

Amazing pet facts

A pet rabbit can have as many as 72 babies in one year!

A goldfish, called Fred, lived until he was 41 years old!

The smallest cat ever, called Tinker Toy, was less than 7cm tall!

Index

Shimmering Waves

&

Dancing Shadows

Iris Clyde

INCA PUBLICATIONS

© Iris Clyde 2008
Shimmering Waves and Dancing Shadows

ISBN 978-0-9558681-0-8

Published by Inca Publications
Voresheed
Berstane Road
Kirkwall, Orkney
KW15 1SZ

The right of Iris Clyde to be identified as the author of this work has been asserted by her in accordance with the Copyright, Designs and Patents Act 1988.

All rights reserved. No part of this publication may be produced in any form or by any means – graphic, electronic or mechanical including photocopying, recording, taping or information storage and retrieval systems – without the prior permission, in writing, of the publisher.

A CIP catalogue record of this book can be obtained from the British Library.

Book designed by Michael Walsh at
THE BETTER BOOK COMPANY

A division of
RPM Print & Design
2-3 Spur Road
Chichester
West Sussex
PO19 8PR

Cover photo by Martin Findlay

CONTENTS

Dedicated to my late husband, Hugh,
still my guide and inspiration

PART I

(May 1993)

1

When Thorfinn saw the trout lying beside the path, silvery cold and firmly fleshed, in prime condition for a tasty supper, there was hardly a falter in his step, he scooped it up and started climbing the hill, pleased with his good fortune. Now the presence of a trout lying in the heather some twenty feet from the loch might cause most people to ponder, but Thorfinn could convince himself, without much effort, that some fishy difference of opinion had caused the trout to leap the distance from loch to path, a gift to any passer-by with a sharp eye and a handy pocket. No doubt the two large glasses of sherry that were warming his blood had played a part in stimulating his imagination.

He had visited the hotel kitchen on his way past Trowsay House to chat with Hanna as she prepared dinner and knock back the cooking sherry on offer. Fortunately his palate was no longer crystallised by the cloying stuff on offer when he first started calling in to see her after his daily beachcombing and hike across the moors. The sherry kept in the kitchen now was lightly golden and deliciously mellow. He would have liked to think that this addition to the store cupboard held some significance but Hanna seemed devoted to her high and mighty husband. Nevertheless, as he continued his climb, he thought optimistically of the day when she might offer him cooking Highland malt.

At the top of the gently undulating hill, he stopped to look back. There was no one about down at the hotel; no one creating a stir and disturbing the peace. The loch was shadowed, the fishing boats drawn up on the shingle at its edge empty and abandoned. He could see for miles, over heath and field, right to the fine veil of mist in the distance where the land merged with the sea. There were few trees because winds coiled over the salty surface of the ocean and whipped the land with destructive force; the trees that survived the salt and the storms had a stunted weary tilt from root to branch. To him, there was an invigorating beauty in the rugged terrain and the sheer doggedness of a land that endured and flourished against the odds. When the clouds were low and louring, the colours were sombre, but when the sun shone the island smiled, the merging greens, browns and greys creasing with light and shadow. He breathed deeply, exhaling with contentment as he turned into the narrow cutting that wound down to the cliff edge between clumps of tough overhanging heather, not yet in flower.

The path he had left followed the contours of the hill for another hundred yards or so before skirting the bay past the Selkie Bay farmhouse which stood high on the headland opposite. Thorfinn wondered how Alec of Selkie was faring. From all accounts he was in a bad way, slowly succumbing to the cancer that was devouring his body. He had got on well enough with the man when their paths crossed, although he had been amused and somewhat wary to find that Alec saw him as a drug-taking voyeur. On one occasion he had asked him if he had any of "those girlie magazines you get from the top shelf", and on another if he had a joint handy. Poor man, he would be chock full of drugs by now, Thorfinn thought, as he negotiated the climb down to his cottage, one half of a long, low, stone-roofed house, built snugly into the side of the hill facing the Atlantic Ocean.

The McFeas lived next door and on his way along the flagged path which ran the length of the building, he could see Mrs McFea sitting at her back window. She was partly hidden by the net curtain but the movement of her hands, rhythmically working her knitting, advertised her curiosity.

Thorfinn's step faltered. Her presence reminded him that it wasn't going to be easy to cook his fish without arousing suspicion. The smell of poaching trout was one with which Mrs McFea was familiar and he had an inkling that her knowledge of the habits of fish was more humdrum than his.

"Hi there, Mrs McFea," he called with a neighbourly wave, intending to keep her sweet, but she drew farther back behind her curtains.

Thorfinn's habit of looking through her window annoyed Flo McFea. "A proper gentleman would have more consideration for other people's privacy and feelings," she said to herself, closing her needles together and folding her knitting over. She stuck her work in the bag hanging on the arm of her chair. "And as for his laziness and slovenly ways …!" Her chins wobbled at the thought.

She knew Thorfinn better than most (as she would say to anyone who saw a redeeming feature and voiced a liking) for the old man had hired him to give her a hand at Trowsay House in his student holidays. She needed the extra help, with the housekeeping as well as the cooking to do by then, but Thorfinn had been a thorn in her flesh most of the time. In fact he had added to her burden rather than reducing it. She could always find him sitting in an armchair in the drawing room, talking and playing chess with the old man, instead of getting on with the work he was there to do. And time hadn't improved him. Hardly a day passed when there wasn't something to tell Callum when he came home from his work.

She could hear the soup gently simmering on the stove. It needed a stir and perhaps a grain more water to keep it right. She levered herself up and found her stick. The table was set and everything was ready for Callum's return. She looked at the mantel clock but there were still a few seconds to go before the minute hand would move forward and he could be considered late. She refolded a cloth and straightened a newspaper, listening keenly for any activity next door that she could interpret. Her days were long with only the radio for company (TV reception was poor to non-existent) and the human presence of Thorfinn on the other side of the wall was tantalisingly close. Finally she decided that another piece of peat was just what the fire needed to keep it bright and welcome Callum home.

On her outward journey to the peat stack, she could see that Thorfinn was up to something because he had closed his curtains; they had been carelessly pulled together, leaving a gap at the top, but there was no need to shut out the light at that time of day.

She collected a piece of peat and was returning with it clasped in her gloved hand, when she was brought up short. His curtains were now tightly shut, the material held taut against the closed window. There was still a streak of light across the flagstones from the jamb of his door but this pencil-thin streak started to disappear, inch by inch, as she watched. Thorfinn was taping up his door when there was no swirl of wind to find a crack. She stood transfixed, trying to work out what was going on, but her imagination could not fathom the depths of a depravity that would require such action. When he pushed something against the bottom of his door so that his cottage was totally blacked out, she felt justified in feeling annoyed. After all these were respectable parts.

The annoyance stayed with her until she had dropped the piece of peat into the scuttle beside the fire and sat down in her rocking chair, then the cold horror of the reason for his behaviour struck her with the force of a blow. She rocked back in her chair, her heart thumping. It was shocking to even think of such a thing, but there could be no other explanation. He would not be taping up his door and making his window fast on a still spring evening unless he was going to put his head in the gas oven.

She tried to get up but she couldn't move her legs. Whimpering in panic and frustration she took the only course open to her. She began to rail against the absent Callum. Where was he. He was never about when he was needed. He knew her health couldn't stand such shocks. She worked herself up into a frenzy of agitation and needed one of her white pills to calm herself down. Gradually she felt better and the strength returned to her legs, but the period of inactivity had not changed the direction of her thoughts. She was still convinced that Thorfinn's life was slowly ebbing away in the cottage next door and only she could stop him before it was too late. The drama of the situation and the personal responsibility involved had their effect; they made her change (as far as was medically possible) into the woman she had been, a woman of decision and authority, a cook who knew how to respond to a crisis. She eased herself up and went looking for her shoes. Crisis or no crisis, she was not going to cross Thorfinn's doorstep in her slippers.

When she had dressed herself to her satisfaction, she gave the soup a last stir and poured half of it into the jug warming on the side.

Thorfinn sat by his hearth in his comfortable armchair, a book on his lap and a whisky in his hand. There was no sound in the room except for the gentle gurgle of the water in the pan as it heated and cooked the trout. He felt relaxed and content. He had faxed off his contribution to *I Browse* that morning, and he could see from the alignment of the planets in his star sign, that there were happy times ahead. He always took a look at his own star sign when he was working. The horoscopes he mapped out on his astrological wheel for *I Browse* were less exact. It was a satirical magazine and the editor wanted fantastical predictions that would amuse rather than enlighten her readers. She seemed to be satisfied with his efforts. At least she was still boosting his bank account with a modest sum each month and she sent him an occasional reader's letter to inspire his imagination.

He thought of the most recent communication. It had read: "Dear Skylarker, I am a Pisces and you were spot on with your last prediction for me. Could we be in telepathic communication?" The signature was an illegible scrawl.

Thorfinn chuckled to himself. He had predicted for Pisces the previous month that they would return from an exhilarating weekend with Caressie and Sukey, lead performers in The Shuddering Gaspers, to find that a noted philanthropist had left them his fleet of hot air balloons with no strings attached. He wondered if his correspondent was a madman or a fellow humorist. He was curious but had resisted the urge to respond.

He lifted his glass to his lips but stopped in mid-swig. He could hear the tap of Mrs McFea's stick and the shuffle of her feet against the flagstones outside his door and his throat closed against the soothing liquid. He could feel her listening but that was not unusual and he waited for her to go away. Instead she knocked. The unexpected sound startled him and he choked on the unswallowed whisky, the remainder shooting from his glass, soaking his trousers, and splashing on the floor. At that very moment, the water in the pan boiled over, extinguishing the flame of gas.

Mrs McFea took her ear from the door.

"Are you there, Thorfinn?" she called. "I've got a nice jug of soup here for your tea."

Thorfinn got up and rescued the pan, quickly putting it in the cupboard under the sink before turning off the gas.

"It's my thick vegetable and it was always your favourite as a lad," Mrs McFea cajoled to tempt him. "I minded on that when I was making it for Callum."

The gentle, coaxing voice and concern for his welfare were quite out of character, obviously a ruse to get inside his kitchen and catch him out. Thorfinn reached for a towel to dab his streaming eyes and wipe the sizzling water on the strove.

Mrs McFea waited but when there was no response, she changed her tactics.

"Thorfinn," she enunciated loudly and precisely, "open this door at once." The command was accompanied by a rattling of the latch.

Thorfinn wiped himself down with the towel he was holding and settled his expression into a look of astonishment and innocence before removing the knife that was slotted along the latch. It clicked up and he was knocked sideways as Mrs McFea thrust her stick and foot forward, heaving the door ajar with her substantial buttocks. She moved heavily forward and put the jug on the table, sniffing the air and shaking her head in incredulous satisfaction.

"How could you think of doing such a thing?" she asked, turning to look at Thorfinn with reproach.

He met her look without flinching. Her abrupt entrance was quite intolerable.

"What an unexpected pleasure," he drawled.

Mrs McFea ignored his sardonic tone. "It's a good job for you that I'm not one to put my own welfare first," she told him, lowering herself onto a kitchen chair.

Thorfinn moved to close the door with an air of resignation.

"Leave that door be. The smell in here is something awful and a piece of fresh air will do you no harm."

She looked about her and Thorfinn was acutely aware of the dirty dishes in the sink and the general untidiness. He was even sure that she could see his unmade bed in the other room. But he was wrong in thinking that Mrs McFea was viewing the squalor with disgust. She was seeing it all as a symbol of despair, especially the empty pad of lined paper lying on the dresser. She knew that he professed to be a writer but she also knew that he was not successful. There was no book with his name on it in the library van that visited Trowsay once a week and the librarian had never heard of him.

"Get yourself a plate, Thorfinn, and have my soup," she said more kindly. "There's nothing like a good, hot plate of soup for settling the stomach."

Thorfinn smiled. "I am sure this delicious and fulsome nourishment will do more for my stomach than that," he flattered, extracting a plate and spoon from the pile of dishes and running them under the tap.

Mrs McFea watched him closely from behind her thick lenses.

"Are you not happy then, Thorfinn?" she asked.

Thorfinn assured her that he was and she had to admit to herself that he looked and acted much the same as usual. In fact if it had not been for the evidence of her own eyes and her own nose, she might have thought that she had been mistaken.

"You can't fool me you know, Thorfinn. I've known you too long."

"And not always to my advantage, I fear. But bygones should always be bygones is what I say. Let me pour you a glass of whisky and we can drink to our future cordiality."

"Indeed you will do no such thing!" Mrs McFea puffed up her chest, ready for battle. "That there," she pointed at the half-empty bottle on the fireside table, "is half your trouble. You never saw the old man always at the whisky bottle. When I think of him now, as fine a gentleman as ever walked this island …" and she was off down a familiar path of memory.

Thorfinn drank his soup and let her talk. As he saw it, death and time had affected her memory. The old man had enjoyed his drink as much as Thorfinn did. He had been a whiskery, charming sort of fellow, well-informed and a dab hand at chess, but he was also a demanding autocrat whose prime interest in life was his own comfort. But Mrs McFea did not choose to remember him that way. It could be that she needed a clean and shiny yardstick against which to measure his faults.

He finished his soup and settled back in his chair.

"Did you enjoy that then?" she asked, breaking off her fond reminiscences.

"I did indeed. No one can rival your culinary skills, Mrs McFea. You're still the best cook on Trowsay."

Thorfinn patted his stomach, thinking that he had given her the reply that would please her most. But Mrs McFea could spot flannel even when it was hidden under a silky tone. She straightened her back and folded her hands in front of her, to support her indignation, and told him so.

He assured her that her homemade soups were second to none but she was not ready to be mollified when there was an opportunity to tick off his faults and add up the score. As he was only half-listening it was he, not she, who heard the familiar step on the flagstones at the end of the close.

"Callum's back," he interrupted.

Mrs McFea stopped her railing and cocked an ear.

"It's him all right," she flustered, looking round for her stick and making to rise. "He'll be wanting his tea and it not on the table."

Thorfinn murmured agreement, with an inward sigh of relief, and moved towards the door to usher her out; but his relief was short-lived. Mrs McFea had sat down again.

"Now you'll promise me, Thorfinn," she said gravely, taking off her spectacles and fixing him with her large, heavy, brown eyes, "that you won't be doing the like of that again. It's a mortal sin as you well know."

Thorfinn was amazed at the drama of the words. Being a finder and a keeper might be a sin but hardly a mortal sin. Fortunately he was spared the need to reply by the appearance of Callum at the open door.

"Hi, there, Callum," he greeted, fetching a glass from the dresser. "Come in and join us." He poured a couple of drams and held the bottle over the glass, offering more. Callum laid his cap on the table and took an extra nip.

"You're right late home the night," his wife accused. "And if you knew the goings-on here …" Thorfinn recoiled. "… but we'll say no more about that. Thorfinn has given me his word that he won't do it again."

Callum was relieved to see the relative tranquillity between his wife and his neighbour and did not question her meaning. He was a peaceable countryman, not given to stirring a calm but stagnant pool.

"Aye, I'm late," he agreed, toasting Thorfinn's health and knocking back his whisky. "There was a bit of a to-do down at the house. Mr Bartholomew ... are you acquainted with the man, Thorfinn?"

"I am." Thorfinn chuckled. "Our eminent visitor always has a store of fishy tales to tell, the tales and the fish getting longer by the hour." He refilled Callum's glass as he was speaking. Two generous whiskies could make Callum mellower and thus more amenable to accepting Thorfinn's belief in fishy athleticism.

"Aye, well, he dropped his trout on the way up from the loch. It was only the third he'd caught this week and the biggest, if he's to be believed on that score. Two pounds he was saying."

Thorfinn's amusement at this exaggeration was tempered by the fact that he thought he'd been caught in possession. Nevertheless he was quick to see an advantage in the fact that his bar acquaintance had got more poundage in the telling than he would have got in the eating. It could be, he mused to himself, that the purloining of his fish was a service rendered. He was thinking about that as a defence when Mrs McFea asked if the trout had been found.

"It hasna. I was over the ground twice looking and there wasna a sign of it."

"And he wouldn't be grateful for the trouble you took, I'll be bound. You shouldn't allow yourself to be put upon like that, Callum."

Callum sipped his whisky and let his wife have her say.

"I can see no mystery anyway," she went on. "It's quite clear to me why there was no trout lying about."

Thorfinn rose to state his case. "Now, Mrs McFea, you may have suspicions, but you've no evidence." He was hoping that she wouldn't have the gall to go over and open his sink cupboard door.

"Evidence? You've just given me the evidence yourself," Mrs McFea told him smartly. "Besides which I have a nose for these things." Thorfinn was silent. He had to admit that there was a faint smell of cooking trout. "In my opinion, a man who lies about the size of his trout will lie about catching one."

Callum raised his eyebrows. "What are you saying, Flo?"

"I'm saying that he was ashamed to come home with an empty basket."

Thorfinn was taken aback. Was it possible that she didn't suspect that he had the missing trout. But if she didn't suspect that, why had she come calling.

"He caught a trout all right," Callum said with certainty. "The man was fairly vexed at the outset. No, no, I was glad to help him, although I couldna see an answer to it then." But Callum had battled with the problem on his way home over the hill. "It would've been one of they bonxies that got it and I'll be telling the boss that the morn's morn. Right menaces they are and useless birds forby."

Gentle Callum's whole demeanour changed when he thought of the great skuas and their malicious taste for young grouse and hare. He saw them as vermin but they were a protected species and he could not shoot them as he did the other vermin … at least not when anyone was looking. In different circumstances, Thorfinn would have indulged in mild argument with his neighbour, the swooping and calling of the huge birds in graceful flight giving him intense pleasure. He longed to say: "they kill to eat not to compete" but he thought it wise to leave well alone.

"That's as may be, Callum," Mrs McFea was saying, leaning on her stick and rising from her chair, "but it was providential that the fish got taken this night and you were kept beyond your time. I'm sure Thorfinn will agree with me on that score now that his reason has returned."

And with these words, mysterious in their obscurity to both men, she took her husband's arm and made her way back to their end of the building.

Thorfinn rescued the pan from under the sink (where the trout had been poaching nicely in the hot water) and sat down to enjoy his meal. He laughed out loud as he eased the flesh from the bone. Mrs McFea was right. It was indeed providential that the fish had got taken that night.

But the night was still young.

He had been up on the cliff path in the late afternoon when the hotel's Range Rover had splashed across the causeway on its way back from the airport. One of the passengers had waved. He was too far away to judge if it were a child, just waving in happiness to any stray passer-by, or a girl from his past.

With his planets favourably aligned, he felt optimistic.

2

Hanna Treatham sat up in bed and listened, feeling uneasy. A gale had been raging for most of the night, wailing and screeching in ferocious gusts and raising the waves on the shore below to a rolling crashing height. In the quietness after the storm, all she could hear were the shrill cries of cruising gulls and the intermittent kee-kee of swooping terns. She wondered if there was something down in the bay that was making them agitated. A storm always took its toll, depositing on the beach beside Trowsay House all kinds of flotsam and jetsam, including old oil drums, plastic containers and other unwelcome rubbish thrown from boats at sea. The faint chimes of the stable clock striking four was a reassuring nightly sound and she lay down, curling into Rupert's back and settling her arm along his length; it was probably just the lack of rattle in the turret windows or a sharp unconscious thought that had disturbed her sleep.

Rupert groaned and stretched out, turning towards her. She resettled herself and relaxed, sleeping deeply until the hiss of boiling water steaming into the Teasmade dragged her up from the depths of a forgettable dream. She sat up and poured the tea into a prepared cup, drinking it slowly as she organised her thoughts for the day ahead. Rupert turned over and she looked down at him, ready to talk. She gently stroked the silver wings of his silky-black hair, but he flipped her hand away and she returned to her solitary contemplation.

The sun shone brightly now, making irregular patterns on the rounded walls and highlighting a stream of dust motes in its beam. She slid out of bed and sat down at her dressing table, loosening her thick hair from its nightly plait and separating the strands with a quick shake of her head. She brushed slowly down its length, watching it ripple like flowing honey.

There were four long windows in the rounded part of the room where she sat, the part that was within the turret. In one direction, the view was out to sea and round the bay to The Mains. Today all was sunshine and light but on a wild day, when the wind was in the east, the waves would rush into the cove below, hit the low cliffs, and send spray rising in irregular gushing spires, to fall gently down on the road and ease away. She spotted Gemma Martin driving the cattle home for milking, flapping a tea towel and running frantically from side to side of the wayward kye. They took little notice, trundling along at their usual pace and in their own way, their swollen udders swinging in rhythm with their steps. It was usually Tavish Martin who brought in the milkers, whacking reluctant rumps and bellowing curses in relaxed command. She wondered idly where he was.

In the other direction, she could see the road running north to the village. It was fringed by the hotel's rough grazing ground and a scattering of ewes and lambs bent to the ground in feed. She got up, still brushing her hair, and went to the farthest window where she had a clear view of the loch, the familiar octagonal church at its edge, and the shadowy hill that rose and fell in sharply marked contours to the sky line. She could just make out where the path started at the edge of the loch and she followed its meandering way upwards, remembering every curve and surface, even when it was out of sight from where she stood. On most days she was climbing the hill at this time, feeling and smelling the quiet freshness of early morning. In her mind's eye, she could see Slavers bounding ahead, only his feathered tail visible as he pushed his way through the wiry dormant heather, sniffing in moving ecstasy. He would wait at the top for her to catch up, lying on the path with his tail straight out behind and his pink tongue lolling. And at the top, she could look down at the long, low building below and the darkened end room where Thorfinn slept.

She stopped brushing, feeling the magnetic warmth of Thorfinn's presence.

"What time is it?" Rupert asked from within the bedclothes.

His voice startled her and brought her thoughts back to reality.

"Quarter past seven," she guessed, going back to her dressing table and putting her hairbrush down.

He turned over and sat up, smoothing down his hair. His moustache had been trimmed neatly to follow the curve of his upper lip and he combed it upward with his fingernails.

"Happy Birthday," she said, reaching over and giving him a hug.

His immediate response was: "Don't remind me."

She had bought him a Georgian quaich and had it wrapped ready in the cupboard at her side of the bed but she would give him it later. He was always huffy first thing.

"It's a lovely day," she went on brightly. "The storm has cleared the air."

"So I see." He leaned on one elbow and reached for his heavy gold watch. "Aren't you doing your lady bountiful stuff this morning?" he asked, sliding the watch on to his wrist.

"I wanted to be with you on your birthday, Rupert," Hanna said evenly, ignoring his taunt. She poured his tea just how he liked it, with a dash of milk and two spoonfuls of sugar, and carried the cup round. "I told Alec yesterday that I wouldn't be over early."

He took the proffered cup and smiled in contrition. "Sorry to be such a bear, dearest." She kissed his raised lips and forgave him. "How is old Alec anyway?" he asked, stirring the sugar round and round until it dissolved.

"Ursula wants him to go into hospital."

"She is quite right. He needs proper care."

"But he doesn't know anyone over in Wick and fears dying alone."

"It's not that far away."

"But the tides could be awkward when the final call came."

Rupert gave a contemptuous snort. "The wretched tides are the bane of all our lives. I can't think why they don't build a bridge across to the mainland."

"It wouldn't be the same," Hanna said, tidying the top of her dressing table. She looked at him through the mirror. "Having a tidal causeway gives Trowsay the romance of an island without the inconvenience. The guests can still drive on and off for much of the time."

"Tell that to those who have to put their gastric juices on hold because they're caught on the other side."

"They've no excuse. The tide tables are prominently displayed in every room." She walked towards the spiral staircase which led to the bathroom below. "You're remembering your appointment this morning?"

"Wait a minute, Hanna. Don't rush off. I wanted to speak to you about that." He drank the last of his tea and set the cup down on its saucer. "We don't need to wait for the final accounts to know that we're in queer street."

"Don't exaggerate, Rupert. We're doing all right."

He reached round and made room for his cup and saucer on his bedside table.

"I think we should put more effort into selling the place."

"Little & Little have got it on their books."

"But we asked them to be discreet. If we want to get things moving we should start advertising. It's better to do that now rather than wait for the winter."

"Would you really want to go back down south, Rupe, and start all over again? We've put down our roots here now."

"You have."

"Yes, I have. But you could too if you put your mind to it. You mustn't be so superior. It doesn't go down well."

He shrugged. "I haven't got anything in common with the people round here."

"You don't try. If you did, you'd be surprised."

"There's little that would surprise me now. What I hear in the bar most evenings drives me to screaming boredom."

"Where would you want to go?"

"Anywhere but here."

Hanna turned away in exasperation saying: "You're being unreasonable," and started to wend her way down the spiral stairs. It was a dead end conversation. She knew that he was exaggerating his dislike of Trowsay, although hands-on hotel work suited her more than him. He preferred to address his mind rather than his muscle to hotel management and was bored now that everything was running smoothly.

She turned on the taps for her bath and listened to the water gurgling down from the high cistern followed by bursts of burping steam. The antiquated plumbing system had not been replaced in the tower and the hot water tap belched out as much steam as water. Ten minutes of trickle would give a reasonable measure but the walls would be running with condensation. While she waited for the bath to fill, she did a quick clean round, thinking about the happy days when Rupert could be daring and fun-loving. He didn't need to try to be more energetic and playful than the men of her age then, he just was. She hated to think that that had gone forever. She wiped round the basin and over the glass shelf above, replacing and stacking the miscellaneous array of bottles. Their reflection in the mirror reminded her of the champagne cascade that Rupert had set up on their first visit to her parents in Norway after they married. She had never seen that done before and it had delighted her nineteen-year-old self, but her parents had disapproved of such ostentation. Of course they would have disapproved of anything he did; it was inevitable.

The water in the bath had reached an acceptable level and she turned off the taps. The old-fashioned, claw-footed bath was stained with age, but it was deep, long and luxurious. She stepped in and lay back, relaxing into its warmth. "Rupert," she called, going deeper and letting the water touch her chin. "Bath ready."

Rupert was the last to bath but he was the first to be ready. He waited at the top of the spiral staircase for Hanna to make the bed and collect the cups. When she had finished fussing (as he put it), he took the tray from her and they followed the spiral down, treading carefully on the narrow uneven stone steps. The door at the bottom opened into their private sitting room, a shabby room, mostly furnished with pieces that were not good enough for the hotel. The chintz covers on the seats were of different patterns, the large oriental carpet threadbare, the red silk curtains faded, and the hard furniture antique because it was old rather than fine. In the past, this part of Trowsay House had been the nursery wing, far enough away to contain the noise of childish high jinks but not too remote. The benefit was reversed for the Treathams.

"It's stuffy in here," Hanna said as they came out of the stairwell. She moved quickly across the room to open a window, picking up newspapers and plumping up cushions.

"Come on, Hanna," Rupert called with asperity. He had gone straight to the door and was holding it open with one foot, the other already in the corridor. "You can do that later."

"If I don't do it now, it won't be done," she replied evenly, finishing her quick tidy round and collecting a full ashtray containing Rupert's stubbed-out cheroots. She put it on the tray that he was holding and followed him along the wide, deeply-carpeted corridor with its long windows and comfortable armchairs, past the drawing room (now the cocktail lounge), to the main hall. Rupert went straight to the kitchen to have breakfast but Hanna stopped in the hall to speak to two of their regular visitors. They were turning over the pages of country magazines in a desultory sort of way, waiting for the breakfast gong to sound.

"My goodness, that fire isn't giving off much heat," Hanna said, moving smartly towards the stone fireplace with its shining brass fire irons and deep peat basket.

She lifted the heavy poker and set to work.

"Mrs Treatham!" she heard Tim Pinkerton exclaim in distress. "Mrs Treatham, please!"

He had jumped up from the hall settle and his hand was looming, ready to grab the poker; Hanna did not relent until the carefully stacked peats had been separated to allow a flame to rise. She laid the poker back on its rest and brushed her hands free of ash.

"That's better," she said, looking up into Mr Pinkerton's long-boned face. His bushy eyebrows had risen to a peak of anxiety and his moustache was drooping over his pursed lips.

"But short-sighted, if I may say so."

He spoke severely, hovering close by, just waiting for her to leave so that he could build up the fire again. Hanna knew that it was a losing battle to attack the fire in Mr Pinkerton's presence. He saw the poking of a fire as a womanly foible, which the provider and more prudent male must endure and redress. He always kept the home fires smouldering during his stay.

She turned to speak to Arthur Bartholomew, a round and florid man who generated his own heat. He was a retired archdeacon, although the only evidence of his calling was the monkish fringe of iron-grey hair that circled his head and the creaking in his knees

"I was so sorry to hear about the loss of your trout," she said in a suitably regretful tone.

"I wanted to speak to you about that, Mrs Treatham," he said, closing his magazine and putting it neatly back on the refectory table. "When we were coming up from the loch yesterday evening, we passed that Thorfinn man. You know whom I mean?"

"Yes?" Hanna questioned warily.

"Could he have taken my trout d'you think? He was in the bar last night and he was evasive when I asked him if he had seen my fish. In fact he was amused when I spoke of my loss, putting forward outlandish theories in explanation."

"His humour is not to everyone's liking."

"But could he have stolen my trout?"

"Extremely unlikely," Hanna said smartly, her confident tone belying her inner thoughts. "In fact I can vouch for his honesty."

Mr Bartholomew still looked doubtful but responded gallantly: "Ah, dear Mrs Treatham, I am sure you would never think ill of anyone."

Hanna smiled in acceptance of the compliment, turning to greet two other guests who had arrived, fresh from an early morning walk. Mr Ayesh, the taller and more substantial of the two, was effusive in his re-

23

peated "Good mornings", proclaiming on the beauty of the day and the anticipatory delights ahead. He was always charming and Hanna found his warmth infectious. (The elderly fishermen had closed ranks when he appeared, murmuring responses to his greeting but barely lifting their eyes, unable to face such excessive friendliness.)

"Where did you walk this morning?" Hanna asked and Mr Ayesh was responding with enthusiastic half-sentences, augmented with explanatory gestures, when Betty Pinkerton trod lightly down the stairs trilling a morning greeting with a wide, red-lipped smile. She was dressed in sunny yellow trousers and matching shirt, the colourful scarf at her neck tied to show an expensive monogram. Mr Ayesh shook her outstretched hand and patted it benignly as she asked him about his plans for the day ahead, looking up at him with a coquettish tilt to her head, her faded blue eyes widely spiked with mascara. He indicated, with a bow, that they were in her hands (she had appointed herself their adviser on places to visit in the surrounding area) and she smiled happily, suggesting that they consult the map on the board. Mr Ayesh agreed and guided her in that direction.

The two men stayed silently in front of the fireplace watching them leave the hall.

"Hal is late," Hanna heard Mr Pinkerton saying as she rummaged in the drawers underneath the reception counter for some old menu cards to give her ideas for the evening meal.

"He went out last night," Arthur Bartholomew replied, rocking on his heels in front of the blazing fire

"No doubt he's making it up with the wife."

"Wives not coming today?"

"Not mine, anyway."

"That new boat has a good rudder. I'll get them to put an engine on it for us."

"I told you yesterday, Tim. Jack is coming with me."

Mr Pinkerton grunted. He was reputed to be the wealthier of the two but he seldom gave his wallet an airing. He never hired the ghillie.

"Perhaps Hal will come."

"I doubt it. He likes to be on his own."

"Beats me."

Hanna found an elastic band and stretched it round the menu cards she had selected thinking, with sympathy, of Hal Yearts' desire for solitude. An old buffer like Tim Pinkerton could not see past Lily Yearts' bright-eyed vivacity and fragile beauty but it was different for her husband. He was there when the drink took hold and her mood turned nasty.

"Ready, now, Mrs Treatham."

Jean Glover was standing beside the gong, the mallet in her hand

Hanna nodded agreement and was leaving the desk when she felt she was being watched. She looked up and found Mr Bartini waiting halfway up the stairs for the hall to clear. He met her gaze with startled eyes. She wished him a good morning and he bowed in agreement murmuring "delightful". Delightful was his favourite word. In the public rooms he would sit with an open newspaper on his lap, watching and listening, but he never voiced an opinion. It was assumed that he was a birdwatcher because he left the hotel each morning with binoculars and a long-lens camera over his shoulders, but he could not be drawn on the subject. He was a little man, inoffensive in appearance and dress. An ideal hotel guest, in fact.

Hanna couldn't understand why he made her feel uncomfortable.

In one of the large front bedrooms upstairs, Isabel Pritchard swung her legs out of bed and stood up, allowing her silk, lace-trimmed nightdress to fall discreetly to her ankles. She stretched her arms and rotated her shoulders to ease her neck muscles, before putting on her negligee and going through to the bathroom. The mirror was covered with a white bath sheet that fell lopsided from the light fitting above. She had hung it there the night before when the surface was still steamy from her bath. She always did that, not wanting to face herself in the morning until she looked respectable. She shuddered at the thought of facing strangers before she had had breakfast.

Her morning ritual completed, she got back into bed and lifted the telephone on to her lap. There was no reply from Marigold's room. Her niece was not an early riser so she could draw only one conclusion, a conclusion that never ceased to shock her. Marigold had just laughed and teased the last time she had reprimanded her for staying out all night, saying that Isabel was out of step with the modern world. Isabel's tart response to that was that the modern world was not on its feet long enough to march in step. However she was reluctantly accepting that she could not make Marigold toe the moral line. She doubted if Marigold's mother could have done better. She seldom thought of her sister-in-law (her late husband's twin) with the affection and gratitude that she had shown to her during her lifetime, remembering instead the irritation she had felt at Marion's acceptance of ill-health and dismissal of financial good fortune. Her lack of sense had also been hard to bear. Isabel could still see her now, lying on cushions in front of the fire, listening to Simon's latest escapade with incredulous eyes and bated breath. Egging him on, in fact. Her nostrils pinched at the thought. It had been Simon's addiction to feats of daring that had led to his early death and her dependence. But she was quick to remind herself that she was no parasite. She had her pride and earned her position in the Wentworth family as a role model for Marigold and a companion for Bertie, her housewifery skills bringing order and comfort to their lives.

At the thought of Bertie, she reached for the telephone again and pressed the digits for his London flat. He had been delayed in town on urgent business.

"Bertie?"

"Good morning, Isabel," was the sleepy response.

"Marigold is not in the hotel."

She could hear the sigh. He always sighed when she tried to get him to intervene in a dispute, but it was her duty to keep him informed.

"I presume that she went off with the young man she was making eyes at for most of the evening. Totally unsuitable, I need hardly add."

"She's a big girl, Isabel." Bertie was easy going and it was not in his nature to offend if it could be avoided.

"She's only seventeen," Isabel retorted. "Really,

Bertie, what chance has she of making a good marriage if this sort of escapade becomes known. When I think of her mother and me at that age …"

"The young think differently nowadays, Isabel. She'll be all right. Stop worrying, love." The endearment went some way to mollifying her. She was no fool. She knew that Bertie would run for cover as long as he was agile, but time was on her side.

"Very well, but I cannot approve." She lifted her lace-edged handkerchief and inhaled the deliciously expensive perfume that he had given her for Christmas. "Have you completed your business yet?"

"It's possible. Just a minute while I check." After a blanked-out pause, he continued: "I think I should make it today all right."

"Don't overstrain yourself," she responded tersely, waving her hand towards Hanna who had come in with her breakfast tray.

Bertie chuckled and said that he wouldn't. His voice quickened: "I'll speak to Marigold when I get there."

"I think you should, Bertie. She'll listen to you."

"Bye love."

"We're missing you, Bertie."

"And I you."

Hanna called, "Give Bertie my love." She was standing at the window waiting for Isabel to finish her call.

"Hanna sends her regards."

When Isabel had replaced the receiver, Hanna went over and settled the breakfast tray over her lap. "Why didn't you pass on my love to dear Bertie?" she asked with a smile.

"I felt it would be over-indulging him," Isabel replied without inflection. "He was getting his full quota of that commodity from his urgent business."

Hanna came slowly down the curving staircase, looking up at the Victorian paintings and down at the banisters, making sure that there were no visible signs of dust. When she reached the hall she crossed to the fireplace and poked the fire, throwing on some more peat. Slavers pulled himself up and retreated a few feet, watching her straighten the fireside rug. He slumped back down, resting his head on his paws and raising his eyes to follow her movements as she restored order. His head came up when she crossed the hall, but she stopped again to lift the empty enamel tray from the refectory table; it would be returned in the early evening to hold the daily catch, the stiff, slippery remains laid out for the admiration (or envy) of fellow fishermen. She stood there, holding the tray and looking up at the plaster cast of an enormous trout which was displayed in a cabinet on the wall above. A dry, scaly, skin-like substance was stretched over its swollen belly and its glass eye twinkled coldly in the filtered sunlight.

"It's a fine fish is it no?" a voice said from behind her.

She turned in surprise and wished Callum McFea a good morning. "Personally I think it is quite revolting," she went on. "I was thinking of having it removed to an outhouse."

"You don't like it?" Callum asked in amazement, looking up at the fish uncritically. "The trout put up a good fight and has been honoured. I remember the day fine."

Hanna noted that the date underneath was 23 June 1947. "You must've been only a boy then, Callum."

"I'd been working a year or two. Fourteen was the leaving age then."

Hanna looked at Callum's kindly face, now deeply etched with the lines of age. He had been working on the estate for nearly half a century and would be retiring soon. He wouldn't be easy to replace.

"Were you wanting something, Callum?"

"I was after the boss."

"I think he'll have gone. Come through to the kitchen and we'll see."

Slavers saw Hanna disappearing into the back quarters without him and bounded across the hall, skidding round a pillar and reaching the swing door just before it closed. He slunk past Callum, who had stopped in the doorway of the kitchen, and rubbed himself against Hanna's legs, before settling down in his favourite place at the side of the Aga.

"You've missed him, I'm afraid."

Callum moved his cap round and round between his fingers. "He won't be back till the afternoon I'm thinking."

"Late afternoon, I should say. Can I help with something?"

Callum pondered on that for a moment before making up his mind. "I'll be having a word with him then." He put on his cap, and with a nod to Hanna, left the way he had come, a tall stooping figure, bent by wind and toil.

Hanna wondered what it was all about but she was not over concerned. She knew that Callum considered work on the estate men's business and gave the matter no further thought. She sat down on the fireside chair with the menu cards on her lap. Lizzie Hope had set the chicken carcass from the previous evening's meal to simmer before going home and a faint aroma of stock was mingling with the last of the breakfast smells. The table was damp and she could hear water running in the scullery; there was also the clatter of pans being scrubbed and laid to dry. She would miss Jean Glover when she went to college after the summer.

While she was considering what to offer as the main dishes for the evening meal and shuffling through the old menu cards to get ideas for the other courses, there was a clatter as a disc fell on the bell indicator and started a noisy chain reaction. Hanna got up and replaced the number.

"That's room 2," she called out to Jean. "Did you forget to put something on Mrs Pritchard's tray?"

The tap in the scullery was turned off and Jean came through, drying her hands on the sides of her jeans. She was tall, with an adolescent slouch, her fair hair cut in a pudding-bowl style; bright, violet-blue eyes peaked out from beneath its fringe. She said that she was sure she had not forgotten anything and was about to give her opinion of Isabel when Hanna forestalled her.

"Would you give her a ring and check for me, please?"

With a shrug and an ok, Jean sauntered through to the front of the house.

Slavers pulled himself up and stretched, laying his muzzle across Hanna's knees, his eyes appealing for attention. She stroked his head, murmuring apologies for delaying his morning walk and making promises as she wrote out her menu. When she had finished, she tidied everything together and stood up, straightening her skirt. Slavers quivered on his hind legs, his muscles tense and his eyes alert, waiting for the call to action. The word came and he leapt back, his claws scratching on the stone slabs as he ran hither and thither round her legs, lifting his head and giving joyful yelps to encourage her forward to the swing door and out into the hall.

Jean was sitting on the stool behind the reception desk, her elbows on the counter and the phone to her ear. She replaced the receiver carefully and looked round at Hanna with large, innocent eyes. "Mrs Pritchard only wanted to know the time," she said, the colour rising in her cheeks.

The idea of Jean having a riveting conversation with Isabel upstairs made Hanna smile but before she could think of a suitable response, the phone rang.

Jean grabbed it quickly. "Trowsay House. Can I help you?" she enquired, her lilting voice warm and eager, but when she heard who was at the other end of the line, she quickly dropped the sizzling receiver into Hanna's hand.

Rupert broke off his frustrated tirade, to ask Hanna without preamble: "Have all the guests had breakfast,"

"I'm not sure. Why?"

"Just find out for me, Hanna. It's important."

Hanna turned to Jean and asked her to check with the dining room.

"What is it, Rupert?"

"I'm at the causeway and there's evidently a car in the water."

"Oh, my heavens!"

Davey is with me and he says that a passing boat saw it in the early morning but it has been taken farther out by the tide and has fallen into a hole. They can't see the number plate or the type of car."

She heard Davey say loudly: "The divers have been sent for, Mrs Treatham, and a freighter with lifting gear is on its way." She could picture him with his arm on the open window and his head thrust forward towards the car phone, determined to tell her the news himself.

Rupert thanked him and she could hear the window being wound up.

"That's better," he said. "Old Davey's breath is to be avoided." The noise of the engine starting and the car moving off made his voice less audible. "I don't know how he knows so much. The lifeboat is there but it's a good hundred yards out. I've been up to the headland to see." The line was still open but it started to fade as he changed gear and started to negotiate the slope down to the causeway

"Are you still there, Rupe?"

"Yes, but I must keep moving or I'll be late."

"Has Davey no idea who it could be?"

"Well, he's touching the side of his nose with a knowing look but if he knows anything he's not saying."

Hanna said wryly: "If he did know something, he'd be saying." She half turned, hearing Jean's running footsteps. "Here's Jean now. I'll let her speak."

Jean took the phone eagerly, her eyes wide with curiosity.

"Mr Treatham? Yes, the only ones who were not at breakfast were Mrs Pritchard who has had a tray in her room, Marigold Wentworth whom I feel fairly sure is across at Thorfinn's and Mr Yearts …"

"Mr Yearts is usually one of the first down," Rupert interrupted in alarm.

"Yes, but Mrs Yearts says he's feeling poorly and has stayed in bed."

"Oh, thank goodness for that. So they're all accounted for." Rupert mused for a moment. "It must be someone from the island then."

"Someone from the island?" Jean's voice rose in alarm. "What do you mean?" The line went dead and Jean turned to Hanna for an answer.

Hanna had been jolted by the news that Marigold was with Thorfinn and could still feel the blood throbbing in her cheeks. She cleared her throat and forced her voice to be steady as she told Jean about the car in the sea, adding gently: "That does not necessarily mean that it belongs to an islander."

Jean was not reassured. She began to run through the names of those who might have been on the mainland the previous evening, her voice trembling with fear and excitement. Then an awful thought occurred.

"It couldn't be Karen, could it?"

That was very unlikely as her sister Karen lived in Inverness, but the remote possibility that Karen had decided to come home for the weekend, had its effect. Jean's hand reached forward and hovered over the telephone.

"I'm sure Karen is quite safe," Hanna said confidently, having regained her composure, "but ring your mother anyway to make sure."

Jean nodded and pressed the digits on the dial, setting the calls rolling.

3

Davey followed the Range Rover down the slope to the causeway. Heidi went after the tyres with yelps of fury and kept at her barking until the Range Rover was at the other side of the crossing. Davey didn't whistle her back. She knew the score. A right pain in the arse that one; everyone said so. All smiles and friendly enquiry when you were needed and hardly a nod when you were not. And their airs and graces were only the half of it. If they got the chance, they would dispose of you like a piece of old garbage. Aye, and with fine righteous talk into the bargain. Davey knew the kind well.

He settled himself back on his boulder, which was set snugly against the rocky bank, embedded in sand. Heidi sank at his feet, resting heavily against his leg, her tongue lolling hotly. Davey sat there most days when the tide was out. It gave him a good view across to the mainland and he could keep a watch on the comings and goings.

"A danger to mysel, they said, just because I was calling down the wrath of God on those uppity busybodies who wouldna let me be." He leaned over and lifted Heidi on to his knee, needing an ear to hear his spleen. She licked his hand, yawned and closed her eyes. She'd heard it all before. "And I'd good cause to be raving and cursing. Aye, that I had, Heidi. I was minding me own business, lying here on this boulder wi the feel o Anna in me arms, welcoming death." He looked around him listening to the piercing cry of a gull in dispute with its neighbour and the gentle lap of the sea against the rocks. The ebbing tide had left the causeway wet and shiny, with a fringe of heavy seaweed and abandoned dark, living pools. "Hard to say why now but it would've been welcome then."

He shifted Heidi closer into him.

"Did I tell you my Anna was a rare beauty, a lass in a million. Did I tell you that, Heidi?" Davey thought for a bit, trying to remember why Anna was special but his mind was a blank. They had stolen the best parts of his memory as well as twenty years of his life. "It was their kind that made the bomb that killed my lovely lass." He rubbed the hollow under Heidi's ear rhythmically. "But they couldna get at her soul. No, they couldna get at that. I gathered it up and carried it home wi me. I wasna going to leave it in that hell they'd made o God's earth." He paused in thought. "Aye, that's the way it was, Heidi. She was wi me, my Anna, from the day her body was desecrated, to the day they rattled me brains in that loony bin south. Obsessed, they said I was." Heidi moved her head and he left off his rubbing, stroking her silky ear instead. "That's as may be. I'm no disputing that point. But they were me obsessions, Heidi. They belonged tae me. I had a right tae them." He munched away on his tongue, looking across the causeway to Talhaugh as he rehashed in his mind the injustices he had suffered at the hands of men who wielded their authority. "A criminal offence it was then tae tak the life God had gaen you and deprive the state o your labours. But I wasna takin my life, Heidi. I was jist showing God that I was willing like."

Heidi pricked up her ears and jumped down from Davey's knee, yelping and running to and fro on her short legs, encouraging Davey to his feet. There was no mistaking the throbbing sound of a boat on the move.

"Aye that'll be them now," Davey said, pushing down on his boulder and pulling himself upright, staggering a bit until the muscles in his skinny legs took hold. He gave himself a warming rub and climbed back up to Trowsay Point to see what was going on.

Sure enough, the freighter was working its way into position, with the skipper leaning out from his wheel-house and shouting instructions until the anchor held. He cut the engine and the oily churn of water at the stern calmed, leaving the rusty tub, with its high crane and ungainly boom, rocking gently with the movement of the sea.

Davey stood at the edge of the cliff watching. He gave a wave to the skipper as he left his wheelhouse and to anyone else who looked in his direction. A crew-man and a couple of divers in wetsuits were lounging at the rail and the police were standing close by. There was a peaceable discussion going on until the skipper joined them on deck. Then a dispute broke out. Davey thrust his neck forward, trying to get nearer to the action and hear what was being said, but he couldn't catch the words and had to guess. From time to time one of the divers would look over the side of the boat and the argument would start again.

Cars, trucks and tractors were arriving at the cause-way and their occupants climbing out to greet each other and speculate about the identity of the car's own-er. Trowsay's population had been over four hundred at one time but was now half that. Most of the islanders were related in one way or another, although there were those who did not choose to remember the connection.

Ted Vale from the shop joined Davey on the headland. He acknowledged Heidi's boisterous welcome and the two men exchanged greetings.

"That was quite a storm last night," Ted went on, "but you wouldna expect this."

Davey agreed, keeping his eyes on the activity below. "I hear you were up at Selkie yesterday seeing Alec."

"Aye, he's taken to his bed permanent like."

"The man isna long for this world."

Ted shrugged, not committing himself, and after a pause for reflection went on: "A fine farm going a-begging."

Davey gave him a questioning look. "I dinna ken about it going a-begging," he said. "His mother's brother out in Canada had a lass, I am certain sure of that."

"Aye he did, but the brother was never back to see Alec or the family at Selkie."

"That's nae surprising. He was one step ahead o the law when he got on the boat."

Ted laughed. "So Cissie was saying. She's related to the family, you know. Takes Alec's shopping up to the farm and sees to him these days."

"Is that a fact!"

"Not close mind, but still related."

Davey chewed on his tongue but he couldn't keep his words in check. "There'll be plenty others when his time comes," he murmured to himself, and changed the subject by directing Ted's attention to the drama unfolding in front of them. "Still a lot of barney going on down there. No doubt the skipper'll be in a hurry to get back to sea."

"Maybe so, but the divers won't go down in that patch of water until the tide is steady." Ted was a fisherman, going after lobster and crab, and so was wary of the tide when it was on the turn. "There was talk of it being Sarah Mac's car. She's always in a hurry that lass. Not a great timekeeper." Sarah had a reputation for careering along the lochside at top speed, scattering wayward sheep with a blast from her horn

"Na na, it isna her down there," Davey said with certainty. "She crossed afore I went home for me tea."

"Is that so?" Ted looked down at Davey in surprise. "Her Ma was creating something terrible in the village. She was ringing the hospital and all, just to make sure that the lass was at her work."

"Her Ma's aye one for pushing herself forward."

"You're right on that score."

"More than likely it's a car from the ither side any road. There were two across there efter the tide was in."

"Two of them?"

"Aye, there were the two." Davey could remember seeing headlights going away from the causeway. "They didna hang around though."

"The Gunn girls were unloading their bairns when I drove up. They're feart it's their lads."

"Is that a fact!" The Gunns were connected to Davey through his granddaughter, Patsy. She came round and sorted him out once a week. "I didna see Stevie Gunn's rust bucket crossing back," he said thoughtfully. "Mind you Stevie and Pete dinna always come home on a Friday night. Patsy was telling me that they just roll out their sleeping bags wherever they find themselves and their Mums are the last to know where they are."

He looked about him, acknowledging a nod and a greeting here and there. Tara and Madge Gunn were standing farther along the headland, looking towards the freighter with their bairns close in by their sides. They were fine looking lasses. Tara was a raver with harsh blonde hair and packed curves, always shouting her wares. Her cousin, Madge, was different, more to Davey's liking. She was just as God had made her and He hadn't been spare with his favours. She was a lovely looking lass with a nature to match. It was a downright shame to see the worry lines already showing on her forehead. Alf Strachan had a lot to answer for.

"Things are starting to move," Ted said, and Davey's attention was refocused on the boat. The divers were strapping on their weights and shrugging into their backpacks, while the derrick was moved into position and the boom lowered. As the divers fell back into the moving sea, Alf Strachan joined them on the headland.

"Jill Jimson's up to high-doh," were his first words on reaching them, His ruddy, amiable face was glowing after the climb up to the point. "Sweyn watched the match to the end last night."

"It didna finish till near eleven."

"Ronald's been trying to get news of him but no luck so far." Alf turned and pointed to a stranger who was standing apart from the islanders with binoculars and a long-lens camera slung round his neck. "The tourist over there has one of those cellular phones and he lent it to Ronald but Ronald can't reach Sweyn's skipper at the boat and his friends aren't answering. Understandable, I suppose, on a Saturday morning."

"I'll away and have a word with them," Davey said, lifting Heidi gently off his foot.

Nora Mac (Sarah's mother) saw him passing and called to Heidi, who leapt through the heather to have her head patted and her ears scratched. Heidi belonged to her, or had belonged to her; Davey was never quite sure which.

He tipped his cap in greeting.

"She's a beautiful bitch," Nora said. "A very high pedigree, of course. We should breed from her, Davey."

Davey lifted his greasy cap and scratched his bald head. "Aye, maybe so." He knew that it was the money that the puppies would bring rather than the puppies themselves that she wanted. "Scott's collie shows an interest from time to time."

Nora straightened in horror. "You're joking, of course."

Davey put his cap back on and gave a low whistle. Heidi came back to heel. "She's grand as she is," he said. "Besides I couldna manage a littler of puppies in my caravan and you'd find them a right nuisance till they're trained." He knew that the mention of puppy piddling would reduce Nora Mac's enthusiasm for having Heidi mated, and he was right.

She sighed and said regretfully: "It seems such a waste of good breeding stock."

"Ah, weel, that's the way o it." Davey gave her his best smile. He was always a bit wary in case she took it into her head to reclaim her property. Heidi had a big heart and was not one to hold a grudge but he re-membered fine the day Nora Mac had cast her out. He had been passing through the village, his head lowered against the wind, when the little dog had dropped at his feet. A gift from God he had thought at the time, but it was not God that he had seen when he lifted his head but Nora Mac, standing on her doorstep with tearful eyes and trembling lips, babbling away about Persian rugs and stretched nerves. He had gathered up the small quivering puppy and continued on his way, feel-ing her silky head caressing his neck. The heartless wife hadn't called him back, contenting herself with making up a fine story to explain Heidi's change of abode. A waste of breath, of course. Everyone knew what had happened, just as they had known that she hadn't ap-preciated her husband's choice of gift. Poor old Mac had died of a heart attack a few days after coming home on leave with the six-week-old dachshund and the talk back then was that the two events were linked.

While he was thinking back, Nora Mac was jabber-ing away. He came in at the end of it: "… having so many puppies could upset her. You were right to point that out, Davey." Davey knew that he was right and wished her the time of day before moving along to the Jimsons who were standing close by.

"Whit like, Davey?" Ronald enquired in greeting and Davey gave the expected response, tipping his cap to Jill. He liked Jill. She was a comely woman, not a weight watcher, and she always gave him a slap-up meal and two cans of beer when he was mending dykes up at Greybarns. It bothered him to see that she was not her usual neat and cheery self. Her bonny dark eyes were wide with fearful foreboding and the clasp that held her hair high on top of her head had fallen loose. Besides that, she still had on her apron and was wearing the old, stained farm coat that she kept on a peg at the back door. He had never seen her outside the farmyard in that.

Jill overlapped her coat to conceal her apron. It was as though she had read his thoughts. "I was doing my weekly bake when Daphne Glover rang," she explained, tightening the belt.

"Dinna fash yersel, lass," Davey said soothingly. "It'll be a tourist from the ither side that's come to grief, you'll see."

"It couldn't be a tourist in the middle of the night, Davey," Jill pointed out reasonably, and went on blaming herself for not turning the television off and shooing Sweyn out of the house at least ten minutes before. "He was always driving across when the water was inches deep."

"Now, Jill, you know very well that Sweyn just says these things to get a rise out of you," Ronald said, his mouth soft with indulgent affection. "He wouldn't cross if it wasn't safe."

"Aye, Sweyn's not that daft," Davey stated, unaware of the implied implication.

Ronald changed the subject, starting to discuss with Davey the symptoms of a sick cow that he had left in the incapable hands of his teenage daughter. Davey commiserated with him and suggested applying a paste made from docken stalks to the cow's udders. He swore that he had been successful with that in the past when a cow had had mastitis. Ronald was not convinced, and his scepticism set Davey off on a series of anecdotes to prove his point.

Jill wasn't listening. She kept her eyes on the sea below, waiting for the divers to surface. With the movement of the tide, the freighter had swung round on its anchor and when the divers reappeared, they had drifted away and had to fight their way back through the strong pull of the current, helped by the crewmen who held their lines. One of them spoke to the policeman on deck and then prepared to dive again.

"Jimmy," shouted Tara Gunn as loudly as she could.

Everyone stopped talking to see what would happen.

"Whose car is it," she yelled through her cupped hands.

Jimmy called up to the policeman (who was already on his radio phone) pointing to the cliff top and the waiting islanders, but he must have got a negative reply because he only gave Tara a shrug and a wave before disappearing under the water again.

"It would be improper to broadcast the details prematurely," Nora Mac said to Tara, who was two children away.

Tara turned her head slowly and gave Nora a look. She asked why, but it was clear from the tone of her voice that she thought it none of Nora's business what she chose to do or ask.

"There could be … unpleasantness in the car."

Tara turned to her cousin and indicated Nora with an extended thumb. "Listen to the unfeeling bitch," she said with a jeer. "It's plain to see that she has nothing to worry about now."

Davey stopped talking to Ronald and gave his full attention to the exchange of words between the two women. Nora Mac made much of her sensitive nature and he watched to see how she would react to Tara's blunt speech. But Nora wasn't going to waste her sensitivities on the likes of Tara Gunn and contented herself with a haughty glare. Tara responded with two fingers and an insolent shrug, before cuffing one of her boys who was trying to get at the sweets in her pocket. He started to howl. Tara ignored him but Madge gathered him up and called to the others to come with her. Her bundle immediately stopped crying and wriggled free, racing with the others down the slope to her van. While they were fighting over the different flavours of crisps on offer, she poured two cups of coffee from her thermos and carried them up to the Jimsons. Ronald refused the offer but Jill reached out and took a cup with a small grateful smile, and Davey took the other.

"I'm sure Sweyn is safe," Madge said gently, speaking to Jill: "He was a good driver and wouldn't have taken any risk."

Jill drew in her breath in the middle of swallowing a mouthful of coffee and choked. Davey thumped her back. He knew that she was put out at the thought of Sweyn getting involved with one of the Gunn girls, who were seen by doting mothers as walking honey-traps.

"Thank you, Davey," Jill gasped, withdrawing herself from his attention. The tears were running down her cheeks and she let them run. She tried to stop crying, apologising all the while, but the tears kept coming.

Ronald put his arm around her and patted her shoulder with clumsy words of comfort.

"Look! They're lifting it now!" shouted Tara, grabbing one of her children who was running towards the edge of the cliff to get a better view.

Sure enough, they could see the crane wires under tension and the hydraulic spindle starting to turn. Then everything stopped. The islanders stood transfixed unable to understand what was wrong. But the lifting had only halted to allow the divers to surface and be helped on board.

"Jimmy's giving the thumbs up," Tara said in delight, turning and hugging her cousin.

Jill dropped her coffee cup and turned her face into her husband's rough dungarees, unable to watch.

The crane started again, the spindle slowly rotating until the roof of the car lurched through the undulating waves. With a rush of falling and spurting water from every opening, the car rose above the water and circled on the derrick for all to see.

It was a silver grey Ferrari.

"Hallo."

"Sweyn, is that you?"

"Yes."

"I've been trying to get through all afternoon."

Jill listened keenly but there was nothing but the echoing void of an open line and intermittent static. "The sound is awful. I can hardly hear you above the crackling. Are you there?"

"Yes."

"I just wanted to hear your voice. Are you all right?"

"Yes."

"Did you hear about the accident at the causeway?"

"Yes."

"I thought it was you in the car. I thought you had drowned."

"Why?"

"You know why Sweyn. You're always taking risks with the tides. Your Dad and I spent a good part of the morning out at the causeway waiting for the car to be lifted. It wasn't yours, thank goodness."

"No"

"I was practically sick with relief, I can tell you. We tried to get in touch with you all morning. We rang the boat and your friends but no one had seen you. Where were you?"

"About."

"Did the boat not sail on the tide?"

"No. I must go Mum. The skipper wants to use the radio."

"Does he?"

"Yes."

"You have no idea how awful it was Sweyn. I kept thinking of you trying to get out with the water pouring in through the windows and no one there to help. You will take care, now. You promise me, you will take care."

"Yes. Bye, Mum."

4

Callum McFea pushed his way through the deep, wiry heather that stretched from the hotel boundary dyke westward to Lowacres. Willie Kylison of Lowacres had been a policeman before he retired back to the family farm with his pension; he would know what to do. Callum trudged on, stopping from time to time to get his bearings and contemplate the uncared-for land all around him. The Kylisons had never seen this part of their farm acreage as worth anything and the whole moor and hillside had been left to nature's will. It needed a good burning to bring colour and life back to the place. By the thickness of the grey stalks and the height of the straggling heather, Callum estimated that the land had not been burned for nearly thirty years. He could not remember the last time he had seen any part of it alight. There were no signs of fresh heather shoots and without new shoots to feed on and thick growth to hide in, the grouse and hare had deserted the place. The hill at Trowsay House had benefited from the desertion. Callum smiled to himself with satisfaction as he plodded on. He managed that land, burning a few strips every spring and covering the whole area in five to seven years.

The heather got sparser as he neared the coast but the ground was still poor, mostly peat and moss. Now he could hear the intermittent sound of waves breaking on the shore and see the block of farm buildings clearly on the skyline. The farmhouse had been a ramshackle place with a sagging roof, no windows, few doors and weeds growing out of the walls when Willie came home for good. Now it was wind and watertight, with new stone slabs cemented in place on the roof, glass in the windows and a bit of paint here and there on the exposed wood. The surrounding buildings still left everything to be desired but Willie had seen to his garden out front. Callum knew that because he had given him a hand, enjoying Willie's stories of life south in the police force. He could hardly credit the dangerous situations Willie had found himself in and the bizarre crimes that he had had to solve, some of which Callum had read about in his newspaper. After one of his exclamations of surprise, Willie had stopped digging.

"Ah, but this is a tonic after a working lifetime in the city," he had said, leaning on his spade and looking out to sea. Atlantic breakers crashed and sucked at the soft sand below and only a ship in the distance interrupted his view of a wide, empty ocean. "When I draw back my curtains each morning, Callum," he went on. "I sigh with contentment, glad to be home."

Callum had much the same view from his cliffside house just along the coast but he wasn't one for sighing over his surroundings.

Willie's contentment had not lasted. A year or so after he came home, a gale had brought massive waves rolling up his beach and over the dunes, to pummel his solid stone dyke with rhythmic exploding violence. The sea had been coming over the dunes at Lowacres during Spring tides for some years but the waves had never got so far nor had such force. This time Willie's dyke had slipped from its foundations and the sand dunes had fallen away, exposing strong roots of marram grass in long uneven clefts. It was the talk of the island at the time, Callum remembered, as he jumped a ditch and crossed the home field to the farmhouse, the curious sheep watching his progress as they chewed. Most people agreed with Willie that someone should have been guarding against the island falling into the sea (God was not seen to act any more in the accidents and disasters of the world) but that 'someone' had not been found.

There was no sign of Willie working on the farm but as Callum passed the kitchen window on his way to the garden, he spotted the round dome of his head showing above the armchair. He knocked on the back door and moved to the side of the house, so that Willie would not feel crowded by his presence when he lifted the latch.

Willie had not long finished his second breakfast (always a substantial meal) and he was reading his day-old newspaper from under closed eyelids when he heard Callum's knock. He closed his mouth abruptly into the chasm between the purple-crescented and crannied crags that dominated his face. Slowly he laid his newspaper aside and raised himself to his considerable height, pulling his braces up into place. He checked his appearance in the mirror, smoothing down the quarter-inch hairs that circled his dome.

He expected to find the man from the electric or a travelling salesman when he opened his door and so was pleasantly surprised to see Callum standing at the side of the house. He put on his jacket and took down his tweed hat from its peg beside the door. "There you are, Callum," he said by way of greeting. "It's a grand day to be out and about."

"It is that," Callum agreed, his mind still focused on the fortifications that Willie had constructed. There were walls and tiers made of cement blocks all round him, with a jutting ledge at the top to stop any wave at its height. Willie's house had become an island in a sea of hard concrete. "You've fairly made a change here since the last time I was across."

"Aye, it's coming along nicely," Willie replied with satisfaction, and started walking Callum round the boundary wall, pointing out different features for him to admire.

"Are you planning to do much more?" Callum asked, unable to see much more needing to be done.

"Bits and pieces here and there," Willie replied, looking out along the beach with a glint of fervour in his eyes.

Callum surveyed the half-circles of concrete steps rising to the supported overhang. He could barely see the roof of the house. "I hear you fell foul o the men from the council."

"I wouldn't say that. They seemed satisfied enough"

"Is that so?" Callum had heard a different story from Davey. Davey had seen the emblazoned van waiting to cross the causeway in the morning and had upped and given Willie, and all the other islanders dicing on the edge of the law, prior warning. At the end of the day, he had waved the van down on its way back to the mainland to talk about this and that and find out all he could. Of course Willie's fortifications were only at an early stage then.

"They just need a letter from time to time to keep them happy," Willie said placidly. "They say that they haven't the money to sort it themselves which isn't surprising. Our taxes go to all those talkers and hangers-on down south who justify their fat salaries by keeping us at the form-filling."

Callum agreed. He was not of a political turn of mind and agreeing kept the peace. "I was hearing that Jimson of Greybarns wasna so lucky," he went on, and they spent a few minutes discussing Ronald's problems with the planning authority as they walked along the shore.

As the conversation wound down, it was time for Callum to ask for Willie's help. The body was well hidden and would still be there when Mr Treatham arrived home, but he felt uneasy about keeping the tragedy to himself. He cleared his throat, the words taking shape in his head, but when he looked up to speak, he saw that Willie's attention was directed elsewhere.

"Is that Thorfinn Dukes climbing over those rocks with a lassie in tow?" he asked, lifting his hand to shade his eyes from the sun.

Callum saw that it was. Thorfinn and Marigold Wentworth were fooling around near the point, splashing through rock pools and decorating each other with fronds of seaweed. He could hear their laughter as they reached the shore and walked towards them, dragging their bare feet through the spent waves and moist, dark sand.

"He's always up to something that one," he told Willie. "It upsets the wife no end. There was a real shemozzle yesterday afore I got home from work ..." Callum's sentence tailed off. His eyes widened in disbelief at the sight of Marigold prancing along the beach in nothing but her underclothes. "Goodness me, Willie, the girl is wearing nothing but a pair of silk camiknickers." he said, shock vibrating his voice.

Willie had seen it for himself. He was giving Marigold the once over when she spotted them and shrieked. Thorfinn quickly moved in front of her, shielding her from view while they rummaged in his rucksack.

"Is that what camiknickers look like, Callum?"

Callum coloured from the base of his stringy neck to the rim of his cap. He could see that Willie was more taken with his knowledge of such ladies' nether garments than he was with the vision itself. He felt that he had let Flo down by mentioning such a thing.

Thorfinn called a greeting as the two barefooted lovers reached them. Marigold was now clothed in a silky dress with narrow straps and a skirt that only just covered the garment beneath. It was plain to see that she had not been back to the hotel since the night before.

"I'm sorry about that," she said, tilting her head and looking from Willie to Callum with a beguiling smile. "I didn't want to spoil my dress."

Callum shuffled a bit with embarrassment. He would have preferred it if she had not drawn attention to her undressed state, but Willie was smiling a welcome, obviously taken with her. Marigold was elfin in size and feature, with long, brown legs and a delightfully merry face. Her mass of blonde hair was tousled and her eyes were opened wide in innocent appeal.

"It's a grand day to be out and about," he said and put out his hand to be shaken.

Marigold slipped her hand into his but her mind was preoccupied. She was looking up at the sea defences in amazement. Willie explained the purpose of the stepped construction and was pleased to take her round on a tour of inspection, enjoying her girlish enthusiasm. He even invited her in for a cup of tea and there were few who got over Willie's doorstep.

This was refused.

"I must get back to the hotel soon," Marigold said in explanation. "My father may be arriving today."

"And I must get home to do some work," Thorfinn added, although what Thorfinn did beyond propping up the bar few knew.

"But you're still taking me to the famous cave, aren't you?" Marigold asked with a provocative pout. She smiled at Thorfinn and turned mischievously to the two men. "Thorfinn was going to take me to the cave last night. There was a full moon and he was sure that it was windy enough to see the trows dancing, but we didn't get there."

This revelation did not go down well. You could practically hear Willie's false teeth gnash. He was outraged that Thorfinn should have stooped to such a ploy to get a well brought up girl like Marigold out of the hotel and on the road to his house. Callum, who knew Thorfinn rather better, was not surprised that he had used this tactic and wondered how many times he had used it before.

"I did explain that I had not actually seen the mirage myself but I was always hopeful," Thorfinn said in an attempt to mitigate his guilt. The myth of the trows, or trolls, was well documented. It was written in ancient tomes that when the sea was high and the full moon was in the right position to shine through a gap at the front of the cave in question, the moving waves and the shimmering light made the shadows from a circle of rock stacks within the cave, dance against the back wall, like a troop of trolls planning their mischief. "There must be something in it when there is a whole page in the tourist guide devoted to how Trowsay got its name."

"Stuff and nonsense all of it," Willie spluttered. "There's no doubt pages devoted to the Loch Ness monster in the tourist guide down south but no one with an ounce of sense would believe such rubbish."

"I'm an optimist by nature," Thorfinn drawled languidly, swinging his rucksack on to his back, "and Alf Strachan is not the only one to have seen the shadows dancing."

"Charlatans all of them," Willie pronounced with heat and authority.

"The trows wouldna be the only ones reeling when Alf Strachan and his cronies were out and about," Callum put in.

Thorfinn chuckled. "I didn't know you were a wit, Callum."

This merriment was greeted with scowls from both men and Marigold became flustered. "It doesn't matter. It's not important at all," she said, looking up at Thorfinn apologetically and taking his hand to draw him away. "I know that trolls are pure fancy… fairy-book stuff … but I have always wanted to see the cave for myself."

She waved as they continued on their way, watched by the two men.

"Can you credit a man using such enticement," Willie said. "It's not far from being a case of abduction."

Callum felt that that was going too far and said so – he had heard the laughter from the adjoining cottage the night before – but both agreed that Thorfinn was a smooth-talking scoundrel.

As they walked up the cool, green garden leaving the concrete monstrosities behind, Callum rolled back his sleeve and looked at his watch. He was beginning to feel anxious about his absence from the hotel and knew that his introduction of the subject that had brought him to Willie's door was now long overdue.

"Willie I've got a bit of a problem."

"And what would that be?"

"It's like this: I was cutting the grass out front the day and when I went o'er the dyke to spread the clippings on the waste ground beside the shore, I saw something caught in the rocks." He looked up anxiously. "It was a man's body, Willie."

Willie stopped walking and straightened to his full height, the muscles in his face tense and his pale blue eyes hard and piercing. "Had the man drowned?"

"Aye, he had."

Willie took off his hat and passed his hand over his bald pate. "And what did you do with this body? You didn't just leave it there?"

"No, I couldna do that. A lassie might have passed that way. I pulled it up and placed it under that rickety old boat that's there on the shore."

"And is it still lying under the boat?"

"Aye, it is."

What Willie thought of discovering a corpse and just leaving it under an old boat to rot was made clear by his piercing and unwavering stare of disapproval.

Callum hastened to explain: "I went into the house to fetch the boss but he wasna there. He'd left for Thurso and the tide's in now. I couldna land Mrs T in it without a man beside her to give her support."

"Did you know who it was? Was it someone from hereabouts?"

"I wouldna be troubling you, Willie, if it had been a Trowsay man. I could've visited the widow mysel and plenty would've helped with the body." He stood for a second or two, thinking of a past tragedy, before getting down to the crux of the matter. "I thocht you might come across and help Mrs T do the necessary."

Willie stroked his chin thoughtfully. It was an unbelievable situation and all very unorthodox but perhaps understandable in the case of Callum who had an old-fashioned sense of female fragility.

"Did it look to you like a simple drowning?" he asked. "Nothing unusual about the body?"

"What else could it be but a drowning, with the body stuck right there at the cliff side?"

"Well, we'll see. I'll go and change."

Callum waited in the courtyard, peering inside Willie's derelict buildings and noting that all the outmoded machinery, rolls of rusty wire, old sacks and other useless junk were just as they had been the last time he was over. He looked at the sea through the gap between the house and the steading for a bit and then leaned against the back of Willie's car, contemplating his boots. The Jaguar's obtruding rear was well covered with seagull droppings and the inside was little better to look at because the back seat had been used to carry bags of cement and the messy trickle from leaking bags had got down the sides of the leather upholstery and over the floor.

Water gurgled down the waste pipe over at the house and Callum looked at his watch. He had been away from the hotel for nearly an hour and he was getting restless. He knew that the journey that had taken him little more than fifteen minutes on foot would take longer by car. There was no road over the heather from Lowacres to Trowsay House. A car had to follow the coastal track north to the village, skirting bays and passing in front of stone-slated cottages, some in ruins, with the occasional boundary fence to open and shut along the way.

In his own good time, Willie appeared, all spruced up and carrying two polythene bags. "There you are then, Callum," he said coming across to the gig shed and squeezing his bulk along the side of the big car jammed into its small garage. "You stay right there until I get it out."

"Aye, fine that."

Willie opened the driver's door and covered the seat with the polythene bags before manipulating himself in through the crack between the door and the uneven stone wall. Callum waited at the entrance, listening to the starter whining and dying with declining impetus until a spark caught and the engine wheezed its way up to a steady roar. When the sound decreased to a sustainable throb, he moved behind and started waving his arms about giving directions, but Willie took no notice, going back and forward at his own pace until he was clear of the hard edges.

"All set?" he asked as Callum got in.

Callum agreed that he was.

Willie adjusted his mirror and opened his window to give his elbow a ledge. He let out the clutch and the sleek car left the courtyard at speed, bumping over the waste ground outside and scattering protesting hens, interrupted at their scratchings.

5

Hanna wheeled the boxes of bedding-out plants from the stable, across the courtyard and through the side garden; a shrubbery crouched in the elongated shadow of the house. She pushed her heavy awkward load between the shrubs and down the slope to the walled garden. It was always wet underfoot there and the single wheel of the barrow gathered mud and left its mark on the sparse grass. She had expected to see Callum somewhere about but she was quite happy to have the place to herself.

The garden had been a wilderness when they bought Trowsay House. Callum had only turned over a few patches of ground to give the meagre supply of vegetables needed for the old man's meals. The rest of the area had been left to return to nature. Dark menacing nettles had been everywhere and the number of spent dandelion heads bespoke of a myriad of floating seeds in past summers. The fruit garden had been a tangle of thorny tentacles from unpruned bushes, and there had been no visible paths. It would have filled most people with despair but Hanna enjoyed gardening and had set to work, turning over the soil and sowing the spring seeds.

The patch of ground she was passing reminded her of Thorfinn. He had come across nearly every day to help her that summer and she often thought of him as she worked, going over in her head what they had talked about and savouring his peculiar, but endearing, idiosyncrasies. She remembered how he would commiserate with a plant that had been flattened by the wind or got entangled with its invasive neighbour, and he always started digging a new patch of ground with his hands, rubbing the soil and sniffing it ecstatically. The first time he had done that he had said, "the warm and loamy smell of the earth reminds me of bed," adding, with mock solemnity, "a flower bed naturally." Every time he smelled the earth after that, he had given her an intimate, caressing smile; the reliving of that time brought the heat to her body. She really didn't know why he got to her like that because he wasn't really her type. She had always been attracted to dark men, solidly built and dependable. He was fair, lanky and frivolous. His hair was his best feature, thick and bleached with sunlight, but it was never properly cut and he wore it far too long, through laziness rather than vanity, she was sure. She smiled to herself at the picture created in her mind. He seldom visited the garden now and the creak of the opening garden gate was no longer associated with his arrival and the leap of pleasure in her heart.

She left the barrow on the circular path beside the bed she was going to plant and did her rounds, the quiet of her surroundings restoring tranquillity to her mind. She was thankful to see that the overnight storm had not wreaked much damage. A branch had been broken off the apple tree, and the resultant wound would require attention, but there was still little growth. A tramping round the neck of the winter caulies and a resetting of some stakes in the herbaceous border was all that was needed to restore order.

Callum had dug over and prepared the ground in the raised bed at the centre of the garden and she surveyed the rich black earth with a sense of both excitement and trepidation as she put on her gloves. She had worked out a plan in her head and could see the end result in her mind's eye but it would be weeks before she knew if she had chosen her plants well.

She laid a piece of old sacking on the soil and climbed up over the low whinstone dyke, which was softened with trailing, variegated ivy. Once started, her concentration was absolute. She didn't hear Willie and Callum coming into the garden, despite the gate's chronic creak.

"My goodness, Callum, you startled me!" she exclaimed, rocking back on her heels. "Mr Kylison." She nodded a greeting to Willie as she wriggled down from her perch and straightened up. He was looking round the garden with curious eyes and she wondered if Rupert had arranged for him to visit and had forgotten to tell her.

Callum cleared his throat. "Mrs Treatham, I'm afraid there's been an accident … a fatal accident like …"

Hanna gasped. Her legs gave way and she slumped down on the earth-spattered wall, dropping a plant from her trowel.

Callum was immediately apologetic. "No, no, it's not the boss. He's fine … as far as I can tell, of course." Callum was always canny in his speech. "It's a Mr Yearts who's dead."

Hanna gasped. "Mr Yearts! Are you sure?"
"Aye, I'm sure."

She stood up and brushed the soil off her apron, taking a moment to regain her composure. "He was unwell at breakfast time," she told them.

The two men exchanged looks, at a loss to understand what she was talking about.

"Was it an overdose?"

"He has drowned, Mrs Treatham," Willie said, speaking for the first time. "Callum here found his body on the shore beside the house early today and I've just heard that his car has been lifted from the sea down at the causeway."

Hanna glanced from Willie to Callum in bewilderment. "But Lily Yearts said that her husband was in their room."

The men gave that contradiction of the facts a moment's thought. Willie was the first to speak: "She no doubt had her reason," he said without inflection and offered Hanna his support in breaking the news to the widow.

"That's kind of you," she responded automatically, still in shock. "What a dreadful thing to happen." She bent over and lifted up the fallen plant, putting it back in the box and laying the trowel beside it. "If only Rupert were here. He has more experience of this sort of thing than I." She gave the men a look of anguish as she took off her gardening gloves and apron. "But it can't wait until he gets home, can it?"

Willie agreed that it couldn't, stepping off the path and allowing her to lead the way along the cinder path with its edging of upright slates.

"A grand garden you've made here," he said, as he held the creaking gate open for her. "The last time I was this way, you couldn't see the soil for weeds."

Hanna barely acknowledged his praise. She was no longer thinking of her garden but was wondering how she was going to break the news of the tragedy to Lily Yearts. As a couple, they had never seemed very close, but who could tell. At the very least it would be a shock.

She climbed the steps from the garden ahead of Willie and made her way back through the shrubbery to the side of the house, her head bent forward in thought. "I'm not decent like this," she said, turning and indicating her old jeans and gardening boots. "Would you wait for me in the hall, Mr Kylison, while I go up and change?"

Willie nodded and went round to the front of the hotel, while Hanna crossed the stable yard to the back entrance.

When Jean saw Hanna and Willie coming upstairs, she stopped vacuuming the top landing and looked at them with a surprise and curiosity that she made no attempt to hide. She watched Hanna knock on Mrs Yearts' door.

There was no reply.

"She's in," she told Hanna. "She answered her cell phone a while back and hasn't gone out since."

Hanna knocked again and Mrs Yearts opened the door a chink. She looked from Hanna to the tall, authoritative figure beside her, waiting for them to state their business.

"May we come in?" Hanna asked.

Mrs Yearts left the door as it was and returned to her dressing table where she refilled her whisky glass, lifting the bottle and offering drinks all round. These were refused. She saw Hanna looking at the neatly turned-down second bed and was quick to explain.

"He usually puts in an appearance during the morning," she said, making a sweeping gesture and slopping whisky on the carpet. She rubbed it into the pile with her slippered foot.

Hanna looked down at the stain on the carpet and then up at Mrs Yearts momentarily lost for words. She had no idea that Mr Yearts sometimes slept away from the hotel, and the assumption that he would be returning soon did not make her task easier. Besides that, she had expected Mrs Yearts to connect their presence to his absence. That had not happened and she was beginning to wonder if Mrs Yearts was in a fit state to grasp reality. She decided that it would be best to approach the subject obliquely, telling of the car's discovery and recovery, hoping that this would penetrate the drink befuddled brain and get Mrs Yearts to ask questions and voice the obvious tragic outcome herself.

The glazed expression in Mrs Yearts' eyes slowly dissolved as Hanna was speaking. She turned away and put her glass down carefully on the dressing table, flopping down on the stool, her head bent and her arms outstretched.

Hanna let the silence lengthen.

Eventually Mrs Yearts lifted her head. "Thank goodness he managed to save himself," she whispered, looking at Hanna and Willie through the mirror as she reached for her whisky glass.

Hanna had not expected her to jump to that conclusion.

"The car was empty …," she began, but before she got any further, Mrs Yearts had knocked over the whisky glass and rushed through to the bathroom, covering her mouth with her hand. They heard her being sick, followed by the sound of a running tap and splashing water. She came back with a mumbled apology.

"Where is he then?" she asked, mopping her face with a hand towel; damp hair clung to her forehead. "Why has he not come back to the hotel?" She looked from one to the other and, seeing the expression on their faces, gasped: "He is dead? Is that what you're saying now?"

Hanna nodded and Mrs Yearts turned on her, her face contorted and her voice shaking. "Why did you yatter on and on about his car when you knew he was dead. As if I cared about the car. It's his car not mine. You can have it if it means so much to you."

Hanna was shocked. She had braced herself to offer comfort in distress, but instead she was being blamed and abused.

Willie took charge, telling Mrs Yearts the details surrounding the discovery of her husband's body and offering to escort her to the back quarters where the body had been placed until the ambulance and police arrived.

They waited for her response but when it came, it was not what they had expected.

"I can see him lying in his grave with the water shimmering over him," she said in a dreamy voice, turning away and lying down on her bed.

"As I was saying …"

"With the steering wheel piercing his heart."

"No, nothing like that. He managed to get out of his car."

"Mumma," she whispered. "It wasn't father." She curled her legs up into the foetal position, her head resting on her pillow and her left arm shielding her face. "And a wish is not enough."

"Would you like me to contact your mother?" Hanna asked. "Perhaps she could come up to be with you."

"Mumma is dead."

In bewilderment, Hanna looked to Willie for guidance, but he had said his piece and was moving towards the door. He held it open for her. Hanna repeated her willingness to help but she only received a dismissive wave.

On their way downstairs, Willie tried to lessen her distress by relating the many strange responses that he had had to bad news over the years.

Hanna listened but she did not think that a flash of anger followed by a retreat from reality was in any way normal. She wished that Rupert had been there. He would have managed it better.

"Perhaps I should get Ursula to come in."

"I would leave her to sleep it off and then see."

At the front door, Willie took his leave, saying that he would telephone round and be back later when the causeway was clear. He assured Hanna that she had done a difficult job well.

"The drink is not conducive to rational thought," he finished, putting on his hat.

6

Kneading dough with the heel of her hand, folding, turning and repeating the process, was a soothing task at the end of a stressful day. The loaf was ready for its tin but Jill went on with the kneading. She was thinking of the man at the causeway who had lent them his cell phone. She would have liked to speak to him again but he had left the headland as soon as the car was raised and was already far along the cliff path when she looked for him.

"We'll have him up for drinks tomorrow," she said to Ronald who had come into the kitchen looking for his slippers.

Ronald stopped in his tracks and turned to her in bewilderment. "Who?"

"The man from the hotel. The one who lent us his carry phone."

"Those south country folk like to keep themselves to themselves."

"I could ask Ria. Perhaps Nora Mac."

"God forbid."

"Well, Daphne then." Jill shaped her loaf in its tin, covered it and put it on the side of the Aga to prove. "I'll ring the hotel and see." She wiped her hands clear of flour and poured herself a soothing cup of tea before dialling.

Mr Bartini was not in but she left a message and he returned her call in the early evening. When the phone rang, Christina, the Jimson's teenage daughter, leapt down the stairs, a landing at a time, shouting that she would get it. She slid into the kitchen and lifted the receiver off the wall with an eager breathless enquiry, full of excited anticipation. This instantly changed to huffy coldness when the caller asked for her mother. She shouted through and dropped the phone, letting it swing on its flex.

Mr Bartini was a bit put out by Christina's rapid change of tone and introduced himself to Jill tentatively, but when Jill heard who was speaking and that he would be delighted to come to her drinks' party, she put him at his ease, smiling and gushing with pleasure.

Christina listened to her mother's cooing, making imitating faces as she flounced around the kitchen, banging drawers open and shut, and generally showing that life at Greybarns was not worth living.

"I'll ask Aunt Ria to bring Yvonne across and you can listen to your tapes," Jill coaxed when she had finished the call.

"Yvonne is years younger than me," Christina responded sulkily.

Jill forbore from pointing out that Yvonne Strachan was just a year younger. "But you like her?"

"I suppose so."

"That's settled then. You can tell me what you would like to have and I will make everything special for you."

Christina mumbled something, which her mother took to be agreement, and returned to her room with enough food and drink to see her through the night.

Greybarns was to the south-east of Trowsay House with the farm of Shaws bordering it to the south and the hotel's rough heather land encroaching from the north. The house had been built on rising land, giving good sight of grazing cattle in the fields below. It was also in an ideal position to get prior warning of visitors' arrival.

"Daphne is nearly here," Jill called, crossing the landing from her bedroom and shaking her head to make her earrings jangle. She came carefully down the stairs in her high heels, looking over the banister. Ronald was sitting at his desk in an alcove between the stairs and the kitchen passage.

"She's always early," he complained, taking off his spectacles and laying them down on the open page of his farm accounts. "Another ten minutes and I would've been done."

They could hear Daphne's car approaching but she was a slow, careful driver, changing right down to the lowest gear before taking the last incline to the gates. She smiled and nodded a greeting when she saw them standing on the doorstep, but she didn't take her hands off the steering wheel until she had swung neatly round the turning circle and come to a stop. She climbed out and gently pushed the door firmly into place.

"What a beautiful day," she called, walking with dainty steps across the gravel towards them, her long skirt falling unevenly from non-existent hips. She had won a beauty contest in her youth but she was now a shadow of her former self. In fact she had become so thin that the belt of her jacket circled her waist twice and still left a flap at the back to tuck in.

Ronald pointed out that the day was changeable, indicating the rain clouds hanging threateningly over the sea. "You've inherited your family's optimism," he added, putting an arm around her shoulders and giving her a squeeze.

"Better than gloomy pessimism," Daphne retorted with spirit, patting her tightly-set hair to make sure that it had stayed in its spray-starched condition.

"Quite right," Jill agreed. She linked her arm through Daphne's and guided her towards the front door. "Don't mind him."

Daphne said she never did, adding in a stage whisper, "he must have his little bit of fun." Ronald was a cousin of sorts and a generation back Daphne's father had sold Greybarns a bull that was all but sterile. The feud that had raged between the two families then had passed, but Ronald could still be tempted into a remindful dig.

"Come on in," Jill invited when they reached the shallow steps leading up to the front door, but Daphne was in no hurry to go inside. She had spotted Jill's display of miniature tulips on either side of the steps and was redirecting her enthusiasm. They were still outside exchanging gardening anecdotes when the Strachans drove up with John Bartini sitting on the back seat beside Yvonne.

Ria Strachan unwrapped her long legs and slid out.

"Wasn't it fortunate that we saw your guest near the bottom field," she said in her low, husky voice, lifting her silky-black hair over her shoulder and putting up her cheek for Ronald to kiss.

The fact that Mr Bartini had had to walk from the hotel put Jill into a fluster.

"I didn't think to ask if you had a car. We would've come down and collected you had we known, wouldn't we Ronald?" She shook hands with a protesting John

Bartini and introduced him to Daphne, who was quick to establish her connection with the hotel.

When that conversation had run its course, Ronald shepherded the men towards the back of the house saying: "We'll just take a look at the fields first."

"Don't be too long," Jill called, following the others up the steps.

Ronald lifted a hand without breaking step, but their guest stopped and turned to give her a small bow.

"Indeed not," he said with a gallant smile.

In the porch, Ria swung off her loose wrap and folded it over her arm. "Where did you find him?" she asked Jill with amused curiosity.

Jill told her about the borrowed cell phone as they walked through the house to the conservatory, elaborating on the awful fear in her heart before the car was lifted. Daphne added her recollections of the tragedy, while Jill poured the drinks and handed them round.

"I didn't know anything about it until later," Ria said regretfully as she made a choice from the variety of homemade nibbles offered.

Daphne took a tiny morsel from the plate and changed the subject.

"I love your choice of plants, Jill," she flattered. "So cool and relaxing,"

On the shelf below the glass and rising from the floor on all sides, were pots of leafy plants in a wide variety of shades and foliage, interspersed with bowls of flowering bulbs.

"The narcissi are a bit whiffy," Ria murmured.

"Are they annoying you?" Jill asked, and fussed about moving the bowl outside. She opened the conservatory door, her loose floral dress catching the draught and billowing into a tent as she reached down to set it on the patio.

Ria turned to Daphne: "What's the gossip?" she asked. "Things must be buzzing down at the hotel."

Daphne took a sip of her diet coke and put her glass down, making herself comfortable against the cushions. "Where would you like me to start?"

"Did the widow really say that her husband was upstairs in bed when he was already dead and lying on the shore?"

"It sounds extraordinary," Jill said, rearranging the plants to fill the space on the slate shelf.

"Not so extraordinary. You see he had gone off in a huff the evening before and she hoped he would be back before he was missed."

"Off on the randan?" Ria asked with a laugh.

Daphne pursed her mouth at the bluntness of Ria's speech and spoke to Jill: "He sometimes went off on his own."

"For the night?"

"He was on his way back, remember."

The telephone started to ring, a distant but insistent sound. Jill ignored it. She knew that Ronald's "look at the fields" was only an excuse for the men to have their first drink in the kitchen and that he would answer it.

"Go on, Daphne," Ria urged when the ringing stopped. "What else?"

Daphne dabbed her savoury on the plate picking up the crumbs while she collected her thoughts. Jean had not actually seen or heard what had gone on in Mrs Yearts' bedroom but her imagination could fill in the gaps.

"Willie Kylison broke the news," she said. "He has experience of that sort of thing, you know."

"Didn't she have any friends staying at the hotel?" Jill asked.

"If she did, they weren't in. There was only Hanna there to give comfort."

Ria said languidly: "I almost feel sorry for the 'oh-so-perfect' Hanna" She lifted the plate of appetisers from the table beside her and offered it to Daphne.

Daphne shook her head. She was a vegan and ate little more than flavoured lettuce leaves. "Mrs Yearts was quite out of her mind with grief."

"In what way?"

"Don't be obtuse, Ria," Jill remonstrated. "The woman was bound to be devastated, especially as they had had a row. How would you …"

She was interrupted by a hesitant voice speaking from the doorway.

"Hello. Anyone at home?"

They turned to see John Bartini looking round the glass.

Jill was at once the hostess, inviting him in as she wriggled forward in her chair and pushed herself up-right with the help of the armrest.

"Come and sit by me," Ria invited, patting the place beside her on the couch.

"Delighted, of course," Mr Bartini murmured with a small bow, looking to Jill for agreement.

"Yes, you sit there."

Jill plumped up the scatter cushion and smoothed the surface of the seat cover, while Mr Bartini exclaimed on the country view and the luscious surroundings. By the time the other two men came in, he was comfortably ensconced.

"I poured your drink through by, John," Ronald said, handing over a well-filled glass with a questioning lift to his eyebrows. He was clearly surprised to find that their guest had joined the ladies prematurely.

Mr Bartini took the glass and toasted the company, smiling serenely, unaware of his faux pas. The colour of the golden liquid revealed the whisky's strength and he sipped warily, but he was tempted by the smoothness on his tongue to drink more deeply. The resultant mellow glow radiating from his throat and warming his blood was having a tranquillising effect until Ria hit him with the full force of her magnetic personality.

"Now tell me, Mr Bartini … John," her voice became huskier as she used his first name, "what brought you to Trowsay?"

He was stunned into a shocked silence.

Jill came to his rescue. "Mr Bartini is a birdwatcher," she said in a reassuringly normal voice, remembering the long-lens camera and the binoculars that he was carrying down at the causeway. "Tell me, have you seen our puffins?"

He came out of his trance. "Delightful."

"And did you hear the tittering call of the whimbrels?" Daphne asked.

He thought he had.

"Twitchers like coming to Trowsay," Jill said cosily. "We have such a wide variety of seabirds nesting on our cliffs."

"Indeed you have."

"Sometimes there are rare and unforgettable sightings."

"Excuse me."

"Migrating birds losing their way and fluttering down here."

"It's not the right time of year for that, Jill."

Mr Bartini looked from Daphne to Jill with a set smile but did not take the opportunity to elaborate on a hobby that was usually an addiction. Jill began to wonder if she had been correct in assuming that he was a birdwatcher.

"There are so many other things to do, besides bird-watching," she said, offering the plate of nibbles. "As long as you've enjoyed your holiday. That's the main thing."

Mr Bartini put his glass carefully down on the table beside him and accepted a savoury. "Your beautiful island is quite delightful," he said in an unexpectedly sombre tone, "but my visit has been marred by events. I do not wish to speak of death at your delightful party, Mrs Jimson, but finding oneself close to tragedy and grief does not create a happy atmosphere."

There were sympathetic murmurs of agreement.

Ria looked at Donnie with raised eyebrows. He shook his head imperceptibly but it did not restrain her from saying: "What if it was not an accident?"

For a fraction of a second the stillness in the room was palpable; it was as though everyone was taking part in a tableau. Lips stopped supping, jaws stopped chewing and hand muscles froze in suspended action.

"According to Davey it was not."

"What has Davey been saying now?" Daphne asked, recovering from her surprise, "He told the police he was all tucked up in bed by ten o'clock."

Ronald's ruddy face glowed with amusement. "I must say that sounded unlikely."

Donnie agreed. "He was certainly telling my brother a different story this morning."

"You'll have heard that Alf's on the prowl again," Ria interrupted. "An older woman over on the mainland who won't stand any nonsense. She puts him out first thing."

"Like the cat," Jill said with a smile.

"Precisely."

Mr Bartini joined in the laughter with polite bewilderment.

"So what was Alf saying?" Daphne asked, leaning forward eagerly.

"He said that he nearly ran Davey down," Donnie replied, looking round at the curious faces before slowly selecting a savoury from the plate beside him. "Alf was in a hurry to get home and didn't want to stop at the causeway but Davey stepped right out in front of him waving frantically and Heidi barked and bit at his tyres, so he had to brake. No doubt he let fly some choice words."

"But what about the accident?"

Donnie flipped the savoury into his mouth and chewed, keeping his audience in suspense. "It seems that Davey's conscience was troubling him."

"His conscience!"

"That's what he said. Alf told him to go home and sleep it off, and was letting out the clutch when Davey said that there were weird things going on down at the causeway on Friday night."

Ria interrupted: "Davey wasn't in bed at the crucial time but out on the hill looking for Heidi."

"In that storm?"

Ria shrugged. "You know how besotted he is with the animal, Jill. Anyway when he was climbing the Brawtoon hill whistling for Heidi, he glanced across to the mainland and saw two cars on the slip over there with no lights on and the occupants jumping about like fleas in a market."

"An exaggeration, I think, Ria."

"Well, he saw enough to believe that there was something suspicious going on."

Donnie threw up his hands and let his wife finish.

"Heidi was found – God only knows what she was doing – and on his way back down the hill, Davey saw the lights of the bigger car driving away but the other car had disappeared. He's now sure that it was in the water by then because he has remembered hearing a howl in the wind that made him feel uneasy. A shriek for help he's saying it was, thus the nagging conscience."

Mr Bartini had been following the conversation with close interest. "Who is this man you are speaking about?" he asked.

Ronald gave him a thumbnail sketch of Davey and his lifestyle.

"It would upset the widow very much to hear such suspicions."

"Relax, John. Davey has just peppered things up for effect."

Jill reminded Ronald that Davey had said the day before that the car belonged to a tourist.

"I thought he was only trying to comfort you."

"I thought so too."

"So he did see cars over there after the tide was in!" Ria exclaimed in triumph.

"But he has added a lot more to it since yesterday."

"Perhaps it was all lying deep in his subconscious and only surfaced during the night, thus the agitation."

Ronald got to his feet, offering to refill glasses. "I can think of at least one reason for Davey being agitated the morning after the Saturday night before."

Donnie agreed. "His home brew is lethal stuff."

Jill said placidly: "He probably was hung over but, in truth, he is just a lonely old man who likes to enliven his life with storytelling." She reminded them of the time when his boulder was moved from the bank down on to the shore to make room for the new shelter. "He saw the ghost of his lost love lying in the crater where the boulder had lodged since time immemorial."

Daphne smiled. "Wasn't that the place where he nearly died of exposure when he was a young man?"

"Curled up with his ethereal sweetheart in his arms, so the story goes."

Ria was not interested in something that had happened long before she came to Trowsay. "How droll," she said languidly, "but such an anticlimax. It would be much more fun if Davey had really seen something sinister on Friday night." She held out her glass to be refilled with an unsteady hand. "Perhaps the little people were out and about, wreaking their vengeance for some fiendish reason or another."

Ronald took her empty glass with a smile. "Wreaking it on Davey as he was lying asleep in his caravan or on the poor unfortunate tourist?" he asked, reducing the quantity of gin and upping the tonic.

"Take your pick." Ria waved her hand languidly. "The trows are meant to have inordinate strength, aren't they? They could have lifted the car and deposited it in the middle of the bay if they'd a mind to."

Talk of the trows, or trolls, reminded Daphne of Thorfinn Dukes' seduction tactics. His outrageous behaviour was always an absorbing topic of conversation so Davey and his writhing conscience were soon forgotten.

Mr Bartini listened to the conversation, nodding his head from time to time. His whisky glass was refilled and he relaxed against the cushions, responding to enquiries about his work and lifestyle in a vague sort of way. Their lives were far more fascinating than his, he assured them, which encouraged the telling of further colourful anecdotes. When a suitable time was reached, he looked at his watch and exclaimed in amazement. He was devastated at having to leave the delightful party but he had a prior engagement, and with apologies and compliments all round, he shook hands with the ladies, acknowledged the men with a bow, and moved toward the door with his host and hostess.

Upstairs the two girls lay on Christina's bed in contentment. They were smoking purloined cigarettes, spiked with cannabis that Yvonne had scraped off a lump of resin found in her brother's room. The blood in their veins throbbed deliciously as they listened to the screech of their favourite pop singer, fighting to be heard above the repetitive rhythm of guitar and drums.

The heavy cumulus clouds had moved steadily from sea to shore and by early afternoon the rain was tapping on the glass roof of the conservatory. Ronald knew that his Friesians would be standing around in churned up mud, looking up the road for him with gentle, patient eyes. He needed to change and get across to the upper field to open the gate so that they could plod homewards, their heads pulled low by the weight of milk they were carrying.

Donnie no longer had dairy cattle (for which he was thankful) but he knew the mid-afternoon signs. He moved forward in his chair, gripping the arms.

"Come on Ria, it's time we were on our way."

Daphne immediately sprang up, apologising for overstaying her welcome.

Jill assured her that she had not done so.

"Time flies when one is enjoying oneself," Daphne went on, looking for her handbag and then remembering that she had left it in her car. "Could I perhaps...."

Jill showed her to the bathroom and by the time they reached the front porch, Ronald was holding her jacket with a smile of resignation. Daphne tied it round and accepted the shelter of his umbrella as far as her car.

Inside the house, Ria called up the stairs: "Yvonne, we're going."

There was a muffled response, which sounded like, "Coming", and Ria returned to the conservatory to collect the glasses and plates.

Jill offered a cup of tea but this was refused.

"Just let us collect our bits and pieces together," Ria said, calling to Yvonne again and going to find her wrap.

In the kitchen, Donnie put his arm round Jill's soft and ample waist, giving her a friendly squeeze and a

smacking kiss. She had been his girlfriend at the local primary school but their young love had waned in
adolescence.

"Now, now, you two," Ria said, coming back. "What
do you think they're doing up there, Donnie?

"Better not ask." He released Jill and went through to
the hall to give a parental bellow. Christina's bedroom
door opened, releasing a cacophony of mindless sound,
and the girls came down the stairs, two at a time, full of
beans. They were reeking of cigarette smoke. Donnie
and Ria cast their eyes heavenward. They were more
upbeat than the Jimsons, considering rebellion against
authority normal at the girls' age. Jill was less sanguine,
and when the Strachans had left, she lectured Christina
about the evils of smoking.

Christina went all sulky, saying that her mother
was trying to drive her out of the house. She knew
well that that was the last thing her mother wanted
to do.

Ronald was wet to the skin when he came in from
the byre. He stood in the doorway of the kitchen in his
stocking soles, shaking himself like a dog, his hair and
shoulders dripping rain.

"You should have put on a coat," Jill said in reproach,
getting up and laying her tapestry on the armrest. She
took a hot towel from the rail in front of the Aga and
handed it to him.

"That cow's mastitis is no better," he told her, shivering as he wiped his face. "I'd best get the vet in the
morning." He rubbed his hair, tangling the strands into
dishevelled spikes.

"Who was on the phone earlier?" Jill asked, sitting down and lifting up her tapestry.

"The police. They wanted to know the name of Sweyn's fishing boat"

"Whatever for?"

"Nothing to worry about, love. They just wondered if he had seen the Ferrari on Friday night."

"But he was driving in the opposite direction."

"Only a routine enquiry, no doubt." He folded the towel and put it back on the rail. "I'm sure Sweyn won't be able to tell them anything anyway."

But Sweyn was able to tell them quite a lot. He had passed the Ferrari about a mile from the turn-off to Talhaugh; it was travelling at speed and on a steady path.

More significantly, he could swear that there was someone sitting in the passenger seat.

7

Davey opened his caravan door to let Heidi out and stood there rolling and smoking his first cigarette of the day. He could see one or two cars moving along the coast road opposite and recognised a few. It was workers rather than tourists who were on the move at that time of day. A mist of low cloud was touching the sea to the east, but there was no rain or chill in the wind to keep him indoors. He flicked the butt of his cigarette away to join the many lying round his door in various stages of disintegration, and went inside to make his breakfast. The porridge pot was in the sink from the day before and he gave it a clean round. He liked a pot of porridge for his breakfast, with a dollop of cream to give the newfangled milk a bit of colour and taste.

It was Patsy's day for coming round and seeing to his cleaning so he needed to tidy up a bit before then; that way there was less complaining. He took his over-flowing ashtrays to the bin outside while his porridge sucked and exploded steam, thickening nicely, and he managed to get some of his empty beer bottles washed and put away for next time. There was always a batch of home brewed beer maturing in a cupboard and another gently bubbling away in a corner.

He didn't take long to eat his breakfast and finish his minimal chores and he was sitting at his open door reading his newspaper when Patsy Gunn's car started up his track. He had been hearing it from some way off but waited until she slowed for the turning before laying his paper aside and taking off his glasses.

"Has that lazy good-for-nothing not seen to your exhaust yet, Patsy?" was his greeting on going to meet her. Les Gunn had been taken on at the garage in Talhaugh during a government work scheme. The job hadn't lasted but Les had acquired a useful skill to stretch his unemployment benefit.

Patsy did not take offence. She had called her husband worse herself.

"He's getting round to it," she said, lifting up Davey's clean laundry from her front seat. She headed for the caravan at a brisk pace, leaving Davey to walk round the car and peer underneath it. She fitted Davey in between her care work at the Manse and cleaning for the two men up at Atlanticscape.

"It's needing more than a repair job now," Davey said gloomily, coming to the caravan door and watching Patsy work.

"No doubt." She opened the door under the sink to dispose of some mouldy food and saw the scraps of an official letter on the top of an overflowing refuse pail. "They'll be after you one of these days, Granddad. It doesn't pay not to answer their letters."

Davey loosened the top set of his teeth and let them fall on to the lower set. He worked them about a bit, making a gnashing sound, which was an adequate reply. Patsy didn't let it drop. She kept at him, even when she was round the other side of the caravan depositing the contents of the pail in his bin. Davey surveyed the scenery and let her have her say.

His ramshackle half-blocked-in caravan was beside one of the island's prettiest beaches and in a prominent position about a hundred yards east of the causeway.

Over the years Davey had collected together all sorts of old junk that he thought he might have a use for one day. This clutter lay round and about with grass growing through it. His son Scott wasn't complaining and it was his land now, but a man in a suit had been snooping around. After he'd gone, his sidekick had come knocking, saying that Davey's caravan wasn't fit for human habitation. Davey had been flabbergasted. He had stood there at his caravan door with the blood rising through the network of veins in his face, erupting into a patchwork of puce. On regaining the use of his vocal chords, he had given the slanderer short shrift and sent him packing, cursing the police for taking away his shotgun. The letter in the bin had been the last of a series he had received. All had been torn up and appropriately filed.

Patsy was at the brushing now. "What's this I've been hearing about you witnessing a murder on Friday night?"

Davey pushed himself away from the jamb of the door and turned to Patsy with his mouth hanging open.

"Didn't you see the man from the hotel being bludgeoned to death and his car pushed down the hill and into the water?" Patsy asked, turning away to hide her smile.

Davey bellowed in outrage. "I've never heard the like! That Alf Strachan's been taking liberties with me story." He started creating such a hoo-ha it was as though one of Scott's bees had stung him in a sensitive place.

Patsy went on with her brushing while Davey told her his version of events. Now that others had given his story

an exciting slant, he needed to add one or two embellish-
ments to brighten the dullness of truth and reinstate himself in the unassailable position as sole witness.

"If I didna see the man being bashed about and his
car sent rolling, no one else did," he finished. "I'm no
saying, mind, that that couldna have happened. The
way the men o'er there were shouting and menacing
each other, it could've been a fight to the death. In
fact it was an embarrassment for me to see grown men
behaving like that."

"How many men would that be, Granddad?"

"There were three for sure, maybe four."

Patsy pulled her long brush out from underneath
Davey's bunk and collected the accumulated debris into
her dustpan. She lifted the dustpan to empty it into the
pail and stopped. A small plastic envelope, covered with
fluff and dust, had caught her attention. She lifted it up
and shook off the clinging sweepings, staring down at
the mottled yellow pill visible through the dirty plastic
surface.

"What's this?" she asked, turning to Davey in question.

He had gone.

She went to the door and called after him but he
paid no heed. He continued on his way, with Heidi
dancing round him. When he got to the causeway, he
sat down on his boulder with relief. He would still get
a nagging when Patsy came the following Monday, but
she needed something to keep her tongue moving and
if it wasn't that it would be something else.

He felt foolish rather than guilty about his sojourn
into drugs or, to be precise, drug in the singular. (If

illicit drug it had been.) He had found the small plastic packet in an ashtray over in the pub at Talhaugh and had pocketed it to think about later. He'd licked one of the pills a bit to see if there were any ill effects but it didn't put him up or down so he'd swallowed the licked one, with dire results. He'd had a nightmare to end all nightmares and his heart had beaten against his ribcage like a hammer on an anvil. To crown it all, he'd been left with a dose of the skitters. Patsy could throw the other one out and good riddance to it.

He started rolling a cigarette. There wasn't much moving. Two strange cars came over from Talhaugh but they didn't stop. The driver of one was so taken up with turning his steering wheel this way and that to find the most even surface for the wheels of his shiny new car, he didn't even notice Davey hanging about. The occupants of the second car gave him a smile but weren't looking for a conversation. The passenger had a map spread out over her knee and was talking to the driver, planning their route. If they had stopped, he could have put them in the picture nicely. Sarah Mac came back from her weekend duty and gave him a wave, and ten minutes later Bill Steed crossed over on his way to Brawtoon to visit Alan.

Davey lowered his eyes until the car drew level and then gave a sideways glance to see if there was any acknowledgement of his presence, but the chiselled profile was as hard as ever and the stony eyes stared straight ahead. If Davey ever let his shame slip from his memory, the Steed family was always around to remind him. It would be fifty years or more since he'd left Betsy Steed to face the music. A gye long time by any count and the disgrace of Scott being born out of wedlock was long since forgotten. Besides Betsy had done better for herself by taking his brother Alan – Alan had the farm. "And I paid for my sin twice over," he mumbled to himself. "There's no need for Bill Steed to be so ill-tempered." He lifted Heidi up and held her close, taking comfort from her warmth and devotion. "I wasna welcome at Brawtoon efter the war, Heidi, and there was nobody caring about me or wanting to fetch me home from the asylum. I'd be there yet if the place hadna closed. Aye, that I would."

After a pause for reflection on these half-forgotten years away, he lifted his well-licked hand and said gently: "Enough now, lass."

He vaguely remembered Betsy's letters coming thick and fast to the place where he was stationed at the start of the war, begging one minute and accusing the next, tormenting him with guilt. Now he couldn't even recall the high jinks they'd got up to in the accommodating hay over at Matlock. No doubt she'd been a willing lass and a bonnie one too, if the photograph Alan had on the mantelshelf in the best room was anything to go by, but her young face was the face of a stranger. All he could remember of her was the crabbit wife she'd become when they sent him home. She was always complaining about his argumentative nature and personal habits, not like his sweet-tempered Anna.

He was musing about his Anna, muddling the two relationships in his head, when he felt a spot of rain. He shielded his cigarette paper and looked up at the grey sky wondering if he should seek cover in the shelter.

But it didn't come to anything. It was just a few drops squeezed out of a heavy cloud in passing.

Ria Strachan stopped on her way over to Tongue and rolled down her window. She always went over on a Monday and came back in a couple of hours with her hair all fancy like. Davey got up from his boulder to lean on the roof of her car and pass the time of day, but he found that she wasn't just stopping to be friendly, she wanted to hear more about his outing on the hill on Friday night. He clamped his mouth shut and pulled away, showing that he was not willing to feed the curiosity of another member of the Strachan family.

He sat back down and watched her make the crossing, feeling a bit out of sorts. The day wasn't going well. His gloomy mood wasn't helped when a police car came over the brow of the hill opposite. He was not one to push himself forward when the police were about and so retreated into the shelter, finding a seat in the shadows. Heidi slunk along behind him, jumping on to his lap.

The minutes ticked by but there was no sign of the police. No doubt Ria Strachan was talking to them, putting herself in the limelight as usual. She'd have two of them to impress, that was for sure; they always moved around in pairs to keep an eye on each other.

He couldn't see the causeway from where he was sitting and eased himself further along the bench to have a better view, clutching Heidi to him. He ducked down when the police car started to move and, in his crouched position, listened to the low throb of its engine as it slowly made the crossing and glided to a stop.

He peered over the window ledge. The distinctive car was right below him. Five minutes passed and it still sat there. Davey strained to hear what was being said but he couldn't hear or see anything clearly. There was just the confused sound of a radio telephone. Eventually the car door opened and two constables got out, a man and a woman. They came up the steps and opened the door of the shelter.

"Davey Petersen?"

Davey looked at the woman through his rheumy eyes and thought about it. "Aye."

"Of The Caravan, Brawtoon?"

Admitting his address was going too far. Davey waited.

"I take it that's right?" the woman said and the man, who was local and whom Davey knew from past encounters, went on: "I hear you've been changing the evidence you gave me on Saturday evening, Davey."

Davey went on scratching beneath Heidi's floppy ear. "It wasna a right time to be calling."

The constable didn't show any exasperation. He was used to the sort of wariness that Davey was showing. "Did you say to me at that time: "I wasn't well enough to be out on a wild night like that. I was in my bed by ten o'clock. I saw and heard nothing."

Davey reran the words in his head to make sure he wasn't committing himself to anything he might regret. "If I said that, that's what I said."

"But you were not telling the truth, Davey."

"What night would this be that you're on about?"

"Friday night. The night that a man drowned here at the causeway."

"Ah, that night." Davey shifted Heidi into a more comfortable position on his knee and concentrated on the wall opposite. The police waited, their gaze unwavering, but they soon realised that the movement of Davey's teeth behind his tightly shut mouth was not in preparation for speech. A more direct approach was needed.

"Were you out on the hill with your dog around eleven on Friday night, Davey?"

"It was a stormy night, I remember that."

"So you were out on the hill late that night?"

"My caravan always rattles a-piece when the wind is wild."

The constable shut his notebook and turned to his woman colleague: "I think we'll have to take him in for questioning."

Davey went all still and then jumped up, spilling Heidi on to the floor. "I've never heard the like o it," he spluttered. "Harassment, that's what it is. It's nowt but a police state we're living in wi talk of throwing an old man and his dog into a cell for minding their own business."

The police listened to Davey's histrionics unemotionally. The woman said: "I must warn you, Davey, that it's an offence to give the police false information and obstruct them in the course of their duty."

"I'm doing no obstructing," Davey said, thrusting his head forward to get nearer to his tormentors without moving. "I'm sitting here all quiet like wi me dog. See! She's gone all a-quiver wi your aggressive questioning." He straightened up as a thought occurred to him, a thought that was stimulated by many idle hours spent in front of the television set. "It's Luke Sinclair we're needing out here. Aye, I'll be getting him to come from the town and spell out me civil rights. That would put a stop to your intimidation."

This was greeted with a thin smile. "Mr Sinclair would tell you to answer our questions truthfully."

When this advice drew no response, the constables called it a day, the man warning Davey again about wilful obstruction and the woman saying that they would be back to take him in for questioning, if it was thought necessary.

Davey waited where he was for the police car to turn and go back across the causeway, but instead of leaving the island, it continued up the road. Heidi was lying heavily against his legs and he stooped to lift her up. He held her against his chest and spoke words of reassurance as he watched the police car out of sight.

He wondered who they were after now.

8

Most of Trowsay's gossip was filtered through Cissie Vale at the shop so it was natural for her to be interested when she saw the police car taking the turning to Lowacres.

She went out to speak to Ted.

"Is that Willie Kylison's order of cement in the store?" she asked, looking up at him on his ladder. He had given the stonework a fresh lick of cream paint the week before and was now meticulously over-painting the sign in bold red: 'Edward and Cecilia Vale – Licensed Grocers'.

He said it was.

"Right you are. I'll give him a ring this afternoon to say it's here." The fact that Sweyn had seen a passenger in the Ferrari on the night of the accident had given Davey's story a boost and with Willie's order waiting to be collected, she had a reason to give him a call and see what the police were after.

As it happened, Cissie did not need to telephone Lowacres because Willie came in to post a parcel. The shop was empty except for Thorfinn who was poking around in the grocery shelves. He always took a long time picking out the same basic foodstuffs and Cissie knew why. He liked to listen to her private conversations.

"Have you got all you need now, Thorfinn?" she asked pointedly, staying behind the shop counter instead of moving round to the Post Office cage to serve Willie who was not a patient man.

"Not yet, Mrs Vale," Thorfinn replied, absorbing Cissie's glare without flinching. "There are still a few things on my list."

Cissie closed the till with a bang and moved round the counter with her slow rolling gait. She was little more than five feet tall and had widened rather than wizened with the years.

"Good afternoon, Willie," she said with an ingratiating smile, taking his parcel and noting the address. "You must miss your daughters with them living so far away. They'll be in their late teens by now, I'm thinking?"

"Nineteen and twenty," Willie said grudgingly, not at all inclined to share his family business.

"Just at the right age to travel before settling down," Cissie said, laboriously nipping the stamps out singly from different sheets to keep Willie talking as long as possible. "D'you think we'll be seeing them over here soon."

"I doubt it," Willie said without emotion. (His ex-wife had remarried and gone to New Zealand.)

The parcel was stamped and Cissie could not delay asking for the money. As she did so, she introduced the subject at the forefront of her mind.

"I hear you kept them right over at the house when the body was found, Willie. The Treathams must've been right glad to have a man of your experience in the neighbourhood."

Willie gathered up the notes and coins that she had given in change and said not a word.

Seeing the way things were, Cissie came to the point: "We were just saying that there could be wheels within wheels as far as that accident is concerned. Did you know, Willie, that there's a man with an Italian name living at the hotel who's been behaving strangely? He was in here on Saturday and he never looked me in the eye when I asked him about the death. In fact I could hardly get a word out of him."

Willie pocketed his loose change and took out his wallet, looking down on the postmistress with an unreadable, unblinking stare.

Cissie was not put off by his intimidating manner. She had known Willie since the days when he had had a snotty nose and holes in the seat of his short pants.

"You'll have heard that Sweyn Jimson saw a stranger in that sports car and the drowned man had no friends in these parts to go drinking with."

Willie still acted the clam.

"It must've been someone from the hotel and that someone could only be the Italian; the other men have wives."

"So is that what the talk is today?" Willie asked, his lips smiling without humour. He put his wallet back in his pocket. "You can tell your lady friends, Cissie, that there is no mystery. It was Darren Shand he had in his car."

"From the garage over by?"

Willie was clearly enjoying Cissie's astonishment.

"He was met in town and given leave to drive that ostentatious car to his road end."

"But Sweyn knows Darren fine. Why didn't he say?"

"No doubt the cars passed each other in a flash, both exceeding the speed limit."

Willie turned away and went across to the freezer to get something for his supper. "The man with the

Italian name, as you call him, never left the hotel that night."

He selected and paid for his meagre purchases, departing with a curt farewell to Cissie and a nod to Thorfinn.

When the tinkle of the bell had faded away, Thorfinn came forward with his groceries.

"Don't upset yourself, Mrs Vale," he placated. "I'm sure there are many deaths with a sinister slant if truth were told by all the witnesses."

"I'm upset Thorfinn," Cissie said with renewed energy, "because Willie Kylison virtually accused me of being a gossip which, God forbid, I certainly am not."

Thorfinn gave a wry smile. "You are merely the island's *Mercury*, Mrs Vale, giving us instant access to news that will be in the local rag at the end of the week."

Far from this statement pacifying Cissie, it made her more irate. Thorfinn should have said that she and her friends were not gossips and that Willie Kylison was an insufferable snob who had got too big for his oversized boots.

Thorfinn knew what was expected of him and obliged, but he couldn't resist adding: "As far as I'm concerned, a dollop of knickerbonker gory goes down a treat."

Cissie was not amused. She glared at him, her mouth tightening and stilling a tongue that was aching to put him in his place. Thorfinn saw the internal conflict and did not push his luck. He waited silently, controlling a smile, as Cissie rang up his purchases and sent him on his way, without the courtesy of a farewell word of thanks or a hope that she would see him again soon.

At the shop door Thorfinn stopped and peered between the notices and advertisements stuck on the glass.

"Another customer, Mrs Vale," he announced opening the door with a flourish.

John Bartini sidestepped into the shop, with eyes lowered and many apologies, trying to make himself as inconspicuous as possible.

"We were just talking about you," Thorfinn told him.

This filled Mr Bartini with confusion. "Me?" he asked in bewilderment, nearly dropping the small rucksack he was taking off his back.

"It was the fatal accident we were talking about," Cissie assured him, giving Thorfinn a look fit to kill. "Shut the door behind you, Thorfinn."

"Adios, Mrs Vale. See you soon."

Cissie turned to her customer. "Take no notice of him," she said. "He's not from these parts and hasn't got the feeling that the Trowsay people have for others." Mr Bartini shook his head slowly from side to side at a loss for words. "We are all very upset. It was shocking to have a drowning so close to our island."

"Tragic, very tragic."

"Were you acquainted with the deceased?"

"I did meet him," Mr Bartini said neutrally, fussing about opening his rucksack and laying it on the counter. "May I please have two bottles of your best local whisky?"

"Indeed you may."

Cissie turned and climbed up the steps that were leaning against the back shelving. "It's a grand whisky this one," she said, lifting the bottles down. "I don't imbibe myself but I'm sure it will be to your liking."

Mr Bartini agreed that it was a very fine whisky, adding: "Always an acceptable present to take home." He took two folded notes from his pocket and handed them over before Cissie had time to tot up the cost.

She flattened the notes out and put them down on the counter beside the till while she made the calculation on her notepad. This gave her time to ask after the widow.

"I cannot tell you," was the murmured response which left Cissie wondering if he was keeping something from her.

"Poor lady. I hear that she stays in her room most of the time."

"She is awaiting the arrival of her friend."

"If you see her, please pass on my condolences," Cissie said, passing over his change and watching him pocket the coins.

"Do you know Mrs Yearts?"

"Well, I don't know her as such, but I feel that I know her."

"Ah!"

"Some say that she is drowning her sorrow but I say that it is not for us to judge."

"Indeed not!" Mr Bartini's voice vibrated with shock.

"Well, I never," Cissie said to his back, affronted by the snub.

She watched as he circumvented Ted's ladder, avoiding any bad luck, and waited until he had disappeared up the road, before going out to talk it over with Ted and decide what to make of it all.

9

Lily Yearts sat at her dressing table, her body slumped forward and her forearms resting on the glassed surface. Her streaked, toffee-blonde hair had been combed and teased into loose curls; the make-up above her eyes and over her mouth had been thickly but shakily applied. She smiled to herself, barely aware of the image she had created in her solitude; she was reliving the happy days of her childhood.

I am sitting on the floor in my Mumma's room watching a programme on television called "Bewitched". The witch is making magical things happen with a twitch of her nose. She is blonde and beautiful, just like my Mumma. Mumma can also make magical things happen. She finds a new hair ribbon in my pocket when I lose mine, makes my favourite doll talk to me when I am crying and produces coins from the lapel of my coat when I am eager to buy something.

She smiled at the memory, touching the mirror lightly, the cold surface and the artificial image of herself bringing her back to shocked reality. She reached for cleansing tissues and rubbed at her skin until it was bare and shiny, the harshly smeared tissues rising in a crumpled heap beside her.

Hal had disliked seeing soiled tissues lying about.

She tidied the mess into her bin. She didn't want to be reminded of him … not yet. It was her mother she wanted to hold close in her thoughts.

Mumma waits for me at the school gate. She is not like the other mothers. She dresses differently. She has a flimsy scarf over her head and she wears long skirts and layers of colourful wraps to keep her warm. She floats towards me as I run down the school steps.

She took a mouthful of whisky, letting the tangy liquid rest on her tongue before swallowing. There was only a little left in the bottle and she tipped that into her glass, dropping the empty bottle into the bin.

It is Halloween and we dress up. I am the witch with the broomstick so that I can pretend to fly; Mumma is my cat. We duck for apples and we cover the scones we baked that morning with treacle, hanging them from the pulley in the kitchen. The paint on my face is smeared with water and treacle. We hunt for nature's treasures in the wood and when I am tired we go to the summerhouse, Mumma's secret place. I can feel the softness of the sheepskin rug where I lie playing with the insects we have trapped. The ceiling is dark and starry and there are brightly coloured hangings and astrological charts on the walls. Mumma is brewing up a potion on her little stove, telling me stories as she drops in the different roots and plants that we have collected.

She opened a drawer and took out a small framed photograph of her mother and herself taken around that time. She held it against her heart for a moment before propping it up against the mirror.

Father burns the summerhouse down. I see the brightly moving shadows behind the panes of glass and I hear the flames crackle and spit as they get hotter and higher inside, until suddenly there is a roar upwards of flaming smoke. The branches of the heavy, overhanging trees sparkle and die.

Her glass was empty. She stood up carefully, testing her legs, and walked slowly through to the bathroom for her last bottle of whisky. She lifted it out of her vanity case and unscrewed the top. Her hand was only shaking slightly as she held the glass to its lip. She poured a generous measure, adding a dash of water and drank deeply. She tried to shut out the ever-recurring memory but it still came.

Mumma lies on the road like a gigantic exotic bird; blood trickles from the corner of her mouth and her gaily-coloured scarves fall like broken wings.

The tears started. The drink was not making her feel better. She returned to her dressing table, carrying the bottle and half-filled glass, wiping her cheeks with her raised sleeve.

She put the palms of her hands on her cheekbones and covered her eyes, looking through the darkness within until the white stars began to fade. But it did not relax her thoughts or make her forget.

Hal is sitting on the long couch in Father's study when I carry in the silver drinks' tray. He jumps up and takes the tray from me. He is tall and tanned with wavy black hair. He smiles at me with large, beautiful eyes and I fall in love.

"I want to marry him," I tell Father and it brings on one of his rages. He is out of his chair, bending over me, his hand raised.

She put her head on the cool glass of the dressing table, her hands over her ears, not wanting to hear the sounds inside her head.

"You foolish, stupid girl. Have you no eyes? Don't you see? That man only wants to get a toe in my door and feather his own nest. Do you think I've brought you up to marry the likes of Hal Yearts. A nothing, a less than nothing. You love him? Blah! Just like your mother. No sense at all." He *splutters and changes tack halfway through every sentence, his colour rising until his face is puce. There are raised veins on his forehead.*

The remote control for the television set was beside her and she lifted it up, fiddling with the buttons. The picture appeared without sound and she flicked through the different channels before turning it off.

She got up and walked about restlessly, finishing her whisky and refilling her glass.

Hal lets himself into the kitchen. He is sitting in the easy chair beside the Aga, waiting for me. I wait for Father to close his book and ask me to pour him his nightcap.

He takes the whisky glass from me and lays it on his side table. I am impatient for him to drink up and go to bed so I am watching him when he takes a long drink and chokes. He pulls at his collar, gasping for breath. I cannot touch him. I never touch him. I rush to the kitchen, calling out for Hal.

I can see the shock on Father's face when Hal appears. He is trying to speak but his coughing and choking get worse. Hal loosens his collar and raises him into a sitting position, speaking in a soothing voice. He sends me upstairs for Father's heart pills. I run to the bathroom then to the bed-room, looking everywhere, but I can't find them.

I come down the long curving staircase, with the red-patterned carpet and the warm wooden banister. Hal is at the bottom, his face flushed. He takes me in his arms and I can hear his heart thumping. I do not cry. I sit there looking at Father as the colour fades from his cheeks. Hal takes a flask out of his pocket and offers it to me. It seems strange to be drinking from a flask in the sitting room and I do not think to ask why he is carrying a flask of whisky when he only drinks Brandy.

She lifted up a lipstick and wrote "Fool" on the mir-ror, smearing it away with the back of her hand and rubbing at the oily mess with a tissue.

Hal introduces himself to Dr Smith as a friend of Father.

It isn't true.

He says that he loves me.

It isn't true.

He says that he likes living in the country.

It isn't true.

I know the truth now.

A bird crashed against the window and the thud startled her, breaking into her thoughts. She jumped up, expecting to see the battered remains spread across the window pane, but there was nothing there. She thought about going to see if it had died and fallen on to the narrow balcony but she did not want to know.

I am alone in Mumma's house, my house. I find her new secret place in an attic above the store rooms. It is undisturbed.

She sat down and started fiddling with her hairbrush.

The low-ceilinged room is airless, thick with ragged cobwebs and muddy-grey powdery dust. On the table under the skylight, there is a jumble of papers and an open book, the writing and diagrams faint under the layer of dust, the edges bitten unevenly by rats or mice. I open the skylight and sit down at the table, sweeping the dust away with my sleeve. Mumma has been sketching a plant and there is a jam jar at the back of the table against the sloping roof, encrusted with the orange sediment of decayed vegetation and dried water. This stained jar stands beside a box that is shaped like a child's treasure chest. I lift it forward and carefully wipe the dust from the beautifully enamelled, intricate and brightly-coloured designs of mythical forest animals. I touch the clasp and the lid opens.

I stare in horror at my gentle Mumma's hidden secret.

I place the box carefully back on the table, and leave.

She ran her hand through the bristles of her hairbrush feeling the pinpricks of pain on her palm.

I see a wet patch on the ceiling and I remember that the skylight in the attic is open. It is cold and fresh up there. The papers and books on the desk are blown about and the heavy layer of dust is swirled and dampened into an uneven pattern on the floor. The jam jar has rolled down the desk and is lying against the open enamelled box.

I focus my eyes on the skylight as I cross the room. I do not look down but it is irresistible. The box is full of water and the male effigy, with the pin through its heart, looks directly up at me. It is only then that I see the resemblance between Father and Hal.

She opened the drawer beside her and took out the enamelled box. She lifted the clasp and the lid sprang open. The inside was still glistening with droplets of water and she took a tissue to wipe round the hinges and polish the inside until the metal shone bright and clean.

I hold out the box for Hal to see. The painted balsa wood figure trembles in the water.

She ran her fingers lightly over the brightly coloured surface.

The muscles in Hal's face tighten and his eyes are full of anger. He knocks the box from my hand and the figure falls to the carpet, lying in a patch of wet, all-askew. He reaches down and crushes it in his hand. I hear him spluttering hateful words in the bathroom as he flushes the effigy away.

She closed the box, wrapped it in its velvet cloth and repacked it in her suitcase, closing the wardrobe door firmly. The stain on the carpet was dry now. She rubbed her bare foot over it, loosening the matted fibres, and started to think of the days ahead.

PART II

(May 1993)

1

Alec Maconachie of Selkie Bay Farm felt a rough tongue licking his eyelids open and a wet nose brushing against his forehead. He pushed Slavers away and told him to behave, but the words and action were just shapes and vibrations inside his head and they slipped away. He could see a cyclamen-pink rose, glistening with dew, gently moving in the wind; a huge bee, the size of Slavers' tongue, was separating the tightly curled petals and the delicate stamens were standing proud. The smell of rose was clean and powdery. Mrs Treatham was there. She was taking him in her arms and speaking to him with strange tenderness. He could feel the warmth of her body and the closeness of her lips.

It was a dream, a lovely dream.

Her face was starting to recede, shimmering and undulating in the moving sea. Waves crashed against the rocks; one towered and raced towards him, its lacy spume rippling and dipping. It engulfed him in its swell, plunging him into a deep and swirling pool. Black icicles clung to him like leeches. He fought to free himself from this silent fearful underworld but his muscles were cramped and frozen. Misshapen stars splattered his darkness, fading and falling away.

It was growing light. The long hours of waiting were nearly over. He could hear the staccato of Slavers' claws as he danced a morning greeting. Mrs Treatham was bending over him. She said that everything would be all right and lifted him forward to plump up his pillows, but his pillows were still hard and flat and his head was aching.

She was going through the door without looking back or saying goodbye. What about his cup of tea. His mouth was parched. He whimpered and she was back, holding his hand and begging him to help her. He said that he would. Of course he would. But what did she mean. His brain wouldn't stay still long enough for him to work it out.

He was lying on the hearth close to the Rayburn with a rim of compacted grey grease close to his nose. He could feel the warmth of a stone slab against his cheek but nothing else. There was a heavy numb coldness where the rest of his body should be. He drifted away but was forced back to wakefulness by the irregular movement of light and shade and sound all around him.

Mrs Treatham was trying to make him understand something. She was bending over him again and speaking urgently and loudly close to his ear. At the same time she was making futile attempts to control Slavers' exuberance with frantic appeals and repeated pushes. (Slavers only retreated a few steps and then came back to give further encouragement with hot saliva breaths.) She had her arms round him and was pulling him up. He struggled to help himself up and at once the blood started to flow through his veins and waken his cramped muscles; an excruciating shudder of pain made him cry out. She laid him down and Slavers barked in sympathy nudging his head under his arm to give comfort. Alec could feel quivers of uncontrollable agony engulfing him and he begged Mrs Treatham to let him be, but she persisted in her effort to get him off the floor and back into bed.

Then it happened

One moment he felt himself drowning in the softness and warmth of an intimate embrace, and the next thing he knew, he was as light and buoyant as a released balloon. Up and up he was going, farther and farther away from his body, until he touched the ceiling and came to rest in the hollow at the top of the dresser, with the hidden and forgotten remnants of his life. He could see his monopoly game in its thick cardboard box, bent and bound with brown tape; his parents' wedding photograph, with its broken glass and frame askew (he remembered breaking it and blaming Flo); magazines confiscated over the years; old keys, curling official papers, and the cruel, thick strap that his mother had used under the direction of her bible. The dust was thick, the surface a grey matted web.

Mrs Treatham was fussing over him in the bed below, scolding gently. The aluminium kettle on the stove was spluttering and hissing against the hot plate. When had she put it on.

Could this be death, he wondered, this colourful happiness that made him feel exhilarated and free and yet left him able to think, see and hear. It was not what he had imagined death to be. There was no sign of damnation or the heat of hell fire that Bess Grant's father, the late Reverend, had told him to expect and fear. Of course it had been different since Miss Silver, the

Reverend's sister, had taken to the preaching, but then it would have been unseemly for her to be possessed in the same way when she gripped the pulpit each Sunday. He could never have imagined that God would leave him here in his kitchen with his own people around him. Not that Mrs Treatham could be thought of as his own people but she was a grand lass, a looker, and a welcome sight for weary, sleepless eyes when she turned up every morning with her dog. "Call me, Hanna", she would say, but he would never have taken such a liberty. Her husband would have had something to say if he had.

That was his body, his remains, lying there below, with blotched and yellowed skin stretched over bones and hollows. What a sight. It was time it went under the ground. And time too that that bed was sent back from where it came. Ursula had brought it in, with its gadgets to lift and turn and push and poke; it fairly cluttered up the place. Aye, there was no doubt about it, his time had come. And none too soon.

But Mrs Treatham was acting as if he were still part of his lifeless corpse. Perhaps he was not dead after all but just taking a turn out of his body – a float-about, so to speak. It would be right aggravating if that were so. There was no use left in that body down there. Good riddance to it, is what he would say, if he were asked. It was strange that he had never seen himself as an old shrivelled-up shell of a man when he had been stretched out on his bed with his head on his pillow and his eyes looking out.

He could hear the distant sound of Dan's pickup careering along the straight tarred road that ran from the causeway to his farm track. He couldn't imagine life without Dan and he knew that Dan would grieve for him sorely. They'd been neighbours and pals since childhood, helping each other out when needed and speaking over their fences as they worked. When he could no longer get out and about, Dan was calling in to see him at all hours and seeing to his needs. Dan was one of the best, there was no denying that. Sometimes he was the first to arrive in the mornings and sometimes it was Mrs Treatham. He liked it when she was the first. She brightened up his day and she never stopped if Dan was already there. Of course she was not accustomed to his way of living but she didn't put on airs or show him up.

He thought about the day when she had first come in. He'd been standing at his kitchen window looking out at the mainland hills, irregular dense contours against the sky above the shimmering Kyle of Tongue, and listening to the waves hushing rhythmically on the shore below, longing for the morning to come. He'd not been able to make her out in the grey light of early dawn but he had heard her calling to her dog and had waved, hoping that she would see him in the lighted room and come in. He was not bedridden and a burden then but he no longer had the strength to do much on his farm and he slept badly.

She had come and knocked at his door thinking that he was in trouble and needing her help. When she found that he was just a lonely old man crying out for company, she could have gone off and not come back, but she had sat down and drunk the cup of tea that he had made for her and she'd been coming in and cheering him up nearly every morning since. Her granddad had been poorly towards the end, she had told him, and she remembered how he had longed for her to get up and break the tedium of the night. Her habit of rising early had started then and she had grown to love the cool quietness of the new day when not another soul was about. He knew what she meant when she said that and they had found common ground. But it was different when there was no work ahead of him. Now the day was as long as the night and he was weary of it all.

Slavers lifted his head and pricked up his ears.

"There's Dan now," Mrs Treatham said, speaking to his empty body on the bed below.

He could hear the grinding of Dan's gears as he slowed for the corner and started to negotiate the track up to the farmhouse. A right mess the track was in. He had never got round to bottoming the potholes the winter past. It was aggravating to leave the place in such a poor shape; no doubt there was worse than that needing attention, if he wanted to think about it.

He tried to float out from his space above the dresser to greet Dan but his mind, or his soul, or whatever he was now, was stuck tight. He should count his blessings, he supposed, but he would've liked to take a last look round the farm without having to drag his body about with him.

Slavers had leapt up from his warm and comfortable position stretched out along the bottom of the Rayburn and had started his usual racket, barking and jumping and slavering, paying little attention to his mistress's commands. She was too soft on him and many-a-time he had had to keep himself from saying so. Her husband should've disciplined the dog long since but her man was not one to see beyond the sides of his thin nose – unless, of course, it affected his own comfort.

Dan Grant knew that something was wrong, even before he turned off his engine and jumped down from his cab. He could hear Slavers barking. That was not unusual in itself but Alec was always quick to call the dog to heel. He stopped at the back door to shake off his boots, as he always did, and had one off and the other half off when Hanna came through. She told him what had happened and he nearly toppled over. His father had been found dead in the byre and no one had known how long he had lain there; that Alec should suffer a similar fate was cruel. He let the second boot fall and walked quickly past Hanna in his stockinged feet, controlling Slavers exuberance with an authoritative command.

At Alec's bedside he took off his cap and brushed his hand twice over his high brow and through his receding rough, wiry hair, as was his habit when he was agitated. He felt for the weak pulse in his friend's neck.

"If you'd rung, I'd have come," he said quietly to Hanna, as he pushed away Slavers' exploring paw.

"I haven't had time to think of anything but getting Alec warm. He's sleeping now but he was like ice when I found him." She lifted the heavy kettle from the hot plate and started to fill one of the stone hot water bottles, set beside her on the range.

"D'you think I should give Ursula a ring?" Dan asked. He lifted his head and looked at Hanna from beneath his jutting brows.

"Let's get some heat into his body first. Have a look around, Dan, and see if you can find some blankets."

Dan went through to the main bedroom. It had not been used since Alec's mother had died, nearly ten years earlier, and was packed with heavy Victorian furniture. An acrid smell of mothballs rose as he opened and shut the drawers in the chests and under the massive wardrobe. They were full of old clothes.

"Why didn't he use his alarm?" he asked as he searched. "I've been out lambing since the back of five. I would've seen the light." He came back through, holding two lank grey blankets that had seen better days. "The batteries couldn't have gone already." He lifted the alarm from the bedside table and pressed the switch. "No, it's working all right."

"He was on the floor, Dan," Hanna pointed out softly. "He wouldn't have been able to reach his alarm from there."

She passed him a stone bottle warmly wrapped in a towel.

"Maybe so, but it's right aggravating to think that he didn't have it when he needed it. He was meant to keep the cord round his neck, you know, but he didn't care for that and didn't see the need. Like a cow with a clatter bell, he would say." Dan fumbled around under the covers to find the right place for the heavy, hot, towelling bundle close to Alec's skeletal feet. He tucked the covers close in. "Why would he want to get out of his bed in the first place," he mused, as much to himself as to Hanna. "He had his night mapped out with a film to watch and letters to write. I passed down his tin box to him before I left." He looked round for the old biscuit tin in which were kept writing materials and family documents. It was a distinctive box, still serviceable although the transfer on the lid of George VI and the Queen Mother on their coronation day had become faded and scratched. "Aye, he's got a letter here waiting for Postie,"

"He fell out of his bed, Dan. His right foot was entangled in the bedclothes."

"Did he take a turn, d'you think?"

Hanna handed over another filled bottle and pulled down the lid of the hot plate.

"More likely he just got too near the edge of the bed," she said quietly, lifting the empty kettle from the side. "You know how deeply he sleeps when he's taken his pills."

Dan looked doubtful.

"He spoke to me and his speech wasn't slurred."

"Ah well, that's a good sign."

"And he was also able to help me get him back into bed."

Dan lowered his head, resisting the urge to look at the buttons on Hanna's open-necked shirt. Alec would inspect the crucial button daily for metal fatigue, speculating lecherously about it reaching breaking point right there in his kitchen. Dan would have been embarrassed if it had done so but this titillating possibility had brought a sparkle to Alec's dull, sick eyes. Dan wondered what had happened during her hauling efforts.

I had my nose in the trough, Dan Boy.

Dan's mouth fell open. "What was that," he said, looking round in bewilderment.

"What was what?"

"I thought I heard …" Dan took a handkerchief from the bib of his dungarees to cover his heated face. "I was thinking, just thinking like, and it was as if …" He couldn't put into words the verbal sensation he had experienced. "Och, I'm just havering." He felt uneasy in a woman's company if the conversation became personal and focused his attention on his thick, hand-knitted socks; they had rubbed thin round the toes and were discoloured with the uneven rust marks of wear.

Hanna saw his embarrassment and did not pursue the subject, continuing on her way to the back kitchen to refill the kettle. When she came back, Dan was rid-dling the stove and topping it up with coke. He picked up the shovel with the spent ashes and shuffled off to dispose of them and refill the scuttle. He was glad to have an excuse to quit the room and cool his face.

Alec's farmhouse was traditional and of modest proportions. Its only claim to modernisation was the removal of the box bed in the mid-1960s. The front door (never used and deep in grass), had a small porch which led directly into this kitchen/living room, with the doors to the two bedrooms on the left and the back kitchen, or scullery, straight ahead. Two large, deep porcelain sinks, with a wringer on the upright between them, dominated the scullery, with floor-to-ceiling cupboards against the wall on one side and a scrubbed table on the other. Under one sink there was an old-fashioned, single-tub washing machine and under the other two pails, one for compost and one for non-degradables. A narrow passage led through to the back door with doors off to the bathroom and the coal bunker.

Dan left the scuttle by the coal bunker door, put on his boots, and went outside to fill one of the potholes in the road with the hot ashes. The pothole he chose was still half full of rain water from the day before and the ashes sizzled and steamed as they sank, leaving a scum of black and grey powder floating on the top. He was feeling weary and was glad to get out and fill his lungs with the fresh morning air. He never got much sleep during lambing and it had been a difficult few days with Alec poorly and Laura coming home in a state to worry her mother. He took out his pipe and fingered its familiar, pleasurable curves with indecision. A smoke would be a comfort but it might be rude if he sought his own company for too long. He put the stem between his teeth and cupped the unfilled bowl in his fingers, looking around as he thought about it. Alec's land was in poor shape, most of his fields needed ploughing, but over on the other side of the loch he could see that the hay was well sprouted and there was good new growth in the pasture. He turned his head in the direction of his own land and saw Laura running over the top field, scattering his ewes as she went, some still in lamb. He sighed, put his pipe away, and went back into the house to finish his morning chores.

Slavers started his barking again. "Enough!" Dan commanded.

Alec hadn't heard the noise and it made Dan feel uneasy. The faint throb of pulse was still there but he was too still for Dan's liking. He was pondering on this and wondering what to do for the best when his step-daughter burst in gasping for breath, her dark eyes wide in fearful premonition. Laura could always find a way to his heart. She was so like her mother, softly slender, with flushed cheeks and jet-black springy curls. He put out his hand and drew her close, murmuring soothing words of reassurance.

Hanna was less forgiving.

"Calm yourself, Laura," she said in disapproval, walking over to close the door quietly. Laura had opened it with such force that it had hit the wall, dislodging a piece of loose plaster and letting in an unwelcome draught. "It doesn't help Alec or yourself to run around in such a demented state."

Laura wasn't listening. Her attention was directed to the motionless body lying on the bed. She started to whimper, lifting Alec's bony hand, blue with prominent veins, and putting it to her cheek. "Forgive me, Uncle Alec," she wailed. When there was no response, she moved closer into the protective arm of her stepfather. "Can he hear, do you think?" She looked down at Alec's cold, expressionless face. "We quarrelled when I came in yesterday and I wish we hadn't."

"He'd not take offence in the long run." Dan offered Laura his crushed handkerchief, none too clean, but she took a handful of tissues from the bedside table instead. Slavers was trying to show sympathy and catch her attention by nuzzling into her side, but she pushed him away. "What were you quarrelling about this time?"

Laura glanced across at Hanna who was standing with her back to them, looking out of the side window. "You can imagine," she whispered with a shrug of explanation and then, unable to control herself, went on: "He said that I shouldn't have given in to Joe's pestering and that he wouldn't want to marry me now. Can you imagine anyone even thinking that today let alone saying it?"

Dan murmured in a non-committal sort of way. His views and Alec's were much the same on that subject but he held his peace. It didn't help that he and Bess knew little about this Joe of hers; they even wondered if Laura knew much herself beyond the fact that he was 'dreadfully clever'.

Laura hitched the door of the Rayburn open with her foot and tossed her tissues on to the hot embers. "Have you rung Ursula?" she asked.

Hanna turned from the window and looked at her watch. "I think you could ring her now, Dan."

Dan agreed. "He's not hearing us at all."

"She's at Shaws, Danda. I saw her car going up there last night?"

Dan pondered on that fact. "Ah, well, that's how it is," he said to no one in particular, lifting the receiver from the telephone on the wall and pressing the familiar digits. He listened to the ringing at the other end, waiting with an elbow on the high mantel, a hand shielding his eyes, until Rob Ballater answered. He confirmed his identity and agreed that there had been a fine change to the weather and that Bess was in good health, before getting to the crux of the matter.

"I'm up here at Selkie, Rob. Alec's taken a turn for the worse." He listened and then went on: "He fell from his bed and lay on the floor for most of the night. No, no, he's back in his bed now but he's right poorly. I was looking for Ursula and wondered if you'd seen her." His oblique question kept up the pretence of propriety although it was clear that Ursula was there because he could hear Rob relaying the message and her response from a distance. "Aye, fine that," he said when Rob came back on the line. "I'll wait here till she comes." He hung up the phone. "She'll be right along to see to his needs. She says …"

He stopped mid-sentence, jerking upright and looking round. He could have sworn that Alec had just chortled with lascivious glee. It was startling in its clarity to him, but neither Hanna nor Laura had heard anything. He looked down at Alec in bewilderment, shaking his head to clear his brain of such a fanciful thought. It must be the tiredness that was making him hallucinate. He was a rational, God-fearing man and he could make no sense of the thoughts that were pushing themselves into his head. He moved around restlessly, looking down at the bed and then up at the ceiling, searching for an explanation.

Slavers' eyes followed his movements.

"It'll be ages till she's here," Laura said, making herself comfortable in the window alcove. She had lifted pots of flowering plants off the sill and was rearranging the cushions on the rocking chair to fit her shape. The largest plant pot made a good footstool. From there she had a clear view of the marbled cliffs on the coast to the west, over the loch to Trowsay House, and along the road to the causeway; that was Alec's favourite place to sit.

Hanna unwrapped the bunch of pale purple tulips that she had picked in the hotel garden that morning and laid them on the oak table, set in the space left by the obsolete box bed. There was a jar of narcissi at its centre, the edges of their frilled heads starting to curl and dry. She lifted that away and took the jar through to the scullery, bringing it back full of fresh water. On various shelves and ledges around the farm kitchen, there were plants and posies of wild flowers. Hanna nearly always arrived with some floral gift to cheer Alec up. As a crofting farmer, his working days had started early and finished late, cut flowers and potted plants had had no place in his life, but when he could no longer get out and about, he found that he enjoyed watching the plants grow and change. He didn't even mind seeing the flowers wither and die. That was the nature of things, as he knew well, and he drew comfort from it.

Dan took his pipe from the bib of his dungarees and began to fill it. He felt calmer now and for no reason that he could put into words, he found himself telling Hanna and Laura about his childhood with Alec.

"Right from the beginning we hit it off," he began, speaking softly and looking down at Alec where he lay. "He was older than me but it didn't seem to matter when we were lads … unless he wanted to get his own way." His mouth twisted in a wry smile of memory, as he reached up and lifted the matchbox from the mantelshelf.

"Dan, I don't think you should smoke with Alec so ill."

"No, no, of course not. I wasn't thinking." He put the matchbox back on the shelf but kept the pipe in his hand, tasting it and smelling the rich pungent smell of the tobacco in consolation. "We didn't stay indoors and watch TV in those days. In fact, there was no television to watch." He turned the fireside chair and sat down. "We were always out and about tracking each other…or looking for birds' nests … or making hide-outs… or damming the burns (he paused as he thought of each activity) or just playing around down there in Selkie Bay, climbing over the rocks and guddling in the pools. If the weather were poor, we would go into the barns and slide down the hay or polish the tackle; there were still some carthorses left then. Sometimes we got into trouble, although it was mild trouble as things go nowadays." He shifted in his chair. "Aye it was a fine time to be young."

Laura called: "The McFeas are coming." She was leaning forward to get a better view. "Trust her to know what's going on. I bet she's got a pair of binoculars over there."

"Now, now, don't be unkind. She's alone for most of the day with no one passing her door."

"Thorfinn passes it," Laura corrected him,

"That may be so, but he's poor company for the likes of Flo McFea."

"She doesn't make it easy for him," Hanna said gently, fiddling with a bent tulip before placing it in the jar.

Laura agreed.

"She's a fine, hard-working body."

"We asked her to stay on at Trowsay House, you know, but she wanted to retire."

"According to Granny Grant, she wouldn't be seen dead down there now."

"So I've heard." Hanna made a face. "It was the making of the drawing room into a cocktail lounge that she resented most."

"A public bar, she said."

"A bar, yes." Hanna put her completed arrangement in the middle of the table. "But it was never going to stay as a private house and alterations were inevitable." She collected together the leaves that she had rejected and the cuttings from the stalks and put them in the Rayburn; they hissed against the hot coke, raising wispy curls of smoke. "Go on Dan, tell us more about your life with Alec." She looked down at the still body on the bed as she dried her hands, folding the towel neatly and putting it back on the rail. She stayed there, leaning against the warmth of the stove. Slavers pulled himself up, shifting his bulk about until he found a comfortable position against one of her legs, and then lay down again, with his head resting neatly between his paws.

Dan offered the fireside chair but Hanna shook her head.

"Sometimes Callum would come with us," he went on, "but his mother was very protective. She thought he might drown if he strayed from her side for too long."

Laura turned to make some comment but changed her mind.

"It's all a long time ago," Dan went on, deep in memory. He smiled to himself, leaning forward with his hands on his knees. "When we were stuck for something to do, there was always the tormenting of old Ma Thompson to pass the time of day. I can see us now in our tackety boots and short trousers, our schoolbags strapped to our shoulders, sneaking over her dyke and zigzagging our way towards her fruit cage, using the cows or sheep for cover. When she saw us, she would go for her stick and we would run hell for leather across her park, before she could get it down from the wall and chase us off her land with yells of rage. Oh, she was a character, was old Ma Thompson." He looked up at Hanna from beneath his jutting brows. "She only died a short time ago. Do you remember her, Mrs Treatham?"

"Did she live in the sheltered housing next door to old Jockie Jay?"

"Yes that was her. She lived there at the last and she couldn't abide Jockie, which kept her fiery to the end of her days. I saw her not long before her time came and she still had the glint in her eye." He got up and went over to see to Alec, feeling his pulse and rearranging the grey blankets, more for something to do than to make Alec more comfortable.

Laura called to say that the McFeas were nearly there. She had been following the progress of their van as it appeared and disappeared round the bends in the road at the south end of the island.

"I wonder if he knows about the potholes," Dan replied anxiously, working his way round the fireside chair to the window. "He's been walking over the hill to see Alec in the evenings."

The three of them watched as Callum slowed at the road end and changed down a gear. He turned into the track and started up the incline in a careful zigzag, but a back wheel still caught the edge of a rut and sank, raising Mrs McFea to an awkward angle in the passenger seat. The wheel spun without gripping and the revving engine petered out.

"Ah, well, there you are," Dan murmured, looking round for his cap and going to help.

Mrs McFea greeted him through her open window and asked after Alec.

"Not great, I'm afraid," Dan told her, nodding to Callum who was inspecting the damage in silence.

"He's a poor soul now," Mrs McFea said grimly, shifting her position on the lopsided seat. "We thought we'd just take a look over to see how he was but we weren't expecting this." She waved her hand in demonstration of their predicament. "There's more holes in that road than surface. What if we'd been the doctor or some other important body who wasn't expecting to be rattled to a stop?"

"Aye, it's needing a bit of attention," Dan agreed.

Mrs McFea changed tack. "You'll need some flat stones for the tyre to grip," she called to her husband, putting her head out of the window and pointing to a number lying on the road and the verge. "There's plenty about."

The men started gathering the stones together, rubbing their surfaces with their thumbs and discussing their worth, before getting down on their hunkers and jamming them round the wheel. They were assessing their handiwork when they heard the distant sound of a car on the road. It was the Postie. They watched him park at the bottom and waited for him to walk up and offer a shoulder. He and Dan got in behind, tensed in readiness, and Callum positioned himself behind the jamb of the driver's door, a hand on the steering wheel and a foot on the accelerator.

"Right then," Callum called and with a roar of the engine and an almighty heave, the tyre gripped and freed itself, spitting most of the loose stones back onto the track, handy for the next time.

Dan took Alec's mail, mostly unsolicited circulars, and was starting to follow the McFeas' van when there was a knock on the front window. Laura opened it a fraction and called to Postie to come up as Alec had a letter waiting to go.

The letter was passed over to him with a few words of greeting and enquiry.

In the back courtyard, Callum had his elbows under his wife's armpits, gently lifting her from the low front seat. Dan had not realised that Flo McFea had got so stout. She had always been a round sort of woman but she had been much admired for her looks and forthright manner when she had first come home. He had only been a teenager then and it was mostly the goodies she kept in her tins that had enticed him over to the kitchen at the big house. Alec had been very smitten, he remembered, and had fancied his chances, but Callum was the one she had chosen.

Mrs McFea straightened up and tottered round into a position to take Callum's arm. She needed his support. Half a lifetime of standing on the hard stone slabs in old-fashioned kitchens had taken its toll.

Dan offered his help but she waved him away.

"You go first, Dan, and open the door," she instructed.

He did so and the couple went in looped tandem along the narrow passage to the kitchen.

"I just happened to be looking from the bedroom window," Mrs McFea said as she hobbled forward on the arm of her long husband, "and there was Alec's light on. How is he then?" She peered down at Alec, pushing her glasses up her nose to get a better view. "My, he looks right poorly." She lowered herself on to the chair beside the bed. "But perhaps it's for the best if the end is near."

Callum stood with his cap in his hand, looking down the length of his friend to his hollowed features and pale mottled skin. Dan could see by the expression in his eyes and the movement of his lips that he was at last facing reality. Callum was always the optimist and had believed in miracles.

"I see you're still here, Mrs Treatham," Mrs McFea went on, acknowledging Hanna's presence. The tone of her voice made it clear that she didn't think Hanna ought to be butting into a neighbourly affair. "Are they not needing their breakfasts over by?"

"Lizzie Hope is in," Hanna replied calmly, looking at her watch. "But you're right, it is time I was on my way."

Slavers perked up his head and thumped his tail in anticipation of departure.

"You did a grand job," Dan said to her gently, "and we're all right grateful."

Mrs McFea raised her eyebrows in question and Dan told her about Alec lying on the cold stone slabs in front of the damped-down stove for most of the night. While he was speaking, she eased herself forward in her chair and heaved herself up, finding a solid stance before lifting the bottom of the duvet and feeling Alec's feet. They were resting against the thickly-covered, stone bottle.

"There's not much warmth coming through that towel, Mrs Treatham," she accused, "far too bulky."

"I've never used a stone bottle before and I didn't want to burn him."

"Not much chance of that," was the brisk response. Mrs McFea rearranged the towelling to her satisfaction and did the same with the other bottle, then she rested her weight precariously on the edge of the bed and found Alec's hand. "We go back a long way, Alec and me," she reminisced, rubbing his hand rhythmically to help the blood flow, "and we never really got on."

"Alec always spoke highly of you," Dan said softly.

"No doubt guilt speaking," Mrs McFea responded dryly, putting both feet firmly on the ground and flopping back into her seat.

"Why was that?" Laura asked innocently from her lookout position in front of the far window and was immediately subjected to the magnified eye and tart tongue.

"Well, miss, I see you're home to bring shame down on your family."

"There is no shame, Flo. We're always pleased to have Laura home."

"Maybe so, but your mother has been given a lot to bear."

"It's my business and no one else's," Laura said sulkily.

"Now, now, Laura."

Dan was not surprised that Flo knew all about the baby. His mother had wasted no time in going across to see her when she heard the news. On her return, she had cornered him in the tractor shed to add another instalment to her grievances. Dan's charity in taking on a divorced woman and a child that had no Grant blood in her veins, he had heard before, but now it was a case of "like mother, like daughter" and the pair of them being a disgrace to the church and the late Reverend's calling. Was Laura, this unrelated stepdaughter, going to produce a son who would inherit Brackenlea? Dan had already thought of that and it had made him sad for the lost years.

"Is that Ursula now?" he asked, hearing a car.

Laura nodded, rocking herself up and pulling her T-shirt down over the top of her jeans. She thrust a hip out and twisted a curl in indecision.

"Are you off then?"

"May as well."

"I must go too," Hanna said, but they both dilly-dallied with their farewells and were still there when Ursula click-clacked along the passage in her high heels and opened the kitchen door. She stopped short in the doorway, a ray of sunlight, shafting through the window, raising sparks in her fiery red hair. The room was full of well-kent faces and she acknowledged each by name, singling Dan out to bear the brunt of her annoyance.

"Turn that alarm light out, Dan," she said brusquely. "I'm here now and we don't want every living soul on the island pushing into this room."

She crossed to the bedside and put her case down.

Hanna told her about finding Alec and what they had done to make him comfortable.

"You should have rung me immediately, Hanna."

"Sorry."

Dan said quickly: "But he was all right in himself then, Ursula. He spoke to Mrs Treatham and was able to get himself back into bed with her help."

"Nevertheless he could have done himself an injury."

Ursula opened her case and gave her full attention to her patient.

Mrs McFea was of the opinion that the Good Lord had sent for Alec and he had heeded the call. She was looking up at the painting on the wall opposite her where two angels were flying across the sky with classical grace, escorting a new soul up into heavenly bliss.

"Nonsense," Ursula said sharply in a voice that boded no argument.

… and Alec found himself back in his unwanted body, feeling the remembered pain in his bony buttocks and the aching, unrelenting effort to inflate his lungs. Despite the warmth of the hot water bottles, the cold- ness in his feet had spread like gangrene up through his wasted muscles to grip his heart. His face contorted. He no longer appreciated the presence of his friends and neighbours. He just wished that they would all go away quickly and leave him to Ursula and the comfort of her hypodermic needle.

But Mrs McFea did not go away. She stayed firmly in her seat, her hands resting on her stick.

"I'll stop over and see to him," she said.

"He needs someone to stay with him all the time now," Ursula told them, repacking her bag. "He should not be left alone."

Dan assured her that he would not be. "Bess will be across and no doubt my Mum will want to come too."

Ursula picked up her bag and headed for the door.

"I'll be back in an hour or two. Ring me if you are worried Mrs McFea."

"Aye, and turn on the alarm light, if you need me," Dan said softly. "I'll keep my eyes open." He leaned over and gave Alec's shoulder a light squeeze. "I'm off to see to the ewes, Alec. I'll no be long in coming back."

"Don't you worry now, Dan, I'll see to him all right," Mrs McFea called as Dan left, with his eyes lowered to shield his distress.

Dan always hid his emotions behind a front of quiet strength. She remembered the merry dance that Bess had led him on, marrying that man south when Dan was waiting for her at home. He had been floored by it all but he had never said a word against her.. His steadfast devotion had paid off in the end, although now he had that little madam Laura to contend with. Many would have shown her the door, coming back in that state and causing a disgrace, but Dan was always the first to help in trouble and the last to call it a day. She looked at Alec and straightened his cover a bit. He had certainly been a good friend to Alec here and Alec was not an easy man to like.

She found her stick and heaved herself up on to her feet. The place needed putting to rights. She moved slowly about the room, dragging the chairs back into place and puffing up the cushions, lifting the pot plants back on to their ledge and straightening the rug with her stick. Each task was an effort but before long the place was looking neat. She was on her way to the kitchen for a duster when Alec spoke.

"Flo," he whispered.

"Aye, Alec, what's the trouble?"

She could not hear a further word, although Alec's lips were moving.

She leaned close to listen and suddenly his arms came up and encircled her, pulling her down hard against him so that her cheek smacked his nose and her glasses were sent askew. Almost immediately his arms slackened and fell back on the covers, leaving her to find her feet and push herself upright. She was gasping for breath as she righted her glasses and fell back into the chair beside the bed.

"You devil, you," she said, turning to Alec in anger, but he was looking straight up at the ceiling, his lips moving with silent words.

"Come see, Flo, come see." he said out loud. "So soft and wee, the blind, sleekit things." He mumbled away to himself. She couldn't hear what he was saying and wasn't about to lean close again to find out. There was a red bruise on the bridge of his nose where her head had hit but there were also spots of colour in the hollow underneath his bony cheekbones and a smile on his lips. Suddenly he said clearly: "You're a bonnie wee lass."

These were the last words he spoke. His eyes slowly closed, his mouth relaxed, and his breathing became deep and regular.

Flo sat on, recalling the episode with the kittens. It was a Sunday, she remembered. Sundays were special days for her because her Mum and Dad came across from the big house to take her out. No doubt she was already excited when Alec opened the screen door dividing their bedroom and whispered about Blackie and her new kittens. She had jumped out of bed and run with him to the hay shed in her nightdress. Blackie was lying there with her six kittens, mewing and climbing over each other to get at their feed. She could picture the two of them, crouching at the edge of the hay in awe and delight, holding the kittens in their hands and smoothing down their scrappy fur, playing happily under the wary eye of Blackie, until Alec's Mum arrived and sent them running. Her Auntie Maconachie had slapped her for coming out from behind her screen before she was dressed and putting temptation in Alec's way. She was only about five or six at the time. She wasn't able to ask what she meant because she was being dragged back to the house, her legs barely able to keep up. Alec had sneaked off. He always sneaked off when there was trouble brewing but he still caught it when he came back.

She looked over at the upright chair against the back wall, seeing in her mind's eye, her Auntie Maconachie sitting there reading the Bible out loud, as she always did on a Sunday evening, with Mr Maconachie dozing in his chair and Alec crouched on the stool with his head bent. His mother had drowned the kittens, she learned later, and Alec had watched while she had put the sack in the trough, the kittens wriggling and squealing all the time. Poor man. She lifted his limp hand from the cover and gave it a squeeze. She had never cared for him but that didn't stop her feeling sorry for him. There was no doubt in her mind that his life had been blighted by his harsh and unloving childhood.

With a sigh, she pushed herself up and fetched the duster from the scullery. The dirt was thick along the mantelshelf, which gave her satisfaction.

"That Hanna Treatham was across here every morning," she said to herself as she wiped it clean, "and she never deigned to help Alec out by doing a bit of house-work."

Once the dusting was done, she brought through half a pail of water and washed down the Rayburn. She was starting on the sweeping when the visitors began to arrive. Bess came across from Brackenlea with her mother-in-law and Agnes Grant stayed on to keep her company. Cissie looked in, staying longer than she was welcome, and other distant relatives came up from the village full of righteous talk and curiosity.

Ursula was never far away. After she had done her rounds, she came in to check on her patient and in the early afternoon she returned, intending to give him an-other injection, but she couldn't rouse him. She stayed on until she was called away. As she was leaving, she said to Mrs McFea: "His body has not been able to take the shock of his night on the floor." Her implication was clear. There was no more to be done. Alec had started his retreat from life.

In the late evening, with his close friends at his bed-side, his breathing started to slow, becoming shallower and shallower until, with a last sighing release, it finally stopped.

2

The Treathams arrived at the church with half an hour to spare. Nearly every pew was taken and Martha Silver was already at the organ, creating an appropriately sombre atmosphere and aiding melancholy reflection with low-key music. Hanna was shown to a seat next to Bess Grant and whispered a greeting, smiling at Dan's mother farther along the pew and receiving a nod in return. Old Agnes Grant was shrunk and shrivelled with age and mental stagnation; she looked for and found fault with nearly everyone.

Bess nudged her and gestured towards Rupert who was standing at the side of the church beside the other men.

"Rupert will be cold without a coat," she murmured. Rupert was only in a dark suit in contrast to the other men who were dressed in long black overcoats, a garment passed down through the generations to thwart the icy winds at the cemetery and avoid Repetitive Death Syndrome.

"It's in the car," Hanna whispered back. She didn't say that Rupert's light-coloured camel coat would only be worn if it turned really chilly. "He was surprised to be asked to be a pallbearer."

"It was Alec's wish," Bess told her and mouthed, so that Agnes would not hear: "Because of you."

Hanna leaned close. "I hope it won't be misinterpreted."

Bess said that it probably would be and they exchanged a smiling grimace.

The coffin lay on trestles in front of the memorial window and while waiting for the service to begin (and between nodding to this person and that) Hanna looked at the impressive window. She knew that it had been donated by one of the old man's ancestors at a time when there was a competition for souls between the Established Church and the breakaway Free Church. It was bordered with stained glass but the central panel was clear and lightly etched, with the scene of Simon Peter and Andrew casting their nets in a grand sweeping movement. The impression given was that the action was taking place on the loch outside and with a little imagination it seemed that the casket was caught in the disciples' net. Thus, in heavy Victorian symbolism, Alec was being gathered up into the heavenly fold.

Miss Silver (Bess's Aunt Chloe) came slowly out of the vestry and mounted the pulpit. She carried the mantel of her late Reverend brother who was a hell and damnation man, but she didn't have the fire in her voice or flay her arms about in wrath or sublimation as he had done. Nevertheless she made full use of scriptural texts to remind her congregation (wretched sinners all) that 'whatsoever a man soweth, that shall he also reap.' She made no mention of Alec's worldly contribution to society. It would have been presumptuous to remind God of Alec's virtues, or even draw His attention to who lay in the coffin underneath the window. God was all-seeing and all-knowing. However it gave Hanna quite a jolt to hear Alec described as 'the remains'.

At the end of the service, Miss Silver came carefully down the spiral stairs from the pulpit, the burden of dutiful chastisement lifting as she descended to the level of her congregation. She faced her flock and raised her right hand, gently giving her blessing to the mostly good and righteous citizens before her.

The congregation stood and watched as the pall-bearers took their places on either side of the coffin. As they lifted it, they quickly adjusted to the weight and their differing heights. Rupert had to stretch a bit to balance with Ted Vale and Dan had to bend his knees to be on an even keel with Callum McFea, but by such manoeuvres, the coffin was held horizontal and steady as the linked men shuffled down the aisle and out into the watery sunshine. The door of the church had been left open to accommodate the overspill and the procession proceeded slowly through this unofficial guard of honour, followed by the congregation.

Hanna became part of the flow of mourners, moving forward from the aisles to the vestibule and out into the open, swerving and altering speed when obstructed. She stood on the steps, feeling a fine mist of rain on her face, and thought of Rupert without his coat. A weak rainbow was coming and going on the hill opposite as the sun's rays broke through the cloud and touched the moisture in the air, but it wasn't cold.

Luke Sinclair beckoned to her. He was standing on the church green to her right, head and shoulders above the rest.

"Would you give me a lift to the cemetery?" he asked when she joined him, bending down to breathe the words in her ear. His face was flushed and glowing with perspiration. "It seemed wise to leave my car at the hotel."

Hanna nodded and mouthed agreement but waited until the coffin had been safely and reverently slid into Tom Nicol's station wagon before greeting and welcoming him. "Rupert has parked right at the end of the track so that there will be no trouble in getting out," she finished, turning in that direction.

Luke acknowledged Rupert's prudence and guided Hanna through the packed crowd. He was lawyer to most of the islanders, coming across from the mainland on occasion to deal with disputes or deathbed wills, and was greeted by each family group as he passed. Now that the service was over, the air tingled with excitement. Alec's closest relative was his cousin in Canada whom he did not know and there was distinct hope that he had not left the bulk of his worldly goods to her but to his more distant relatives living right there on the island.

"How is the farm managing in these difficult times?" Hanna asked Luke, as they walked along the track between the wall of the church and a ditch.

"Ticking over," he replied with a slow smile, replacing his cap. It was an open secret that Luke spent a large part of his day down on the family farm, although this was never admitted when clients rang to speak to him. The pretence was kept up that he was absent on legal business, either visiting clients or pleading for them in court. If the weather were fine for a spell, Luke would fall foul of whatever virus was on the go, the virulent bugs leaving him with a tan and a healthy twinkle in his eye.

"I suppose 'ticking over' is as much as one can expect," Hanna replied in sympathy, stepping farther out to avoid bumping against a car that had been carelessly parked. Cars were at all angles on the grass verge of the track, leaving barely enough space for vehicles to pass. "The wet weather last summer has had a knock-on effect for us all."

Luke agreed and they discussed the precarious nature of their rural economy until Rupert joined them.

At the appropriate time, Rupert eased the Range Rover out from the edge of the track and took his place in the long line of vehicles moving at a funereal pace along the main road north, through the village and up to the island cemetery at the old Free Church. (The Free Church had been deconsecrated in the mid-1960s due to the decline in population and church attendance.)

Alec's friends and neighbours met again at his family lair, gathering round the grave with heads bowed as Miss Silver pronounced the final words of committal and the coffin was lowered. Hanna silently voiced her own personal farewell to Alec as she waited with the other mourners for Miss Silver to finish her private prayer and step back.

The formalities were over. Alec had been laid to rest. Caps were put back on and there was a movement away from the deep narrow slit in the ground. Until the coffin was covered with soil and grass, the open grave was a stark and shuddering reminder of the ultimate human destiny.

Some of those present took the opportunity to visit the grave of a recently deceased member of the family or a loved one who was not forgotten despite the years. Chloe Silver always visited the graves of her parents and brother. She had planted a miniature garden in the shadow of their memorial stone and she tended this lovingly, changing the bulbs and plants with the seasons. There was comfort for the bereaved in this peaceful place, where the living greens of the land tipped over into the ever-changing blues of the sea.

Hanna and Luke had no visiting to do. They walked along the paths between the serried rows of graves, exchanging the odd greeting and murmuring the expected phrases of mourning. The memorial stones they passed were of different ages and materials, some ornate and some simple. Many were deeply pitted, with the loving words of remembrance long since rubbed off by abrasive wind and rain. From time to time Hanna looked at an inscription that was particularly poignant. There was the grave where four of the children had died in the 1919 flu epidemic; another where a father and the only two sons of the family had drowned in the same fishing boat tragedy. She stopped again to decipher with her fingertips the inscription on a very old stone wondering, as she always did, what history time and weather had obliterated.

When she looked up, Luke was a short distance away, speaking to Wilhelmina. Wilhelmina was taking no notice of him, or of the others who nodded and lifted their hats as they passed the old man's raised monumental edifice where she was sitting. She was looking beyond them straight at Hanna. It was an unnerving scrutiny and Hanna caught her breath, exhaling slowly. She felt that she was being touched by a breath of cool air, an odd sensation that she quickly shook off and dismissed as a totally irrational response to Wilhelmina's attention.

Nevertheless, when she stepped down from the smooth spongy grass that separated the graves, she decided to take the route that forked away from where Wilhelmina was sitting.

But Wilhelmina called out to her in her high distinctive monotone: "John and Annie were pleased to have you visit."

Hanna stopped in her tracks. Wilhelmina had never spoken to her before and it gave her a jolt to be the recipient of one of her messages. She smiled and called a greeting as she walked towards her. Wilhelmina was wearing one of her silkiest and most colourful smocks in celebration of Alec's arrival. The silver whiteness of her long hair was at odds with her unlined face. Hanna asked for more information about John and Annie but there was no reply. It was as though Wilhelmina had never addressed her. She just sat there, smiling and nodding to herself, her attention focused on the gravestone that Hanna had left.

Wilhelmina spent most of her days up at the churchyard, walking and running between the stones, speaking and laughing. It was said that she could see and hear the spirits of the recently dead and the long gone ancestors of the islanders. Hanna had smiled on hearing that, believing it to be amusing but fanciful talk. She regarded Wilhelmina's antics as a type of madness, to be viewed with compassion but not taken seriously. Yet there were those who swore that the messages Wilhelmina passed on from the dead to the living were so accurate and extraordinary that it must be true. Hanna would have none of it. She maintained that these uncanny messages were merely an answer to wishful thinking. Even now, she was not persuaded. The words Wilhelmina had spoken to her had no verifiable content. The inscription on the stone was so obliterated, she could not tell if it even commemorated anyone called John or Annie. In fact by the time Hanna reached the exit, she had convinced herself that the vision Wilhelmina had seen was only a reflection from her own mind and not wandering spirits that had been watching Hanna touch the surface of the stone; an amusing story to tell Rupert when they were alone.

There was no sign of him among the few remaining groups moving slowly towards the exit. Luke was talking to Donnie Strachan and she waited beside the massive wrought iron gates for him to join her. A member of the Free Church (who had made his fortune abroad but neglected his soul) had donated these gates, their ornate gilded curlicues now rusting with neglect. Celebration of death was an acceptable gift from a benefactor to a Free Church, etched and stained glass windows smacked of Roman Catholicism and the worship of idols. The biblical message across the top read, "Fear God and Keep His Commandments", a timely message for the living as they buried their dead.

Bess Grant hurried towards her from the direction of the car park.

"He's left with Dan," she said breathlessly. "Didn't he tell you that the pallbearers were going up to our house afterwards?"

Rupert hadn't told her and she felt aggrieved.

"Sometimes Rupert is unbelievably thoughtless," she said, speaking with unusual heat. "I could have been waiting here for ever."

Bess touched her gently. "It could be that Dan didn't mention it to him, just assumed that he would know."

Hanna let her vexation pass.

"It must be a nuisance for you to go to a meeting, Bess, with the men all up at Brackenlea."

"Agnes is there. In her element I need hardly add." She smiled without malice and took Hanna's arm. "Would you give me a lift down to the hotel?"

Hanna said she would. "I must wait for Luke Sinclair though," she added, looking over to where Luke was still speaking to Donnie. "We brought him out from church."

"I saw you with him." They started walking slowly up the road. "It's all rather exciting isn't it," she whispered with sparkling eyes, giving Hanna's arm a squeeze.

They were not the first to arrive in the hotel's private sittingroom where the meeting was to take place. Thorfinn was already there, leaning against the mantelpiece with a glass in his hand. He smiled when he saw Hanna, his mouth widening and his cheeks dimpling, his deep-set eyes disappearing behind radiating laughter lines.

"Really, Thorfinn," Hanna said in disapproval, "I would have expected you to go to Alec's funeral rather than imbibing so early in the day." She was over severe in her manner to counteract the effect his smile had on her pulse rate.

"Don't scold me Hanna, my lovely," he replied in a suitably subdued tone. "Without the light of your smile, I am cast into outer darkness."

Hanna's expression softened. She touched his lips lightly with a finger as she passed by, beguiled by his hangdog expression and way with words; his eyes lit up, sparking with unguarded desire and she could feel him watching her as she directed Luke to the seat she had selected for him.

"Actually I was in church,"Thorfinn went on, putting down his glass to help Bess off with her coat. "I witnessed Alec's soul being brought to the notice of the Almighty, but I'm afraid deep oblong holes in the ground make me feel queasy."

Bess laughed, chiding him for his flippancy.

Luke said wryly: "Following the coffin to the cemetery used to be considered too traumatic for women's sensibilities but men were meant to be stoical."

Thorfinn chuckled. "That was the official version, Luke, but I don't subscribe to it. It suited men to regard their female dependents as fragile."

They were discussing funeral customs when Jean arrived with the drinks and sandwiches, closely followed by Cissie Vale, dressed in sombre black. Hanna knew that she was related to Alec and offered condolences before settling her on the couch beside Bess.

Cissie sipped her vodka and orange and took a good look round.

"I see you've got one of Duncan's paintings," she said, noticing an addition to Hanna's possessions. She put down her glass and got up to peer at it. Duncan's paintings were best viewed from a distance, but it was clear that Cissie could make nothing of this one from where she sat and hoped that a closer look would be more illuminating. It was not. "I can't see anything in them myself."

"It reminds me of spring," Hanna said placidly, taking no offence. Duncan and his partner, Phil, lived at Atlanticscape. "I see spring flowers emerging from the cold earth and surviving, despite the wind and April snow."

No one else saw the expressionist work in that way and a pleasant few minutes were spent while Thorfinn and Bess gave their widely different interpretations, providing mild controversy and laughter. Luke sat back in his armchair with a benign smile and said nothing. It was obvious that he agreed with Cissie.

There was a small tap on the door.

"So sorry to keep you all waiting," Chloe Silver said, hurrying in, her bony frame moving independently of her dark grey suit and her halo of wiry grey hair awry. "Wilhelmina put out her hand as I was passing her and that delayed me."

"I assume that she was not offering her services," Thorfinn ventured.

Miss Silver smiled sparingly. "You assume correctly, Thorfinn. She was not."

Luke pushed himself up to shake hands, settling Miss Silver in a high-backed chair beside him. He sat down again and reached for his briefcase, depressing the springs of his armchair to near breaking point. He laid the briefcase on the low table in front of him and dug deep into the top pocket of his tweed jacket for his pince-nez and folded white handkerchief. The pince-nez was not kept in a case and it was part of Luke's ritual to hold it to the light and give it a polish before clipping it on the bridge of his nose. Hanna smiled at the incongruity of the old-fashioned spectacle settled at the centre of Luke's wide, ruddy face. He had told her that he had found the pince-nez amongst his grandfather's effects, although he had never seen him wearing such a thing. He didn't know where it had come from, but he liked to believe that he was following in the wake of an erudite ancestor. It also helped his image, he had added, with a twinkle in his eye; his clients were more at ease when he produced the scholarly accoutrement.

The silence was becoming weighty.

"Has Alec left a large legacy to the community?" Bess asked, voicing her curiosity.

Luke clicked open the locks on his briefcase and lifted out the envelope lying on top. "Alec has left the bulk of his estate to the community," he told her, glancing over his pince-nez at Cissie who was flicking at a splash of drink on her skirt. "There are only three legacies, one to Isolda Brown, that is his cousin in Canada, one to Laura Smythe, he nodded towards Bess, and the third to a Florence Rose whom, I believe, is an actress in a television serial."

There were exclamations of surprise.

"Fancy old Alec hankering after a soap star," Thorfinn remarked with amusement. He was still leaning against the mantel, warming his whisky in his hands. "Totally in character, of course."

"Now, Thorfinn," Miss Silver reprimanded, her voice severe, "we're not here to make fun of Alec or judge his actions but to discharge our duties as members of the Community Council."

Luke opened his envelope and handed a copy of the will to each of them.

"You will see that his assets are to be spent raising the causeway and joining Trowsay to the mainland."

"Never!" Cissie exclaimed in outrage, dropping her copy of the will on to her lap in a gesture of dismissal.

"You're not against it, are you, Mrs Vale?" Hanna asked in surprise. She could imagine Rupert's elation when he heard the news. "Surely it would benefit the community to have easy access to the mainland."

"It would no doubt benefit some people," Cissie answered tartly, the inference pointed, "but those who've been born and bred on this island will want it to stay the way it is."

"That remains to be ascertained," Miss Silver put in.

"I'm afraid there will be opposition, Hanna."

"Do you really think so?"

Thorfinn nodded and she looked down at her hands, threading and unthreading her fingers, her cheeks flushed. She would have liked Thorfinn to support her but she was not really surprised at his response. His lack of a job commensurate with his academic ability was not entirely due to laziness; he put little store on monetary acquisition, enjoying the natural environment and what Trowsay had to offer.

Bess fidgeted with her short, dark curls in nervous indecision. She never liked to take sides or provoke disharmony around her. "Alec had the support of the farmers," she murmured, and immediately quailed under the glare that Cissie sent in her direction.

Luke was sitting back in his armchair, his hands folded over his stomach, listening to each in turn, his half-raised eyebrows expressing surprise.

"I see that the young TV star ..." Thorfinn began.

"She's not so young," Cissie corrected him.

"I bow to your superior knowledge, Mrs Vale, but as I was about to say, her legacy would appear to be tied to her appearance here to open this new road."

"She will not be needed."

"Rather hard on her to have such a string attached."

Luke leaned forward and opened his briefcase. The click of the locks interrupted the dialogue.

"It's clear that you have much to discuss before you need further assistance from me," he said, putting his papers away. "However you will note that if this road does not go ahead for any reason, the money will go to Cancer Research." He closed his case and pushed himself upright with the help of the armrest. "You've got a room for me, Hanna, I think. The tides are rather awkward today."

Hanna agreed that a booking had been made.

When she returned from giving Luke his room key, she was surprised to see that the meeting was breaking up. Bess had already put on her coat and was picking up her scarf and handbag.

Miss Silver offered reassurance.

"I have not allowed further discussion of the will today, Hanna. It is wiser for us all to go away and give careful thought to the consequences of carrying out Alec's wishes."

Hanna agreed, noting that Cissie was still comfortably ensconced on the sofa, nursing her drink. She sent Bess a silent message which was received.

Bess touched Cissie's shoulder. "Would you take me home, Mrs Vale?"

"Aye, it's time you were back, Bess." Cissie finished her drink and pushed herself up. "They'll be waiting to hear what Luke had to say and we'll have a thing or two to tell them now."

The use of the plural pronoun was noted. Bess gave a half-smile and mumbled acquiescence, responding to Thorfinn's wink as they left the sitting room by casting her eyes heavenward.

Thorfinn was in no hurry to leave the hotel. He lagged behind in the hall and lingered in the porch after Cissie and Bess had driven off, hoping that Miss Silver would also depart speedily. It was a false hope. She stayed firmly in place, eyeing him steadily

Hanna eased his disappointment by saying: "We will see you tonight, Thorfinn. I believe you are dining with the Wentworths."

Thorfinn nodded, and taking her hand held it to his chest. "No hard feelings I hope, my lovely."

"Of course not."

"Old Alec is having his last laugh with his will. He liked to stir things up."

Hanna reclaimed her hand thoughtfully. "Cissie Vale is right, of course. It would benefit us. The tides can be a nuisance for the hotel."

"For us all at times, but you will have guests who choose Trowsay because it has the charm of an island."

"Rupert will support the scheme. I'm sure of that."

"No doubt our estimable laird is thinking of lower things."

"Goodbye, Thorfinn."

He laughed, turning to blow her a kiss and give Miss Silver a parting bow.

Hanna invited Chloe Silver to take a turn round her garden and stay for tea but this was refused. Her sister would be looking out for her, she was told.

As they walked to her van, Miss Silver said: "The joining of Trowsay to the mainland has been spoken about for as far back as I can remember, but the situation is different now that we can pay for it ourselves. We must call a public meeting and consult everyone on the island before we decide. I assure you, Hanna, that that will be done. We will not make a hasty decision one way or the other."

Hanna opened the door of the high-roofed van, converted to take Martha Silver's wheelchair. "If our meeting today is anything to go by," she said with a rueful smile, "there's trouble ahead."

She settled Miss Silver into the front seat and closed the door, waving until the van took the turning on to the main road and disappeared from sight.

By the time Hanna had finished clearing the dishes and tidying the sitting room, Rupert was behind the reception desk reading his newspaper. She asked about the gathering of jolly mourners up at Brackenlea.

"A boozy do," he responded, with a grimace and a shrug. "And you? Everyone is waiting to hear the news. Did Alec leave his money for the Community Council to squander?"

The telephone started to ring.

"You'll never believe it, Rupe," Hanna began, reaching for the receiver. "Most of his estate is earmarked to build a raised road across to the mainland." She watched

Rupert's astounded expression as she put the phone to her ear.

"Is that the Trowsay House Hotel?" the caller asked before Hanna had time to make herself known.

"Yes, it is."

"Sorry to trouble you but I wonder if you could help me. Do you know someone there called Alec Maconachie who lives at Selkie Bay Farm. I've been ringing the number he gave me but without success."

"He's not there," Hanna said softly and told her of Alec's death.

"My goodness, has he really passed on?" The caller's voice was high-pitched with astonishment. "Actually I don't know the man at all but he has written me an extraordinary letter which has just been forwarded." Hanna remembered the letter on Alec's bedside table. "The thing is, he says that if I get in touch with him I will hear something to my advantage. It sounds like legal jargon for a legacy but I've no idea who he is."

"Are you a star in a TV serial?"

The caller laughed. "Hardly a star, I'm afraid, but I have a part as a relative of one of the main characters who visits the neighbourhood from time to time."

"In that case, you should get in touch with the lawyer dealing with the estate. Let me give you his number and you can contact him tomorrow."

"Look, the reason why I'm ringing is that I've just finished doing a play in Inverness and I thought I might drive up and stay for a few days."

"It might be best to contact Mr Sinclair first," Hanna cautioned.

"I think I'll come anyway. My mother came from one of the islands. I have never known which island it was but it now looks as though it could've been Trowsay."

Hanna was startled into silence. Could that be the connection. Could Alec have known the actress's mother. A childhood sweetheart, perhaps.

"Are you still there?"

Hanna came out of her reverie. "Yes, I'm still here. Would you like me to book a room for you?"

"I feel sure your terms would be beyond my means. Is there a decent B & B you could recommend?"

"Gemma Martin, the farmer's wife at The Mains, does B & B. If she can't take you, I'm sure she can recommend someone else. Let me get the number."

Hanna finished the call and slowly replaced the receiver, thinking about the actress and her revelation.

Rupert interrupted her thoughts.

"Is Trowsay really going to be joined to the mainland?"

"If the majority agree."

He chortled to himself. "I should go to church more often."

"There is even more to it than that, Rupert. That call, for instance …" Hanna saw Jean hovering beside the door of the cocktail lounge. "Come through for a bit and I'll tell you all about it."

3

Thorfinn put on his one and only jacket and tie, seldom in use and aged in years. Marigold had assured him that he would get on well with her father but he doubted it. He had no illusions about her Aunt Isabel's opinion of him and he expected her father to take an even grimmer view.

When he came out of his house, he found Mrs McFea sweeping the flagstone path. Relations between the two of them had remained cordial since the episode with the trout. He had no idea why that should be so, but he welcomed it.

"Hi, there," he said, dropping his latch and turning to her with a smile. There was no room for him to pass until she had lifted her broom and given way.

"Off to meet your future father-in-law is it, Thorfinn?"

"You're teasing me, Mrs McFea."

He was not surprised that she knew where he was going. Marigold had gone next door for a chat while he was making the breakfast that morning and had come back with the gift of a cross-stitched wall-hanging and stories about the grand people Mrs McFea had cooked for before returning to Trowsay.

"A right fine lass."

Thorfinn agreed. He loved Marigold's joyful enthusiasm and generous nature.

"Far too good for you, my lad, unless you pull yourself up by your boot strings and get yourself a proper job."

Thorfinn looked down at his loafers, decorated with a twist of leather and said with a chuckle: "Too short and knotty to hold on to, I'm afraid."

"Naughty!" Mrs McFea exclaimed, stopping her sweeping and the blood starting to rise. "That's not what I would call what's been going on between the two of you. Indecent is more like it." She rested on the handle of her broom waiting for an explanation but, for once, Thorfinn was lost for words. He could neither explain his joke nor justify his relationship with Marigold to Mrs McFea's decency standard.

She relented.

"Get on with you, Thorfinn," she said, lifting her broom from his path and squashing herself against the wall so that he could pass. "You mind your manners now."

Marigold jumped up when Thorfinn appeared at the door of the cocktail lounge and ran to give him a quick kiss. She took his hand and presented him to her father with a happy laugh and an upward adoring look. Bertie Wentworth was a round, bouncy man, a Tweedledum of a man, who made Thorfinn welcome. He ordered him a double whisky and sat back in his chair with a contented smile to see how the evening would develop. Thorfinn responded to his easy manner with a relieved grin and turned to Marigold's Aunt Isabel. He enquired after her health before sitting down on the chair that Marigold had drawn up close to hers. He could see that Marigold's merry countenance and light-hearted attitude to life had been inherited from her father (although fortunately she had not inherited any of his other features) and that he was not going to come over all heavy with him.

As they sipped their pre-prandial drinks, Isabel Pritchard probed a bit, trying to find out about Thorfinn's family, his current financial situation and his future prospects. Bertie didn't seem over concerned that his daughter had fallen in love with a bum, even although Thorfinn was a reasonably presentable bum.

"From what you say, I'm not quite sure how you earn your living," Isabel enquired, taking a more direct route to find out about Thorfinn's prospects.

He was tempted by her inquisitiveness to tease a bit. She could guess his present circumstances and he disliked having to rest on the laurels of past academic achievements in order to be accepted.

"I'm afraid I make a precarious living," he said ruefully. "But the pound in my pocket is of little importance when I can gather and eat what the land and the sea have to offer."

"Indeed."

"And there's a bountiful supply if you know where to look."

"What exactly do you eat?" Bertie asked, sipping his whisky to hide his smile.

"All sorts of things – watercress, dandelion leaves, nettles, seagulls' eggs, crabs, wild mushrooms, things like that."

Isabel raised her eyebrows and looked down the length of her nose. "These edibles will give you essential nutrients," she said, laying her gin and tonic on the table beside her, "and they should not have an adverse effect on your digestive system if you wash the watercress in fresh sea water and choose your seagulls' eggs carefully."

Thorfinn's startled expression crumpled and widened into a grin. He thought his tease had boomeranged.

"Uncle Simon was an adventurer," Marigold explained.

Isabel corrected her sharply: "Your Uncle Simon was a retired naval officer."

"Yes, Aunt Isabel, but you would hardly believe it. He was such fun."

Bertie agreed and was developing the theme for Thorfinn's amusement when he remembered that Isabel had been bereaved by Simon's love of fun. He sighed. "A tragic loss for you, dear Isabel."

Isabel acknowledged this with a nod and lowered her eyes.

When the silence lengthened and it seemed clear that Isabel was not going to expand on her unusual life, Marigold went on: "Besides crabs, we're always on the lookout for other things to eat along the shore. Mussels and … what are those tiny, snail-like things called, Thorfinn?"

"Whelks." Marigold's softly manicured hand was holding his possessively and he gave it an indulgent squeeze. "There are also the occasional suicidal birds or co-operative fish that come my way."

"Indeed."

Isabel was not looking pleased and Thorfinn knew that he had gone far enough in reinforcing her image of him.

"Actually I do a bit of writing and research," he told her with an apologetic smile. That was straining the truth through a hair sieve but he could see that a trickle of truth was needed. "I suppose you could say that I am self-employed … in the broadest sense of the word, of course."

"There you are, Isabel, the lad pays his taxes," Bertie said triumphantly and Thorfinn laughed at this assessment of his modest income.

"He is also into astrology, Daddy. He sticks pins into a round board decorated with the signs of the zodiac and can tell everything that's going to happen in the future."

"Not quite everything, sweetheart, there is the odd fact that I fail to predict."

Marigold chortled with delight. "He's had heaps of things published."

Isabel enquired melodiously: "And has your writing been well received, Thorfinn?"

"Tolerably."

"How interesting." There was no doubt by the change in her tone that Thorfinn had climbed one or two rungs up the social ladder of acceptability.

"You don't sound as if you come from this part of the world," Bertie remarked.

"I'm not an islander by birth but I've looked on Trowsay as my home since student days. I was the odd-job man here at the house during holidays and while writing my thesis."

Bertie looked across at Isabel with a merry twinkle in his eye, but she was studying the contents of her glass. "What was your subject?"

"Biophysics. I taught science at a comprehensive to begin with but I'm not made of the right stuff to inspire the reluctant mind. I threw in the chalk when the old man left me a house on the estate."

"And it's a life that you obviously enjoy."

Bertie jumped up to order another round of drinks and get the menu.

"I wish we were staying longer," Marigold said, making a face. "It's such fun finding things to eat and cooking them fresh."

"I'm sure it is."

"I've also learned to gut fish, dress crab, identify edible fungi and lots of other things."

"Good for you."

"And we pull driftwood up the beach to dry so that Thorfinn can be warm in the winter. Today we found a piece of hardwood that had floated right across the ocean." She looked at her father and Isabel with sparkling eyes.

Her father said that he did not doubt that she had been enjoying herself, but Thorfinn could see by his indulgent expression as he passed Marigold the menu, that he knew her enthusiasm for the simple life would not last beyond the holiday end.

As the evening progressed, his enjoyment increased. He found that Marigold's father had not made his fortune as a wheeler and dealer but was an ideas man and an inventor. They discussed all manner of subjects and the dinner was eaten and drunk in a mood of harmony. Even Isabel became more animated as the wine flowed. Thorfinn flattered her and they established a pleasant rapport although she made it clear, through unsubtle inferences, that Thorfinn was not a suitable suitor for her niece and should not expect their romance to prosper. As Thorfinn concurred with her assessment of his eligibility, it did not mar the cordiality of the evening.

Liqueurs were ordered and coffee served. Marigold inspected the plate of sweetmeats that accompanied the coffee and chose a stuffed date. She picked out the marzipan and rolled the odd bits together on her plate. Her father watched her and when she was satisfied with her offering, he leaned forward and opened his mouth, ready for her to pop the misshapen ball in. They exchanged familial smiles as he sat back, chewing with contentment, his hands folded over his rounded stomach.

"I think we should go to the Caithness glass factory tomorrow, Marigold," Isabel said pouring the coffee and handing her a cup. "We can get presents there to take home."

Marigold was dismayed.

"We were planning to climb Ben Hope tomorrow, weren't we, Thorfinn?"

He nodded and asked Isabel pleasantly if she would like to come with them.

"I think not." She looked across the table at Bertie, her eyebrows raised, expecting him to support her wish to have Marigold spend the day with her, but before she could ask him directly to intervene, he was on his feet.

"I wonder what's happened to our drinks," he said and was off.

Thorfinn watched him pass between the tables, covering his cowardice with excessive bonhomie. He stopped beside Arthur Bartholomew and slapped him on the shoulder in comradely congratulations. Two fine trout lay on the enamel tray in the hall and there was no need to exaggerate their size or weight. He was still there, exchanging fishy stories with the two elderly men, when Rupert arrived with their tray of drinks.

"What's been keeping you?" Bertie asked, leading the way back to his table. "I thought you had forgotten about us."

Rupert set the tray down and apologised.

"I couldn't find my twenty-year-old malt," he explained. "Hanna had it in the kitchen."

Bertie relaxed and toasted the absent cook, praising her culinary skills.

Thorfinn reciprocated the toast, swirling his brandy round in its balloon glass with a gleam in his eye and a smile on his lips. He hoped that the whisky would find its way back to the kitchen before his next happy hour with Hanna.

4

Rupert tossed and turned throughout the small hours, pulling at the bedclothes and groaning from time to time. He hoped to waken Hanna but she remained stubbornly still and he had to resort to a two-way conversation inside his head, with Hanna's imagined self pointing out difficulties that became more and more fantastic as the night passed. He woke as Hanna came up the spiral staircase, her cheeks healthily rosy and her step brisk. She was carrying a tray with tea and toast.

"Time you were up, Rupe. It's the most gorgeous day out."

It was only twenty minutes to three and he couldn't understand why Hanna was up and about so early. He opened his eyes and looked at the clock on his bedside table again; the hands were pointing to a quarter past eight. He should have felt grumpy at not being able to make capital out of his wretched hours of sleeplessness but Hanna was smiling down at him and he forgot his ill humour.

"Now let me get you comfortable," she said, fussing over him as he sat up, plumping up the discarded pillows and putting them behind his back.

"You spoil me," he said complacently as she laid the tray on his lap. He could see that the toast was cut how he liked it, in fingers with the crusts cut off.

"Comfortable?" she asked, staying where she was beside the bed and fiddling with the things on his bedside table. "There's a letter from Aunt Liz. I've left it in the office."

"What does she want now?"

Hanna shrugged, not meeting his eyes.

"No need to feel guilty," he said gently, touching her hand.

"I'm not."

But he knew she was. She hated to be reminded of his first wife, her mother's sister, even although he had been divorced for years before he met Hanna at his daughter's wedding.

"Come and sit down," he invited, patting the duvet in invitation.

She sat on the edge of the bed watching him drink his tea.

"Jean was telling me that the police are taking Davey's stories seriously," she told him. "Evidently a grey car was seen in the Talhaugh car park on the night of the accident but there were no strangers in the pub."

Rupert lifted a piece of floppy toast. "No one would have seen a thing if old Davey's ramblings hadn't stimulated imaginations."

"You don't think there's anything in it?"

"Absolutely not. Lots of tourists travel along the north coast at this time of year and stop to take a look at Trowsay." He popped the toast into his mouth and chewed. "What really got me was Alec's bequest to the island being on the Radio last night. That'll bring all the environmental cranks up from the cities to tell us what to do."

"Perhaps." She smiled. "I don't suppose Davey will be trying to stop them crossing or Cissie refuse service at the shop." The islanders' reaction to the protest against seal culling was part of island folklore.

"Mrs Vale will be giving them a warm welcome. Tavish Martin says that she has started a petition against the road."

Hanna grimaced. "Everyone will sign it if Cissie thrusts it under their noses."

"Some counter-action is needed to spike her guns. D'you think we could have a public meeting before the ceilidh on Saturday night?"

"I don't think so, Rupert. It's far too soon and Chloe Silver would never agree."

Rupert's mouth hardened into a stubborn line.

"It needn't be an official meeting. The ceilidh is in our ballroom and I can arrange to have a formal discussion beforehand if I want."

There was the distant sound of the second gong being struck in the hall. Hanna looked at her watch. "I must go," she said, getting up and putting Rupert's cup and plate together. "Why don't you ring Chloe? Say that the island is rife with gossip and it would help to settle things if everyone had a chance to air their views. See what she says." She called back over her shoulder. "I doubt if it will sway her though."

However Miss Silver proved to be surprisingly amenable when Rupert telephoned her acting the role of the concerned citizen.

"You are correct, Rupert," she responded calmly, interrupting him in mid-argument. "There is unhealthy division and discord in the community. It would be wise to let everyone have their say in an open forum where uncharitable views can be seen for what they are."

"Quite so." It was not the angle he wanted to stress. "Personally I never listen to the jabbering of the gossips."

"Nor I," Miss Silver retorted with asperity. "But I'm afraid my sister is slightly deaf and conversations between her and Patsy Gunn are very audible. According to Patsy, Alec's Trowsay relatives are finding reasons for being cut out of his will, some of them most unpleasant."

"That's understandable, I suppose."

"It is not understandable, Rupert," Miss Silver corrected him. "Such attitudes are motivated by greed."

"Quite so." Rupert didn't want to pursue that line, which could push him off the moral height of civil duty onto the rocky ground of personal advantage. "Anyway I'm glad you agree with me ... about the meeting, I mean. Now if I did the arranging, would you be willing to take the chair and keep order? If you could see your way to laying out the facts at the beginning, even better."

"Yes, I will do that, Rupert. I am unable to preach yet again on the ninth commandment but I can try and encourage more tolerance in an opening address."

"The ninth commandment?"

Miss Silver clicked her tongue in reproach. "I shall direct you to the place in the Bible where you can find our Lord's commands."

Rupert had only wanted a few introductory words not a sermon and changed the subject quickly.

"Such a generous gift from one of the island's leading citizens requires fulsome praise."

"A generous gift indeed."

"I'm glad you see it that way."

"I am well aware of the way you would like me to see it, Rupert, but that is of no consequence. I shall conduct the meeting in an even-handed manner."

"Fair enough. 7.30 on Saturday, shall we say?"

Rupert was sure that it was the force of his personality that had charmed Miss Silver into agreement and was pleased with himself. He went off to tell Hanna of his success and accept her admiration. As he was leaving the kitchen, he remembered Miss Silver's clicking tongue.

"By the way, Hanna, what is the ninth commandment?"

Hanna stopped chopping the vegetables for the soup and gave his question a moment's thought. "As far as I can remember, it's the bearing of false witness against one's neighbour."

"That figures."

When he reached his office he found the letter from his first wife propped up in a position where it could not be missed. It was addressed to them both but it was unopened. He slit the envelope across and read the content without expression. His younger son (and the apple of his mother's eye) had yet another business idea that would make his fortune if his father came up with the initial finance. Rupert doubted it and tossed the letter into his in tray. More importantly, a notice needed to be printed giving the time and place of the meeting. He did that on his word processor and ran off thirty copies. Three copies would have been sufficient, one for the hotel, one for the old Free Church (where village meetings were held) and one for the shop, but he thought he would take a walk round the village, ostensibly to leave a notice at each house, but in reality to impress his views on whomever he met.

His first stop was the shop.

When the tinkle of the doorbell had subsided, he lifted his cap and smiled all round, greeting those present. Cissie said nothing, waiting for him to state his business.

"Ah, Mrs Vale, no papers today, I see," he said, looking round and about. He was all set to give her petition the once-over and check who had signed it, but she must have put it under the counter when she saw him coming.

"They'll be in around four," Cissie told him, not moving from her position behind the post office cage

"What a blessing it will be when we have the raised road across to the mainland and we can get our newspapers at a regular time. Don't you think so?" he enquired of the elderly woman whom Cissie was serving, but she had been the local head teacher and was adept at side-stepping a trap that had been laid to catch her.

"I seldom take a daily paper," she said in a crisp voice, collecting the notes that Cissie had placed on the counter with her pink-tipped fingers and putting them carefully in her wallet. She was above average in height with a sharp bone-structure and pendulous breasts. She had burned her bra years before it had become fashionable to do so and gravity had taken its toll.

"Ah, quite so." Rupert peeled a copy of his notice from the bundle he was carrying and handed it to Cissie with a request that she display it on the shop door. Cissie cast her eyes over it without a change of expression and then fixed him with a basilisk eye, waiting for him to leave the shop.

But he was not to be outdone entirely.

"My wife has asked me to get some celeriac, Mrs Vale. Do you have such a thing?"

"I think you'll see that I have not, Mr Treatham. There is no call for that sort of fancy food here." Cissie folded her lips back into her gums and watched Rupert's departure without so much as a flicker of her drooping eyelids.

He climbed back into his Range Rover and sat for a moment lighting a cheroot. He puffed it into a steady glow and stuck it in his mouth before reaching for the starter. Atlanticscape was as good a place as any to start his campaign, he decided. Phil made a proper cup of coffee and was always good company.

He drove round the bay and up to Atlanticscape's open gates. The house had been built by the colonial who had donated the cemetery gates but the estate had changed hands several times since the original family had moved away to replenish its fortune. In their different ways, it was an ideal place for the two artists. Duncan craved silence for his deeply psychological art and was happy to walk over the moors or round the coast with his thoughts for company. Phil, on the other hand, was an extrovert, quick to offer help when needed and happy to pass the time of day, sharing triumphs or listening to grievances. He was a carpenter by trade and made fun furniture.

Rupert turned through the gates and changed down a gear, manoeuvring between the potholes at the bottom of the drive. There was evidence that the drive had been wide and smooth at one time, with neat stone edges, but now it was just a fenceless track winding upwards through sour, over-grazed land, with grass and weeds growing through its broken surface. Resting sheep were reluctant to move from the patches of road that had been warmed by the sun, only pulling themselves up and scattering when it was clear that they had no alternative. By the time the Range Rover reached the top of the last incline, Phil was leaning out of his workshop window on the top floor, his forefinger over his lips and his arm a-flap. Rupert knew that he was being beseeched not to slam his car door and disturb Duncan at his work. He responded with a thumbs up from his open window, turning off his engine and gliding to a halt in front of the house, his wheels crunching on the gravel.

The front door was on the latch and he pushed it open, dropping his cap on a peg in the shape of a butler's obsequious hand and stopping to look at himself in the mirror. The design of the mirror had been inspired by the evil queen in *Snow White and the Seven Dwarfs*. A carved knowing face was stretched over the top, with hair flowing in snake-like waves round the frame and two bony, long-nailed fingers gripping the glass at the sides. Underneath it, a wooden plaque had the words of the fairy tale deeply carved into its surface. Phil's creations could be found in surprising places all over the house, frequently lurking in dark corners or peeking from behind doors.

Rupert combed his hair and refreshed his moustache, reaching the hall as Phil lumbered heavily down the stairs with his hand on the banister. Bernie, his aged

St Bernard, followed along behind at a sedate pace. Phil was a big man with bushy iron-grey hair and eyebrows to match. At one time he had had the muscles of a weightlifter (there were photographs in the bathroom to prove it) but now he drooped all over, the loose skin on his face folded into deep furrows and his eyes softly appealing.

Rupert slapped him on the shoulder and whispered a greeting.

Phil smiled his welcome, leading the way to the kitchen at the back. As they passed the parlour door, he whispered: "You must see Duncan's latest creation," and indicated the large painting on the wall facing them.

Duncan was an abstract expressionist in the style of Jackson Pollock, the relationship between the elements and man's nature inspiring his work. Since coming to Trowsay, it was the changing tones and merging shapes of the clouds that tormented his thoughts and stimulated his imagination: the colourful streaks of sunlight or the moving shadows cast on the ocean; the relentless spitting of life-giving rain or the cuts of destructive lightening. These all reflected for him the different facets of human existence and the ultimate eternal mystery.

Rupert was not a fan. He liked to recognise the subject matter of a painting so that he could judge the ability of the artist. Phil had tried to educate him by begging him to look beyond the surface of the painting into its depth and explore the juxtapositions with spiritual as well as visual awareness. It had not worked for him but it had worked for Hanna. The more she looked, the more she seemed to see and sense, but he could not appreciate the rhythm and illusory quality of the forms and colours created by the lavish use of dripping pigments and the ambiguity of line. Hanna said that it was like looking through a mottled windowpane into a new world. But he didn't see the point, preferring a realistic rendering of this world to a world that was represented by an incomprehensible mess of paint.

This latest creation was a gigantic work, filling a good part of the wall, and it was not painted in the cool blues and earthy range of colours that were Duncan's trademark. This time the canvas was covered in hot splashes of steamy rage and jagged edges of purple despair, tangled and cut by distorted and disjointed black strokes of violence.

Phil was watching him for his reaction.

"Quite shocking," Rupert said with a shudder.

"It is meant to shock. When Duncan was a small boy he saw a mill fire in his home town. There were workers caught on the top floor behind barred windows. He still has nightmares about it. He saw a similar fire in a high-rise apartment block in Chicago recently."

"Surely the tenants were not caught behind barred windows in this day and age."

"No, but the wind was whipping up the flames and the cries were the same."

Rupert could see something of what was described – at least the prominent colours mimicked flames – but he didn't want to be reminded of life's horrors when they didn't affect him personally.

"Not really my cup of tea," he said ruefully, stepping back to get a more distant view and promptly tripping over Bernie.

Bernie yelped and got clumsily to his feet, looking at Rupert in hurtful bewilderment. He could not understand why Rupert would want to kick him. Rupert was contrite and apologetic but Phil ticked Bernie off for getting in the way. (He also patted him with affection to show that he was not really annoyed.) Once that had been sorted out, they continued on their way to the kitchen at the back of the house.

Rupert sat watching Phil as he lifted the heavy kettle off the Aga and set the coffee to percolate. That done, Phil took an assortment of tins out of the side cupboard and started lifting their lids, looking for an appropriate accompaniment. He decided on a rich fruitcake and eased it out on to the bread board.

"You don't usually come visiting in the mornings, Rupert," he said with an enquiring lift to his voice.

Rupert started to explain about Alec's will but Phil stopped him. He had heard all about it from three different sources, he said, with many disgruntled opinions and malicious gossip. Rupert wanted to hear more and Phil repeated a story or two while he cut large slabs of cake and laid them neatly on a plate. (He did not say that some relatives were accusing Hanna of subjecting Alec to undue influence during her morning visits, a reason for challenging the will, and others that it was unseemly for a married woman to visit a strange man so early in the morning when he had plenty of kith and kin to see to his needs.)

Rupert was only half listening; his mind was on his notice. He pulled the bundle out of his jacket pocket and laid it down in front of him. Phil squinted round to see what it was all about and Rupert turned a copy, passing it across the table and pointing to where it said that Miss Silver would be taking the chair. "It has her complete support," he told him, to emphasise the meeting's legitimacy.

Phil was dubious about the merits of bringing the two sides together and thought it would create tension rather than alleviating it. He was cautious when Rupert pressed him for his personal views.

"To be honest, Rupert, I wouldn't want to be seen to take sides." He filled the cups with coffee and offered milk and sugar. "I think Duncan and I will give the meeting a miss."

"I hoped that I could look to you for support," Rupert said a trifle petulantly, taking a slice of cake.

"I can only promise that I won't vote against you in the referendum, which I am told will take place eventually. It is for the islanders to decide." He looked up, sensing Duncan's approach, and when Duncan appeared in the doorway, he asked anxiously: "Did we interrupt you?" He was always concerned in case Duncan lost his inspiration in the middle of a painting.

Duncan reassured him, pulling out a kitchen chair and accepting a cup of coffee. He was older than Phil, well over sixty, and in contrast to his partner was slight of build, with a nervous twitch and a completely bald head. His brains seemed to pulsate when he was thinking deeply.

"To what do we owe this pleasure?" he asked Rupert.

Rupert told him the reason for his visit and explained the need, as he saw it, for positive action to counteract the attitudes of those who had airy-fairy ideas.

"I'd be a bit careful with that argument, Rupert," Duncan said, fiddling with his teaspoon and looking up at Rupert with a twinkle in his eye.

Rupert misinterpreted his amusement, being too focused on his own concerns.

"All right, Duncan, it would benefit us, I'll grant you that, but you must admit that the irregular flow of the tides is an unmitigated nuisance. I've heard you saying so yourself. Remember the time when you had to stay in the pub at Talhaugh because the flights and the tides didn't work well together."

"And the beds were damp."

"There you are!" Rupert exclaimed triumphantly.

"But the landlord was most generous with his toddies and Trowsay looked very fine seen from the other side of the water."

Rupert gave up. He could see that his two friends were not in favour of a permanent link with the mainland. The promise not to vote was as much as he was going to get. They talked of other things.

Over the next hour, Rupert got discouraged. The houses on the Atlanticscape side of the harbour were either empty or the occupants were not answering his knock. On two occasions he sensed a presence behind the door but it was not opened and he was obliged to push his notice through the letterboxes without the chance to have his say. Round the other side of the bay, past the shop and Tom Nicol's joinery, was the old Free Church. After a long spell of hollow dereliction and in an attempt to halt the depopulation of the island, this monumental building had been converted into industrial units of various sizes. An upper floor had been fitted into the awkwardly-windowed space and partitions erected throughout. Half of the units had been let.

Rupert turned the latch ring and put his shoulder against the plain, heavy oak door. It creaked open and he stepped up into a narrow vestibule which was dark and gloomy. There was no light bulb in the socket attached to the long flex hanging from the ceiling and he had to prop the door open with a heavy Bible while he read the notices; some were advertising the commercial activities within, and others informing the public about church or social meetings. There were no spare drawing pins. Most notices swung from only the one pin and it took a bit of reorganisation before he could affix his notice in a prominent position. Once he was satisfied with his skilful adjustments, he followed a directional sign to the laboratory, finding a white-coated researcher in the kitchen.

She gave him short shrift.

The knitting machines were silent and abandoned in the other commercial room downstairs but he could hear a variety of noises coming from above. The top floor was let to the island craft co-operative. Rupert climbed the stairs and found himself in a large, light, airy space. The new wooden floor had not cut the long narrow church windows in half. Instead the window alcoves were cordoned off and made safe with reinforced glass insets. The intricate stonework and starry shape of the rose window at the apex gave a glow of diffused light and brightened the wooden floor with shadowed patterns. Waist-high partitions divided the room into three distinct areas, a workroom, a packing area and a playroom. There were six sewing machines in the main part of the room, four in use, with tables to the right and left of each machine station.

Tara and Madge Gunn were among the workers making Trowsay capes, a traditional long cloak with a double hood, updated for modern use. They were sliding their work into their machines and turning finished rows of stitching at speed. The tables on their left were heaped with work waiting to be done. In the playroom, six or seven children were running about; one had come through and was leaning heavily against his mother as she operated her machine.

When Rupert was noticed, work slowed and the noise of the machines petered out; the children stopped running and collapsed in a heap, righting themselves to stand and stare. He lifted his hat and greeted those present, before walking down the room to the cutting-out table at the far end. This was presided over by a very large, authoritative figure. She looked up briefly when she saw Rupert advancing towards her but she finished cutting before she spoke, and the "Yes" of enquiry was not encouraging.

Rupert took off his hat and introduced himself before starting his charm offensive, but he was forced by the steady gaze fixed on him to come to the point.

The woman listened to what he had to say, straightening her shoulders and putting her scissors down neatly beside the cloth she was cutting.

"I am totally opposed to any such construction," she told him. "It would ruin the cohesion of our island community and our independence. Have you any idea, Mr Treatham, how difficult it is to keep this co-operative solvent?" As this was a rhetorical question, she didn't wait for his answer. "I have great difficulty getting orders and even more difficulty in filling them. Fifty capes must be finished and on their way within two weeks. The material was late in arriving but I know from grim experience that that will not be taken into account if the delivery is late."

During this tirade, the children had left their play area and were now closely packed round Rupert's legs, in curious delight at this unusual diversion. He felt imprisoned. It was a long time since he had had any dealings with children and even in the years when his children were young, he had managed to spend as much time as possible away from home.

"I can understand how you feel," Rupert began, but his adversary picked up her scissors in irritation and dismissal of this banal and false assertion. Rupert persevered, feeling moist, paint-stained fingers taking his hand. He looked down at the winsome upturned face and felt that he could not disentangle them. "The new road could be an asset to your enterprise, Mrs ..."

"Spencer."

"Mrs Spencer, of course." Rupert's small bow of acknowledgement and smile was not reciprocated. "You would be able to get workers from the mainland if they had unimpeded access to the island".

"Really, Mr Treatham, you have no understanding of the situation." Mrs Spencer all but threw down her scissors in exasperation. "I retired up here with my husband and I did not choose to be part of this co-operative. It was my duty to become involved because I was the only one here with experience of manufacturing and marketing."

Rupert would have given up there and then, freed himself from the curious toddlers, and headed for the door if he had not seen Tara Gunn raising her eyes heavenward, mimicking Mrs Spencer's indignation.

"Let the gentleman be, Winnie," Tara said, putting out her hand for a copy of the notice. "Give it here; I'll be along to cheer you at your meeting if my Mum will come in early." Her friends on the adjacent sewing machines said that they might as well cone along early too. They were all going to the ceilidh. He passed copies around, leaving Madge's on the table beside her. She gave him a brief smile of thanks while turning her work, ready to start again.

It had not taken long for Cissie to find out that Rupert was knocking on doors and canvassing support for his position. She had followed his progress from her side windows as he worked his way round the bay and wanted him to know that she was aware of what he was doing so when he came down from the Free Church, she was standing outside her shop with her arms akimbo.

On a devilish impulse, Rupert blew her a kiss.

Later that day, Rupert had cause to reassess his position.

He was in his tiny office behind the reception desk checking over Mr Ayesh and Mr Mann's accounts, when he felt that he was being watched from closer at hand than he would have expected. He looked up to see Mr Ayesh's benign face peering at him from just above the knuckles that were about to make a discreet knock. He got up and opened the door with annoyance. He liked the guests to stay at the other side of the reception desk.

"Could I have a word with you, Mr Treatham?" Mr Ayesh asked pleasantly.

Rupert acknowledged the request and moved to come out of his office, knowing that complaints were better heard in public where the complainer would feel at a disadvantage.

Mr Ayesh stopped him. "In private please."

Rupert resumed his place behind the desk and waved his hand towards the only other chair. It was squeezed between the filing cabinet and the wall and Mr Ayesh had to position himself uncomfortably on the edge of the seat, pulling his bulky shoulders forward.

"I have been in correspondence with Little & Little, the estate agents in London," he said, coming straight to the point. "I believe you have this establishment on the market."

Rupert laid his pen down and regarded Mr Ayesh without expression. His muscles had tensed with shock but he was too old a hand at confrontation to allow amazement to show in his face.

"That is so," he said, when he had regained control of his voice. His mind was working overtime. What in the world would Mr Ayesh want with a hotel in the north of Scotland. He did not even look or act like an hotelier; he was too nice in his manner. "Am I to un-derstand from your enquiry, Mr Ayesh, that you wish to make a purchase?"

Mr Ayesh threw up his hands in protest. "You go too fast, Mr Treatham, but I will say that we have been looking for a property like this for many months now.

Unfortunately we have always encountered one or two problems. Your hotel does not have these problems and may be suitable for our purpose if our lawyers can arrange a mutually agreeable sum."

"Is Mr Mann your lawyer?"

Mr Ayesh laughed heartily. "I don't think he would be flattered to be so described."

Rupert got up.

"Come along to my sittingroom where we'll be more comfortable," he invited. "I'll have some lemonade sent through and we can discuss this matter in more comfortable surroundings." He opened the door. "After you, Mr Ayesh."

"'Ayesh' is not the name I am usually known by," his guest said, with an embarrassed apology. He reintroduced himself.

Rupert assured him that it was of no consequence. "In the hotel business, guests don't always sign the register in their own names."

"I didn't want to mislead you, Mr Treatham, but I was advised to be discreet. However, I see that my name means nothing to you and so the charade was not necessary."

As they came round the side of the reception desk, Mr Ayesh beckoned to his friend who was seated on the hall settle surrounded by luggage. He was reluctant to leave their belongings unattended but Rupert assured him that they would be quite safe and after a voluble discussion, which seemed questioning rather than heated, Mr Mann (or our Mullah, as he was reintroduced) took the briefcase, and the three men moved down the wide corridor to the Treathams' private quarters.

5

Davey sat at his door in the sunshine, with the open pages of his newspaper fluttering around his feet. He always had a bit of a doze when the news was repetitive, but to fall into a deep sleep at ten o'clock in the morning was not to his liking. It was a sign of old age getting the better of him and he wasn't ready for that yet. He moved his head round and about a bit, easing the muscle that had taken the brunt of his abrupt awakening, and got down on his hunkers to collect the pages together, folding them over into a bulky bundle.

Davey was seventy-four but he was still doing a few hours' work if the weather was fine. That morning he had woken at five and taken himself up the home field where he had seen a bit of dyke needing repair. He knew that if he didn't repair the wall quickly, Scott would knock in a few posts and sling a bit of wire across the gap. Scott always took the easy way to solve a problem, though he never grudged Davey his pay if he did the work. He had had his breakfast over at Brawtoon. He didn't go that way more than once or twice a week for the Brawtoon kitchen was a sad place for him now. His mother, his sister Ruthie and Betsy had all passed on over the years, and Alan was a poor soul, just sitting in his armchair beside the stove saying little, unless something stimulated his brain into a miscellaneous memory. Colleen was a good daughter-in-law to both of them but she was no farmer's wife when it came to providing a good breakfast. It was hard to credit that a big strapping lass like her, brought up over at The Mains where the men liked their food, would think that orange juice, followed by a khaki coloured cereal from a packet that chewed like old cardboard, was a fit meal for a working man. The thought of his unsatisfying breakfast brought Davey to his feet to put the porridge pot on. A bit of porridge and cream would set him up nicely.

When he had finished this second breakfast, he stood for a bit at his door watching the waves down in Braw Bay lapping on the shore. They were beginning to pull and swirl in the shallows, which was a sign that the tide was ebbing fast from the causeway. He would have his smoke down there. Heidi was off rabbiting but he gave her a whistle and set off to see what was going on, feeling refreshed by his sleep and his meal.

Within a short time of his arrival, a smart car came down the brae opposite and stopped at the bottom. A woman got out to look at the uneven surface of the causeway. She waved and he waved back. She then cupped her hands and called to him, asking if it was safe to cross. He nodded and got up from his boulder to beckon her forward. When she reached him, she rolled down her window and smiled. It was only then that he recognised the actress from the television, the one that Alec had fancied.

"It was good of you to guide me across," she said. "It's a hire car, you see, and I was nervous about the insurance covering any mishap."

Davey was sorry that his guiding had only amounted to raising his arm. He wanted to tell her that, but he couldn't find the words. He stood there all pink with pleasure, flashing a perfect white smile.

"Would you tell me the way to a Mrs Martin?" the star went on, picking up a piece of paper from the seat beside her. "She lives at The Mains which is not far past the hotel."

Davey found his voice. Giving instructions was what he was there at the causeway to do and he had his spiel ready. "You take the turning to the right at the top of the road," he began. "The first track is the one that leads to my caravan. You dinna tak that one. You go on along the way for a while and the next road end is to Brawtoon. That's where my brother bides ..." Davey gave her a complete rundown of every turning and who lived along it until he came to the turn-off for The Mains. He then went back to the beginning. "Now if you were wanting Alec's place, that's the Selkie Bay farmhouse, you would take the left hand turning at the top and go along the ither side o the loch." He looked down at the beautiful bemused face. "But maybe you winna be wanting to do that the noo."

"Did you know the farmer at Selkie Bay farm? The one who has died."

"I knew him fine. Younger than me by a-piece but a grand lad." Davey had never cared much for Alec or the family up at Selkie but it was not the time to say so.

"I see you've heard about my legacy. Tell me, do you think this Alec could have known my mother?"

She had lost Davey there. He couldn't see where her mother came into the picture. He had been told that Alec had taken a shine to the actress herself. Alec had always had an eye for the ladies but it was the young and shapely ones he liked, especially those who displayed themselves naked in the papers.

"I wouldna know about that," Davey said reluctantly, not wanting to be unhelpful.

"Thanks anyway." The actress gave him a wide smile, opening her eyes and blinking them twice, just like she did when the handsome man on the television took her in his arms.

Davey's voice deserted him but he smiled and waved as she over-revved up the slope and disappeared from sight. He could see why Alec had fallen for the lass and, as he sat back down on his boulder, he savoured the lovely feeling that the special intimate smile had given him. Heidi came and lay over his feet, looking up at him with soft, hurtful eyes. Davey reached down and lifted her up, assuring her that she had not been forgotten. He reminded her of their evenings sitting together in his armchair while the actress played out her role on television, and repeated the conversation he had just had, adding a few bits. (These additions subsequently became part of his reminiscences.)

A car crossed and he didn't even lift his head to acknowledge its passing.

When he had finished discussing it all with Heidi and got it straight in his head, he was anxious to be on his way. He had been the only one there to welcome the star to Trowsay and that was in need of the telling. He waited for the next car to appear so that he could ask for a lift to the village.

Nothing came.

Davey thought about starting to walk but he didn't see much chance of a lift. He knew that neither Scott nor Colleen were on the move that day and it was not likely that one of the Grants or Rob

Ballater would be going to the village before the papers came in. He might as well stay put and wait for someone to cross.

It was all of an hour before another vehicle appeared.

This time it was not a car but a large, high-sided motor caravan. Like the actress, the driver stopped at the bottom of the hill opposite; he hadn't stopped to test the surface of the causeway but to take pictures with his video camera. Davey watched him walking for a bit over the rocks, turning the camera first one way and then the other, before sitting down with his arms over his knees and his camera held loosely against his legs, just taking a look around. When he had had his fill, he returned to his van and climbed up into his cab. Davey got up to watch as the van started swaying and lumbering its way across the causeway. It stopped beside the shelter and the driver jumped down. It was a mighty jump for such a little bit of a man.

"That was quite something!" he exclaimed, looking back at the causeway. "I wonder if I'll make it back across in one piece."

"Aye, it's getting worse."

"I can see that something needs to be done about it. Not great for the island with the tourist season starting."

"Aye, but they still come and go. We only lost the one last week."

The little man's face creased with merriment. "We only lost the one last week," he repeated with a guffaw. "I like that! You're a wag after my own heart." He slapped Davey on his lower back and invited him into his van for a beer. Normally Davey wouldn't have needed a second asking to have a beer and see inside a stranger's campervan, but he shuffled a bit with uncertainty. He had mistaken the word "wag" for "fag", which was a word he knew from his army days, and wondered if this over-friendly gnome-like man with his black pointy beard and tufty hair had designs on his body.

However curiosity got the better of him.

When he appeared round the back, the little man said: "Come on, climb up. You're just the person I want to see." He opened the fridge and took out two cans of beer, pulling the rings to open them. "Rory's my name and you are …?"

"David," said Davey quickly, putting his hand on the edge of the door and pulling himself up. David had a more respectable ring to it than 'Davey', and he wanted to stress his respectability.

"Well, David, it's like this," the man began, sliding in along the bench seat and putting Davey's beer on the table opposite him. "I'm a freelance cameraman, and I've been asked to come across here and do a piece on Trowsay." He lifted his can and wished Davey good health.

Davey sat back in astonishment, forgetting his reluctance to be friendly.

"Well, I never! Is that a fact!" He reciprocated the good wishes and drank deeply. He could not believe that two celebrities had passed him in just over an hour. He looked round the inside of the van but there was none of the bulky equipment that he would have expected the man to have and wondered if he was having him on.

"I'm told that a benefactor has left the island a lot of money and that you're going to raise the road here and stop the flow of the sea."

"I dinna ken aboot Alec being a benefactor but he must've been hoardin his money all right."

"I hear that it's causing a lot of trouble."

"Aye, it is. Would you be working for the films or the television like?" Davey asked, being more interested in Rory's presence on Trowsay than Alec's bequest.

Rory pulled at his beard to hide his smile. "An extended news item is what's being asked for, but if I get good storylines and pictures, I'll develop it into a documentary on Trowsay."

"Is that a fact!"

"Now," said Rory, turning and taking a notebook from the shelf behind him. "I'm hoping that you can tell me where I should start and whom I should go and see."

Davey drank his beer in silence, giving the matter some thought. "I was just on my way to the village," he said eventually. "That'd be a good enough place to start.".

"Fair enough. And who is for and who is against this bridge?"

"Well I would take what Cissie Vale at the shop says with a pinch of salt. She's not one for sticking to the truth. And Mr Treatham at the hotel only came here a year or two back. You dinna want him in your camera shots."

Davey watched Rory copying down the two names and he stressed again that they weren't worth noting.

"Well, who can give me the best line, David?"

"Call me Davey now that we've got to know each other. You'd best start with Jockie Jay. We'll find him in the village. There's not much gets past Jockie. What he doesna know, I'll fill you in on."

Rory smiled slowly and closed his notebook.

"If we're off to the village, it's time we were on our way," he said, collecting the empty cans and putting them in the bin under the sink.

Davey climbed over into the front seat, tickled pink to be sitting up in the cab beside the man from the television, pointing out where this one and that one lived as they travelled along the road. He felt like a king in his coach, waving extravagantly to any islander who came within his vision.

It had been a day full of excitement and it wasn't over yet.

Rory decided that he would do his filming of the two elderly men down at the harbour and he followed their progress from the hill above as they walked slowly down the slipway, catching Jockie waving his stick at low-flying black-backed gulls disturbed at their meal of squashed rabbit. Jockie had just celebrated his ninety-second birthday and was dressed as he always was on weekdays, winter and summer, in a long tweed coat and a bonnet that covered the metal loop connecting a pair of empty bakelite earphones. He had told Rory that the earphones protected his bad ears. Rory assumed that he suffered from earache and had given this explanation a sagacious nod but, in fact, Jockie's ears had been badly frostbitten during his years in the navy, working the Arctic convoys.

Once they were settled on their bench at the water's edge, Rory walked back down the hill for the interview. As he approached, he heard Davey saying: "I was the only witness and I can tell you, Jockie, that was no accident."

Rory started reloading his video camera.

"They've never found the car they were after," Jockie stated by way of reply.

Davey snorted with derision. "Would you be coming forward if you were driving a hot car?"

"Was it a stolen car then? Is that what you're saying, Davey?"

"It's more than likely."

"From the south, no doubt."

"Aye, no doubt."

Rory was curious to know what it was all about but he had already listened to a lengthy dialogue on the history of Trowsay, with contradictions and disagreements, and thought it wise to leave well alone.

"I'm ready," he said and the two men looked up at the camera warily. "Now I would like you to tell me what you think about the joining of Trowsay to the mainland. Are you in favour or not?"

He started rolling the film but it was five seconds at least before he got a response.

Davey brought his loose teeth forward with his tongue and sucked them back before he spoke. "What I say is this: If an island was good enough for our faithers and grandfaithers, it is good enough for us. They're always wanting to change things these days."

Jockie was not to be outdone. "It's of no account to me what they do down in those parts. I'm not a travelling man. Not like Davey here."

"I wouldna say that, Jockie. It's a time since I was oot along Eastside. I remember ...

"Cut," Rory said. It was not a word he would normally use but he knew that it would be respected by the two old characters as being in keeping with the occasion. He could see that they didn't think much about the subject he was there to record, being more taken up with exchanging reminiscences and rivalling each other on memory recall.

"Can I give you a lift?" he offered, packing up his equipment.

Jockie said that he was in need of a bit of company and asked to be dropped off at the shop. Davey thought the shop would suit him fine too; he could pass the time there until he found a lift home.

When they got to the campervan, Davey said magnanimously: "You can sit up front, Jockie," and he watched while Rory propelled the old man up the high step with an almighty heave, before going round the back.

Rory climbed up into the driver's seat and adjusted his cushion so that he could see over the steering wheel. He was checking in his rear-view mirror, getting ready to go, when he saw Davey wandering around behind, testing the slide of the drawers underneath the bunk benches and inspecting the bottle rack attached to the side of the cupboard. He was peering all round the rack as if he was wondering how it was put together; then he took out a bottle to get a closer look.

"Are you fancying my best wine, Davey?" Rory asked, still watching him through the rear-view mirror.

Davey held the bottle away from him to read the label. "I wouldna be drinking this foreign stuff," he said, replacing it. "Breeds sissies."

"Cissie's a fine lass," Jockie said, only the one word penetrating his earphones.

Rory slapped the steering wheel in delight and asked his roaming passenger roguishly: "Are you in the breeding business then, Davey?"

Davey responded grumpily: "You ken fine what I mean," and sat with a miffed stoop to his shoulders during the short journey up the hill. When they got to the shop, he stood up and made his way to the back door of the van without a backward glance.

"Cheers then, Davey," Rory called, which elicited a reluctant "Bye the noo."

In the meantime, Jockie had opened the passenger door and swung himself round ready to get out. He thought better of trying the jump himself.

"Geez a hand," he cried.

Rory made his way round to help his passenger down from his high perch. He got himself into position, his arms raised and his legs tensed to take the weight, but when Jockie made the jump, he was nearly flattened, and they ended up doing a four-step jig before they regained their balance.

Jockie straightened his cap and earphones, reminding Rory of his age.

"You're still a fine figure of a man though," Rory flattered, taking his cue.

"Aye, weel, you havena so far to fall, that's for sure," the nonagenarian countered, taking his stick and lifting it in farewell.

"Are you no coming in?" Davey asked Rory from the shop door, the offence forgotten.

Rory shook his head, waving as he moved off. Davey's denial of the merit in seeking the postmistress's opinion, led Rory to assume that she had much to say on the matter, but he thought it best to wait until the two men had enjoyed their bit of company and gone on their way.

He drove back down the main road to the hotel.

First he visited the Loch Church. He liked churches, mostly for their splendour but also for their architectural differences. The octagonal shape of this one, with its simple bell tower, fascinated him. The extended rounded ends (for the vestibule and the vestry) were in the traditional Celtic cross design, but its size and position were unusual. He climbed the two shallow steps and turned the latch ring, entering the airless, gloomy vestibule with its solid-legged table and church notice board. Daylight only penetrated through a dusty rose window high above the heavy oak door. The dark of this rounded space was in complete contrast to the interior of the church, which was full of sunlight. The windows in five of the agonic walls were made of heavy plate glass, criss-crossed with lead to form diamonds of light, and in the sixth there was the etching of the two disciples casting their nets. Through this window, Rory could see a fisherman throwing his line far out on the loch and was awed by the conception and execution of a work of art that could unite the biblical past with the everyday present in such a simple way.

He climbed the hill and focused his lens on the church and the incredible pseudo-castle behind, with its close-cut terraces undulating to the edge of the loch. The mansion had all the ostentation that he would expect to see in the country residence of a Victorian gentleman. Three and a half storeys high, it had the obligatory tower at one end, the heavily-pillared portico in the middle and a jutting wing. The windows in the ground floor were tall and elegant, as befitted reception rooms; the windows in the two storeys above were shorter, discreetly paned, some with balconies; and in the attic roof space, dumpy slated dormers peaked above the parapet.

His interview with the proprietor of the hotel was disappointing. Jockie had told him that the man was a hundred per cent behind a permanent link with the mainland and had even been round the village canvassing support, but he proved to be lukewarm and would not commit himself on either side.

"Had he changed his mind?" Rory asked.

Rupert smiled slowly, taking his glasses off and using one of their legs as a pointer. "You shouldn't listen to gossip," he reprimanded. "As a hotelier I must think of what my guests want as well as what is most convenient for myself."

It was a very unsatisfactory interview.

Fortunately Rory found a farmer in the bar who was more than willing to speak strongly in favour. Alf Strachan looked just as a farmer should look with the florid face of a man who worked outdoors, and the powerful shoulders that were needed to lift heavy animals and bales of hay. Later, when they were relaxing over drinks, Rory wondered if he had misinterpreted the reason for the healthy colour. Alf could toss back a beer and chaser quicker than most of the drinkers he knew.

By the time he got back to the village to interview the postmistress, she was all of a-flutter, thinking that he was going to miss her out. Nevertheless, despite her uncertainty about his return, she was dressed for the camera, with her hair fluffed out and neatly curled over her forehead.

"Now where would you like to take me," Cissie asked, going behind the counter and pulling down her top so that the rounded neckline was neatly stretched.

Rory stepped back and put his head to one side as he assessed the shot. "Not quite right," he said, as much to himself as to Cissie. She was too short and broad to have the counter cutting her in half. He was looking round for a suitable place inside the shop when he saw Ted hovering in the background. They had met down at the slipway in the afternoon.

"Hello there," he said, smiling up at Ted who was looking sheepish and slouching in an effort to look shorter. "I was wanting to see you again. Could I buy a lobster to take back to my wife?"

"Aye, you could."

Cissie took over. "And we'll have lobster for our supper. Off you go, Ted, and get one from the lobster pond." She turned to Rory. "You'll stay and have a bite to eat with us, won't you?" Rory was pleased to accept. He hadn't eaten since leaving the mainland and lobster was a rare treat.

He positioned Cissie in front of filled shelves. She immediately looked behind her to make certain that he was filming her against the right sort of grocery items. She didn't want to be standing in front of shelves of toilet rolls or worse, she said, and Rory assured her that he would never have considered placing her against such an inappropriate background.

The pointed camera had an inhibiting effect initially. Rory posed the same question as he had to the others. Was she in favour or not?

"I'm not in favour."

Rory lowered his camera and explained that he wanted her to give her reasons for not being in favour.

"There are plenty of reasons," she said and was off. "We're Trowsay people and that's the way we want to stay. Don't listen to what he's saying down at the hotel. He's not from these parts. If Trowsay were just another part of the mainland, it would be nothing to him."

Rory kept filming. "Do you see your shop closing if the road is built?"

"More than likely," was the reluctant response. "But I'm not just thinking of us mind, the government are not going to be paying for our school or our district nurse if they don't have to."

"Is that the general opinion?"

"It is."

Rory left it like that and went out to his van to write up his notes. It was easy to forget impressions and there would be a script to write and editing to be done before he had created a visual story. Shortly afterwards he returned for his supper.

Cissie had been keeping a look out for him and met him at the door.

"Come away in," she said. "No, no, there's no need to lock the door. We're still up if anyone runs short." She ushered him across the shop towards the inner sanctum.

Rory had always been curious about the back room in village shops. On the tinkle of the doorbell, the shopkeeper would appear, offering his services like Mr Benn in the children's television programme. Was there magic lurking there behind the curtained door. He smiled at the thought. In fact the only surprising thing about the Vales' back room was its modest size and the heat from the solid fuel stove. The stoking door was open and a large black pot was hissing on the hot plate. On either side of the raging fire were the armchairs, rubbed down to the thread, their greasy backs largely hidden by sparkling-white antimacassars; a third upright chair had been set between them. There were a wide variety of calendars, photographs, knickknacks and scenic china plates resting on shelves or hanging from hooks, giving a bit of interest and colour to the dull cream walls that had soured with the years. All the surfaces had been cleared of clutter. Rory could see stacks of old newspapers and magazines, even part of an engine and a pile of tools, hidden behind the chairs and underneath the cloths half-covering the fireside tables. The salivating whiff of lobster was in the air.

"You sit there," Cissie said, pointing to one of the armchairs and Rory sank down with the springs. Ted poured beer and the three of them sat round the open stoking door, enjoying the heat and discussing Rory's project. Ted had a few suggestions to make about where to go and what to see and when Rory agreed to follow his advice, he got up and went through to the shop to telephone round and set up appointments.

During his absence, Rory listened to Cissie's decided opinions on island life and the characters he would meet. It was a one-sided conversation. A word here and there was enough to keep her going. He had had a long day and sitting in the soft chair with a drink in his hand, and the heat from the fire relaxing his muscles, he dozed off.

When he opened his eyes, the room had been transformed, just as if Mr Benn had been there all along, performing his magic. A table had appeared in the middle of the floor, covered with a starched white cloth and set with silver cutlery and gold-rimmed plates. Trailing ivy and bright shiny peonies rose from its centre, and candles flickered.

"We didna want to wake you," Ted was saying. "But the lobster's ready for eating."

Rory had been so deeply asleep that it took him a moment to piece his mind together into a thinking whole. He was at once profusely apologetic, knowing that he had fallen asleep while Cissie was talking. She shrugged this lapse off as being of no consequence.

"I laid your drink on the side table," she added in a matter-of-fact tone.

Rory could see his tankard underneath the fringed lampshade and realised that Cissie must have taken it from his hand, avoiding a messy accident. He thanked her and she gave a knowing smile, saying that she had had her eye on him, which was somewhat disconcerting.

He wondered if he had had his mouth open at full snore; if he had, she wasn't saying.

He pushed himself forward in his low, soft chair and got to his feet. The thought of lobster was nauseating with his sour-tasting mouth and woozy head.

"Could I perhaps splash my face a bit and wash my hands?"

"That you can," Ted said, and took him through the scullery and out the back door. It had never occurred to Rory that the Vales would only have an outside privy and he felt embarrassed at having asked to use their facilities rather than going out to his van. But it was no privy he was shown into. Ted pushed the door open against a deep-pile raspberry-coloured carpet in one half of a stone built building across the narrow yard.

"There you are now," he said and Rory found himself in a bathroom fit for a king (should any king happen to be passing and be caught short). "I'll leave you to find your own way back when you're ready."

The bathroom fittings were pink with matching tiles, and the predominantly turquoise wallpaper reflected the colours and shapes of an underwater world. There were frills and flounces everywhere – across the window, underneath the basin, over the tissue box and round the toilet roll. The only indication that this unexpectedly grand room was positioned in an outhouse was the slight dampness in the air, the curling of the wallpaper near the ceiling and the huge spider that had crawled up the waste pipe and was trapped on the shiny surface of the basin. (Rory ran the tap and sent it back down from whence it came.) There was none of the everyday clutter that he would have expected to see lying on the shelf above the basin, and all the matching towels were neatly folded. Rory felt sure that Ted did his shaving at the scullery sink and there was, indeed, a privy next door.

When he returned, they sat down to eat. The lobster had been pulled apart, hammered, gouged and incised with pincers; every last piece of flesh had been extracted to lie pinkly on Cissie's best ashet.

"There you are," she said, putting the prized pieces on a plate in front of him. "Stick in, till you stick oot, as they say."

Rory protested at this favoured distribution but was told to eat up and enjoy it, which he did. The generous tankards of home brew continued to flow, and when the lobster was finished and fingers licked, Cissie brought through plates of scones, a wide selection of cheeses and a festively coloured and decorated cake.

"You shouldn't have gone to so much trouble," Rory protested, noting that the shop stock had been raided to set the feast before him.

Cissie scotched the idea that he could be a trouble.

"You must just take us as you find us," she said.

Rory ate most of the scones and cheese and refused the offer of cake and ice cream. Sitting back, he patted his stomach in contentment and complimented the cook.

Cissie blushed with pleasure, the heat seeping down her neck and over the respectable amount of flesh showing above her scooped neckline.

"You're very welcome," she said. "We're always glad to make visitors feel at home, aren't we Ted?"

Ted agreed and Cissie told Rory about the important people that had sat in their back room, mostly politicians although there had been an ornithologist whose photographs were printed in a tourist magazine.

"Homely fare is always best, I say," she went on. "They've not learned that along by. Fancy names they give for heaped up food that ends up like a high class dog's breakfast, once you've stuck your fork in."

"Now, Cissie, love, Rory doesna want to hear about that," Ted said softly, getting his wife off her hobby horse by gently moving the conversation sideways. He told Rory about the old man and the many times he had taken him out fishing, including a near disaster he had had when the old man was all but pulled overboard with a 30 lb halibut at the end of his line. That particular anecdote led on to discussing the plight of the fishing industry generally and lobster fishing in particular. Thus the comfortable hour after eating was passed, while they bemoaned the decisions of politicians on nearly every issue, touched on world affairs without much enthusiasm and came back again to the important events that took place on Trowsay. It was time for Rory to take his leave.

As he crossed the shop on his way out, he swayed a bit and Ted had to give him a supporting arm.

"That's a strong brew you've got there, Ted," he said, his voice slurred.

"I've known stronger."

Ted might have known stronger but as Rory drove the half mile or so up the hill to the caravan site near the entrance to Atlanticscape, he was thankful that the tide was covering the causeway and that there were no police on Trowsay. Any breathalyser put to his mouth would have combusted.

Before he climbed up into the bunk above the cab, he stood in the doorway drying his face and breathing in the cool night air. It was still gloaming. A rim of deep pink was showing on the horizon where the sun was setting, the colour shimmering low on the surface of the ocean. Above him the sky was fading into night and down at the slipway the fishing boats bobbed gently at rest. All was quiet in the village

6

Callum was leaning on his hoe, resting from his labours, when he saw the actress getting into difficulty in the boggy ground to the north of the hotel. A countrywoman would have seen the reeds and been warned off, he thought, putting down his hoe and climbing over the wall to go to her assistance. He chose his route carefully through the uneven rough pasture and when he was within calling distance, he directed her away from the marshy land and over to the shore path. They met up at the gate leading onto the back terrace of Trowsay House.

"I thought I was going to be jumping from tufts of heather to soggy grass for ever," she said, giving Callum her bewitching smile and thanking him extravagantly.

"Aye, it's always a temptation to take a short cut from The Mains but you would've been just as quick if you'd stuck to the path round the coast."

"And my shoes wouldn't be in this state," she exclaimed in vexation. "They're ruined. I'll never get them clean." She started to rub her thin leather pumps this way and that way on the grass, but the clinging mud just smeared.

Callum cleared his throat to give his bold words space to come out.

"If you come with me, Mrs … um … Rose, I'll give them a going over," he offered, fearful of a rebuff, but his damsel, lately in distress, looked up into his anxious pale-blue eyes and accepted gratefully.

He guided her towards the high, stone-carved archway leading into the stable yard, which was paved with blue-grey flagstones, worn thin and flaking with age. She stopped at the entrance and looked up at the dovecote and belfry, with the coach houses (now garages) on one side of this central tower, and the horse stalls (now gardening sheds) on the other.

"I like it," she said.

Callum found his tongue. "Aye, it's fair enough." He pointed to the small-paned windows in the upper storey. "I lived in one of the flats up there for a while when I first got married. My mother was alive then."

"Are they still occupied?"

"Australian girls come and go to help out."

When they reached the former tack room, he lifted the latch on the green wood-slatted door and stood back for his guest to go first.

"I keep my bits and pieces here," Callum explained, now wondering about the propriety of inviting the star into his workshop, but she smiled in reassurance as she stepped over the threshold.

He turned on a tall brass lamp with an old-fashioned plastic shade, discoloured and stained with burn marks, and invited his guest to sit down in the low armchair; its floral-patterned cover faded to almost nothing. She looked round with curiosity. The room was full of surprises. On either side of the window hung faded blue, damask curtains, held back with blocks of wood to let in as much light as possible through the small-paned window. Underneath the window was a long stained workbench with small items of hotel furniture awaiting repair, a variety of tools, cans of lubricant, rags, bills and other pieces of odds and ends. Beside the workbench were shelves, with the accoutrements for making tea or coffee, and rows of books. Florence Rose wandered round in delight, picking up a tapestry covered footstool with a broken hinge to look at the design, fingering a broken photo frame and leaning over the bench to read the titles of the books.

"She's a grand writer," Callum said and his guest agreed, while admitting that she had never read a Barbara Cartland book. He would have offered her one for her holiday reading but they had all been well thumbed and were not fit to lend. "You'll be thinking I've not got enough to do with books in my workshop," he went on diffidently, "but the work falls off in the winter."

She assured him that she had thought no such thing and, sagging down into the old armchair, took off a shoe.

Callum held it in his hand as he looked round for a suitable rag. He had plenty of rags lying about – torn scraps of old towels, tails of a shirt that had worn out around the neck and woolly material from who-knew-what, but most had been well used and were heavily stained. He went to an old cardboard box in his cupboard and poked around inside it, extracting a teacloth, worn thin in the middle but pristine clean, as it should be for the important task ahead.

"Don't go to so much trouble. Use a dirty rag. It's just going to get even dirtier."

"No trouble."

Callum meticulously took the mud off the shoe and laid it on his workbench. He then started to look for something under the bench, and came up with a scrap of carpet for the actress to put her foot on.

"How thoughtful," she said with a smile as she passed him her second shoe.

"It's a right cold floor and none too clean."

Once the dainty shoes were as clean as he could make them, he found an old tin of dubbin, greasy leather polish that had been used for polishing the tack in the past, and did his best to bring a shine up on the damp surface. The regular movement of his hand back and forward made him feel more relaxed and he became brave enough to ask her about her part in the daily soap and if she was going to go off with the married man.

She smiled knowingly putting her finger to her mouth. "It's a secret," she said, and then gave him a hint, which made him feel very special.

Callum told her that he had visited Alec in the evenings when her story was on and it had been one of his favourite programmes. "I don't get to watch it now," he added sadly, and she voiced her surprise. "My house is built into a cliffside, you see, and there's no signal worth speaking about." He put the first shoe down and lifted up the other. "That's what they say any road."

"It sounds as if your house is in an idyllic position."

"I don't know about that." Callum had lived in the same house for most of his life and took the uninterrupted view of the ocean and the sounds of the sea and the birds for granted. "But my wife could do with the company of a television now that she's home all day."

"Perhaps you could put an aerial up at the top of the cliff and run a cable down."

"Perhaps so."

They chatted on.

When the shoes were polished to Callum's satisfaction, she put them on and admired the cleanliness and shine, turning her feet this way and that in inspection.

"Nearly as good as new," she said, getting up. She thanked him for being her guardian angel, causing the heat of awesome pleasure to rise in Callum once more.

He stood beside his workbench looking at his boots.

She smiled. "I must get on. I'm already late for coffee at the hotel."

Callum cleared his throat and nodded his head but he did not move to open the door. He was plucking up his courage to say something and she waited for him to find the words.

"I was wondering about asking for your autograph." He lifted his head and looked at her with his anxious blue eyes. "For my wife, like."

"I can do better than that. I have one of my signed photographs here." She opened her large handbag and took out a cellophane folder that contained her publicity photographs. She extracted one and put it down on the workbench, asking: "To whom should I address it?"

Callum looked even more uncomfortable. "Florence Rose," he said bashfully.

"But that is my name."

"It is my wife's name too."

She looked at Callum in amazement but he was surveying the toes of his boots again, so she took out her pen and wrote: "To Florence Rose, with best wishes", above her already scrolled name.

"I'm afraid it looks rather odd the two names following each other like that," she said with a smile, handing it over. "I hope I will meet your wife."

"I hope so too," Callum said, his eyes lighting up with pleasure. "I'd have to speak to her first though. Find out how she felt."

Florence Rose was a bit nonplussed by this reply.

"She doesna get about much," Callum explained, opening the door.

"Of course, I understand."

The conversation reverted to the banal as he walked his guest to the front of the hotel and they parted with the mutual hope that they would meet again.

When Callum got back to his den, he lifted up the photograph from his bench and scrutinised the face of the actress. She was much younger looking in the photograph than she was in reality. He smiled happily to himself, letting his rough, dirt-ingrained thumb run over the two names, one after the other: his Florence Rose and her Florence Rose. It was a photograph to be treasured. He looked round for a bag to put it in so that it would be kept shiny and clean.

7

Rory felt himself being rocked gently back and forward. The motion made him feel warm and secure within a happy but garbled dream of summertime and hammocks in the garden of his childhood home. It was well past eight before he woke and it took a moment for his befuddled brain to realise that his van was being swayed by the wind. He threw off his duvet and pulled back the curtains.

The peace and harmony in the village below had gone. Now all was grey and turbulent; the boats at the slipway were bobbing in a higgledy-piggledy fashion and a light rain was misting the view. The temperature had dropped and Rory shivered as he pulled on trousers and sweatshirt. He was thankful that he had done most of his filming and interviewing during the late afternoon and long, bright evening. There was enough already filmed and recorded for the news item, but he had hoped for more.

Before he did anything further, he climbed over into the cab and drove his campervan down to the harbour, where it was sheltered. Only then did he open the door and let in the draught.

There was no sign of Ted Vale down there, but another fisherman was making his boat secure by retying the line to one of the moorings and Rory had a word with him while he shaved. The day would improve by midday, he was told, which was good news, if it were true.

While his breakfast was cooking, he checked his equipment and organised his thoughts for the day ahead. There were two interesting projects in the offing. Ted had phoned a Jemmie Stout who lived out by the Trowsay cave and Jemmie was to meet him there around ten. The tide would be high on that side of the island by then, Ted had said. He had also arranged for a young man with photographic experience to help him with his lights. Later he was to see Professor Fauld at the bird sanctuary. All being well he should have completed his filming and be off the island by late afternoon.

The track leading up to the cave was not made for heavy traffic. The ruts on either side of the central grassy mound were cut deep, the clay binding the stony surface dissolving, freezing over and baking hard with the changing seasons. It took its toll on the springs of the van as it slowly lumbered its way onwards towards the coast.

Les Gunn sat silently beside him clutching the strap over the door. Les said that he had a headache and he certainly looked like a man who had had a heavy night and had got out of his bed earlier than usual. He had many skills, according to Ted. Rory was not sure if six months in a photo lab gave him much experience of working lights and focusing cameras but it was the best that Ted could offer.

They arrived at the beach half an hour late. The wind had dropped and the sky was no longer hidden by low-moving rain clouds but it was still overcast and breezy. Jemmie Stout was waiting for them, sitting on the sand dunes and looking out to sea, untroubled by the time. His boat was pulled up on the beach with its motor attached.

"You got here all right," he said, by way of an opening, shaking Rory by the hand and giving Les a nod. "Tell me now, what is it you're after?"

"I'm told that at high tide the shadows of the rock stacks jig about against the cave wall like whirling trolls. I was hoping to film it."

"Aye, well, that's so. It's a rare sight."

Rory was not sure if his 'rare' meant that it was an amazing occurrence or seldom seen. Before he could ask, Jemmie went on: "It's by moonlight that they take to the dancing but I've got a strong light on the front of my boat and I can take you through the mouth of the cave easy enough."

Rory looked at the boat and wondered about the wisdom of the expedition, but he comforted himself with the thought that taking tourists to the cave and keeping them from drowning was Jemmie's job. He started to unpack his equipment.

"I've got lights we could experiment with," he said, lifting one out of its large holdall and handing it to Les. "Les here is going to take some shots from above and that will give me two camera angles."

Jemmie helped them to carry the lights up to the wooden walkway circling the craggy hole in the roof of the cave and watched while Rory and Les set up and tested the lights. Rory was surprised to find that Les had a good knowledge of working lights. He was also quick to learn, and even suggest what angles would be best. Either the bracing sea air or the concentration of his mind on a job that interested him had cleared his head. Rory left him there with more confidence than the journey out had led him to expect.

They set off out to sea, the boat jumping with a hard rhythm over the waves. Rory was thankful for the padded cushion round his seat which alleviated some of the discomfort. He had his video camera underneath his lifebelt and oilskin, his arms folded round it for protection from the spray.

All was well with him and his stomach until they rounded the point and were in a position outside the cave entrance. Jemmie then spent some time manipulating the boat to the right angle to enter the gloup on a wave and during this process the fish-smelling boat rocked uncontrollably. Up and over they went through the gap and into the cave. The movement of the boat was slower and more undulating in the sheltered water but it did nothing to settle Rory's heaving gullet.

Jemmie turned on the flashlight at the front of his boat and Les responded from above, readjusting one of the lights. This had the effect of creating deeper shadows within the cave, but Rory was too ill to do anything but point his camera in the direction of the stacks and let it run. Ted had assured him that the dancing shadows were a phenomenon worth seeing but he had not seen them and unless Les had fared better from above, he had wasted precious time getting seasick for no purpose. On reaching the open sea again he threw up, toast and tea mingling with half-digested lobster, and endured the additional nausea of seeing swooping seagulls devour his vomit with relish.

He sat on the shore with his head and arms falling slackly between his open knees, waiting for the nausea and cold sweat of seasickness to settle. Jemmie and Les stood awkwardly by, watching him. Les said that he had got something on film but he was not specific about what that something was. Rory only nodded as he got slowly to his feet. He didn't feel much better in an upright position but as he walked about, testing his legs, he decided that if Jemmie would agree to be interviewed on the subject, he could salvage something from the morning's shooting. But Jemmie was reluctant to face the camera. He had not actually witnessed the shadows taking on their full mythical guise although there were plenty on the island who had. While they were arguing the point, Rory saw a man walking along the beach towards them. His stature and bearing marked him down as a reliable witness and Rory went to meet him with a sickly smile of welcome.

"A fine day for a trip out to sea," was the greeting called to him. (Willie was barely concealing his amusement.)

"I'm afraid I've been taken for a ride in a smelly boat," Rory said, with an embarrassed laugh.

The tall man would have none of it.

"So you didn't see them?" he said, his eyebrows rising in mock surprise. "Ah, well, the beam from Jemmie's fishing boat is not the same as a full moon on a dark night. And the sea has not the strength in it today to catch them at their dancing."

Rory's mind was taken off his queasy stomach by the prospect of a good interview. "Have you witnessed the phenomenon?" he asked, reaching down for his camera case.

When he straightened, he was met by a solid hand, which warded off any suggestion that photographs could be taken.

"That is neither here not there," he was told. "I only came along this way to tell you that I own this beach and I won't take kindly to trespassers beyond this point."

Rory had had a bad morning and he was not going to be intimidated by an aggressive individual who was towering over him, trying to fix him in his place with a splintery gaze of icy-blue coldness.

"I have no intention of going your way," he said, giving a contemptuous look at the flat, uninteresting shoreline (Willie's fortifications were just out of sight round a bend in the bay) and started to repack his expensive equipment. It didn't help his temper when he looked up to speak to Jemmie and saw the man giving Jemmie a knowing wink before turning on his heel.

But Rory was not a surly man by nature and as his motor caravan slowly bumped its way back along the track with Les sitting silently beside him once more, he began to see the funny side of the outing. He'd been duped into parting with money for a boat trip and an assistant cameraman to film shadows on a wall. Perhaps with some self-deprecating dubbing he could turn the expedition into an amusing interlude.

After dropping Les back in the village and over-paying him for his morning's work, he took the road up past the gates of Atlanticscape and out towards Eastside Point to see the old professor and complete his assignment. This time the track was better. The surface was still made of loose stones bound with clay but it had been recently graded and was reasonably smooth. He travelled some distance over moorland with no sign of the coast or any habitable house. There was a scattering of crumbling croft buildings, some just a rickle of stones, and the surrounding patches of green that had been cleared with much toil, were now being reclaimed by gorse and encroaching heather.

The journey was taking longer than he had expected and he stopped to check the map. There was no alternative route and, in the silence after the throb of the engine, he could hear the distant breaking of a wave and smell the salt air. He folded the map away and started off again, leaving his window open and breathing the sea-fresh air deep into his lungs. The track deteriorated as he neared the coast, damp moorland on either side giving way to clumps of reed, boggy moss and pits of stagnant rainwater. He changed down a gear, keeping the engine from stalling as he manoeuvred the wheels of his campervan between low-lying rocks and muddy crevices, lurching along until he reached the last incline, which took him up to a firm, grassy surface at the edge of the cliff. The professor's house was built into solid rock, high above the ocean, with only a foot or two of stone wall visible below an overhanging thatch.

Rory leaned over to the back for his camera and jumped down, slamming the door. The abrupt sound made kittiwakes and guillemots rise silently on the updraught and glide round before falling away. He put his camera round his neck and was walking forward to get a better view, when Professor Fauld's lined, weather-beaten face appeared above the cliff edge, his breeze of white hair flying loose from a ponytail.

He welcomed Rory with an arm-shattering handshake.

"Come into my burrow," he invited, ushering him down the cliff path to a wrought iron balcony running the length of a wall made entirely of glass. He was delighted by Rory's amazement at the architectural feat required to build the house where it was.

"There was an old army battery and lookout here at one time," he explained, grinning broadly and showing uneven, discoloured teeth.

Rory lifted his camera to take a shot of the front of the house but his arm was held down in an iron grip.

"Now, now, young man, it's the birds you've come to see and I'd be obliged if you'd not advertise my presence here."

He waited until Rory had put his camera back in its case before sliding the door open. The house was little more than a bothy. It had only the one room, lower at the back than the front, the structure of the rock dictating the shape of the walls and the division of the different living areas. It was scrupulously tidy.

"What about a sandwich and a bottle of beer?"

Rory declined the offer, explaining about his boat trip and adding a bit here and there to make a good story. He got an appreciative response. The professor threw himself about in merriment, finally dropping into a chair in a paroxysm of whooping laughter, thrusting his legs out and exposing long, bony ankles sticking into threadbare plimsolls. When he had regained his cool, he filled Rory in on the background of the characters he had met.

An Alka-Seltzer was dropped into a glass of water and Rory lunched on that while the professor munched on his sandwich and quaffed his beer. They sat on the balcony, hearing the waves breaking against the cliff below and feeling an occasional mist of spray. The sun only appeared intermittently, but the early afternoon temperature was pleasant in that sheltered spot.

While he ate, the professor told Rory about the birds and the life that he had retired to on Trowsay. "I am not going to see that changed with an environmentally unfriendly, concrete-block road," he went on, his eyebrows moving swiftly up and down above bulging impassioned eyes. "There are no weasels or adders on Trowsay to decimate the wildlife and they would be across here in a flash if there was a road down there inviting them in."

Rory looked dubious.

"Besides that, it's been shown elsewhere that the construction of sea barriers results in thousands of tons of displaced sand settling round the man-made structure, bringing coastal erosion in other areas, sometimes a great distance away. In my opinion, and the opinion of those who know, it is not wise to tamper with nature."

Rory listened to the forceful words and determined tone, watching the change in the professor's facial expression with the eye of a cameraman. The man was going to be an ideal subject and an important addition to the film.

After lunch they climbed back to the cliff top and tramped over the heather to a deep ravine where the waves broke soundlessly on the rocks far below. They sat on a cushion of spongy, tightly-packed mosses and the professor pointed out the fissures high up in the rock face opposite where the puffins bred. They waited and watched but it was only very occasionally that one of the toy-like birds slipped from its hideaway and moved gingerly forward on its ledge.

"Why do they stay at the edge for so long?" Rory asked. He kept lowering his camera and missing the flight.

"They need a thermal to give them a lift. See how top-heavy they are."

"They look as though they are plucking up the courage to launch themselves off."

The sheer cliff face was dotted with colonies of seabirds guarding their eggs, and the air was alive with swirling wings as the hunters swooped and chased in noisy competitive forays out to sea. Rory got superb atmospheric shots there but he was not so successful with the embryo colony of whimbrels. They were nesting on a headland round the other side of the bay, and the professor didn't want them disturbed. Rory was only able to shoot moving, inquisitive heads and some quick wing-beats, when the occasional territorial dispute took place.

As he filmed in both locations, Rory recorded what the professor had to say. Later he took shots of him looking across the sea to the north of Scotland, his throat bare and his white hair flying ferociously in the wind. With a bit of prompting, he repeated his dogmatic and uncompromising opinions, demonstrating, with wide emphatic sweeps of his arm, the damage that would be done to the natural environment if a raised road were built and Trowsay was 'flooded with tourists'.

Rory was pleased with his afternoon's work. He knew that the professor would use his eminence in the academic world and his knowledge of wildlife to rally support and enforce his views. The same shots could be used in news items for months or even years to come, bringing in good commission.

The Alka-Seltzer over at Eastside Point had been a welcome lunch, but by the time Rory reached the causeway on his homeward journey, his stomach was touching his backbone. He had hoped to find Davey there to share a sandwich but there was no sign of him and with no incentive to stop, he kept going, nearly stalling when one of his back wheels slipped on the uneven algal surface.

He drove to the viewpoint on the crest of the hill and turned off his engine, resting his arms along the top of the steering wheel and breathing deeply, letting his heartbeat slow down. There was a soothing bar of chocolate in the glove compartment and he reached for that, pulling the wrapper back. The sea was well out, leaving a wide expanse of shingle and wet sand, spotted with debris and fringed with seaweed. Rory watched the movement of the waves as he munched, trying to gauge if the tide was on the ebb or the flow and becoming mesmerised by the rhythm. He knew that there would be many tides to come and go before any bridge was built. If it was built. Who could tell. Most of the houses and farms were hidden by the undulations in the land; only Davey's old caravan stood out clearly to the east. He spotted Davey walking down the cliff path and thought he looked up but he didn't wave and Rory could not be sure if he had seen him. It was too late now anyway.

He forced the wrapper into the overflowing ashtray and reached for the starter. If his assignment was to be completed and ready for transmission before the news became stale, he needed to get moving. There was still much to be done.

8

When he got back from work with the signed photograph, Callum was jumpy with excitement. He could hardly wait for the tea to be past and the washing-up done. He knew that he had to choose his moment carefully and waited until Flo had settled herself in her rocker, with her feet up on a footstool, before he fetched his precious offering from under his jacket, hanging on a hook behind the door.

Flo took the photograph from him and looked at it closely, handing it back to him without a word.

"You see that she has the same name as you, Flo."

"I see."

"Alec and I thought she might be your daughter."

That made Mrs McFea sit up and take notice. She rocked back in her chair, shaking her head from side to side in shocked disbelief, the light from the fire flaming and shimmering on the magnified lenses of her glasses.

"How, may I ask, did Alec know that I had had a daughter?"

Callum knew that the question was rhetorical. It was only he who could have told him."

"Don't take on, Flo. It just came out, and his time was near." His wife's fixed stare did not waver and Callum hurried on with his explanation: "He wasna easy in himself about the days you spent at Selkie when you were none but a bairn."

"I can't see that that has anything to do with your broadcasting my private business all over the place."

"Not broadcasting, Flo. Alec wouldna have told a soul."

Mrs McFea lay back in her rocker, moving it gently back and forward.

"All right, Callum, tell me what this is all about," she said, and he felt relieved that she was no longer gimlet-eyed. He brought the creepie forward and took off the slipper on her nearest foot, starting to massage her toes. She liked him to do that.

"Remember how I'd speak about the television programme that Alec and I watched when I was up there?"

Mrs McFea said nothing. She just redirected his fingers to another part of her foot.

"It was Alec who saw that one of the actresses was named Florence Rose. He remembered your mother calling you that when she came to the farm to take you out of a Sunday and he began to talk about those days. He was troubled about the way he'd treated you, getting you into trouble with his Mum."

"And so he should've been."

"Aye, well, one thing just led to another."

"And you thought it would ease his conscience to know that I had had a daughter that I couldn't bring up myself."

"No, it wasna like that, Flo. It's not common to have the names joined, and the more I saw of the actress, the more I thought that the lass could be your girl. When she came on the screen, I talked about her more than was natural, and Alec teased me. My crush he called her. I didna want him to think that I had eyes for anyone but you, so I told him. I can tell you, Flo, when he heard how you'd been treated by that bigamist, he went near raving mad. He was fond of you, you know. You were the nearest he ever had to a sister."

"That's a laugh."

"It's true. Don't be harsh on him, Flo." He laid his hand on her knee and looked up at her, willing her to believe him. He would have liked her to remember Alec kindly even although his jealousy had made her life a misery when she lived at Selkie. "In the end he also saw the likeness," he went on, forcing her attention. "She looks just like you did when you came back to Trowsay."

"Callum McFea, don't talk rubbish," his wife said, lifting up the photograph and scrutinising it more carefully. "She looks nothing like me. She's a lovely girl and far too young to be my daughter."

"She's not as young as she looks in that picture. She called it a publicity photo and no doubt it's been touched up a bit here and there."

Mrs McFea handed the photograph back to him. "And Rose will be the lass's surname. Had you thought on that?"

"Aye, we had, and it's no. She uses her first names for her acting. Alec found that out from one of his magazines."

Mrs McFea straightened her shoulders. "Was she showing herself in one of Alec's magazines?"

"No, no, Flo, not that sort of magazine," Callum assured her, putting her slipper back on and moving his creepie so that he could massage her other foot. "One that talks about television goings-on. You know the sort."

She said nothing further and he worked in silence.

"I didna know about his will," he said after a bit. "Alec never mentioned to me that he was going to name the girl and get her to come up to Trowsay. I think that was his way of repaying his debt to you."

"What stuff and nonsense! You men can indulge yourselves with fairy tales while watching television but don't get me involved in such fanciful and silly talk. All right, Callum, you can put my slipper back on now, that has eased the pain nicely." She managed to wriggle her toes a bit. "You're a good man," she said, touching his cheek. "But you're sometimes right daft in your ideas."

"I thought I might bring her up for tea the morn's night," he said, helping his wife up. "She's a friendly lass."

"You'll do nothing of the sort, Callum. You've upset me enough already."

And that was that.

Callum took the photograph through to the bedroom and put it with the other family photos in the big drawer underneath the wardrobe. Before he closed the drawer, he looked at it one more time with the low feeling that comes after quashed elation. A ready-grown daughter would have been a nice present for him to give Flo in her old age. She'd had a hard life. Farmed out as a baby to Selkie because her parents couldn't keep her at the big house. No picnic for servants in those days. Easy money for Alec's Mum though. A sour stick of a woman she had been, always quoting the harsh bits out of the Bible. Then Flo had her elderly parents to nurse down south till they passed on. To crown it all, there was that wheedling criminal who took advantage of her. God shouldn't be lenient with him when his time came.

"What are you doing through there, Callum?"

He closed the drawer carefully, even guiltily, for Flo had made her feelings clear, and went back through to the kitchen.

"It's nearly time for *The Archers*," he said, turning the radio on.

Flo had fetched her knitting and was gently moving her rocker back and forward as she knitted one of her squares, a green one this time. He could see four squares on top of her workbox, pressed and ready. When she had done another two, they would decide how to place them on the half-made blanket and he would do the sewing. Flo's blankets went all over the world to help those suffering misfortune in earthquakes or floods. She didn't like doing the sewing part and he was pleased to do it for her. He called them "Flo's blankets" but she always said "our blankets" and he liked that.

He put another piece of peat on the fire and sat down in his easy chair. This was the time of day when he usually nodded off, the food and the heat after his day's work making him doze, but his brain was too active. He didn't expect Flo to change her mind. She wasn't one for changing her mind. But he wasn't going to change his mind either. He was determined that the actress wouldn't leave Trowsay without a meeting taking place.

As they sat listening to the radio, talking a bit from time to time, he thought out a plan of action. The actress was staying at The Mains. He knew that for a fact.

He would give Gemma a ring from the hotel and mention that Flo needed an outing. Gemma Martin was his cousin and she invited Flo down for a cup of tea from time to time. That way a meeting could be arranged, casual like.

9

Bertie lifted Hanna's hand and kissed her fingers. Kissing a lady's fingers when the opportunity presented itself was one of his little ways.

"Don't worry," he said.

"But are you sure she won't delay coming back and you'll miss your plane?" Hanna insisted, looking at the carriage clock on the mantelshelf for the second time.

"I am sure." He placed her hand back on the couch between them, patting it as he spoke, to reinforce his assurance. "I like Thorfinn, by the way. He is a clever man and if he chose to come back into the mainstream of life things might be different, but life in a cottage, living off the land and all that sort of thing, is not for Marigold."

Hanna agreed adding: "You have been very tolerant about their affair."

"Ah, dear Hanna, one must accept unsuitable alliances and indiscretions at Marigold's age. It is all part of growing up and acquiring wisdom."

"Girls are different," Hanna said softly, twirling her wedding ring. "More impulsive."

"Perhaps."

There was a short tap on the door and Isabel came in under full sail.

"Really, Bertie, it is too much," were her first words. She was dressed as she should be for a stay in the country, a camelhair coat was thrown casually over her fine tweed suit and sturdy brown brogues punctuated her slender legs. Her hair and make-up were impeccable. "Down, Slavers, down now." She pushed his sniffing nose away and he slunk back to his previous position, resting his back against the sofa. "Thank you, Hanna, I will have a small gin with plenty of tonic." She dropped her coat from her shoulders. "I could see it all from my bedroom window. Marigold is lying out there on the bottom terrace in the arms of that man."

"Love's sweet dream, Isabel. You must remember how it was when you were young."

Isabel could not remember ever being so indiscreet and said so. "Deep emotion is no less strong, Bertie, when it is manifested in private."

He agreed, adding: "But sometimes passion cannot be contained."

Isabel pursed her lips as she accepted a filled glass from Hanna. "She is your daughter," she said tightly, relinquishing her responsibility.

"It's getting a bit hot and stuffy in here," Hanna stated, passing a hand over her heated forehead. "Why don't we go out and join them on the terrace?"

Bertie thought that was an excellent idea and bounced up, neatly avoiding Slavers who was quicker off the mark. "I'll take an extra glass and the bottle of whisky. I've no doubt Thorfinn will be needing a snifter by now."

Isabel was less keen to abandon her comfortable armchair for hard, messy and probably damp grass. "I presume you have a rug or some chairs that we can sit on, Hanna," she said, recloaking herself and lifting up her glass of gin and tonic.

When they trouped out – Bertie with the whisky, Hanna with the tray and Dodie Hope with a folding table and two rugs – Thorfinn was resting on a forearm looking down at Marigold and caressing her hand in a distracted sort of way.

"Hallo, there," Bertie called down and they looked up in surprise.

"We thought we would have a farewell drink together," Hanna said as the two lovers parted and Thorfinn got to his feet.

"Let me help, Hanna," Thorfinn said, coming up the short slope. "We can't have you slipping and falling."

As he took the tray from her, she was startled to see the expression in his eyes. She had expected to see the hunted look of a man trapped in the awkward situation of a lengthy farewell, not the distress of a lover facing separation. She turned away, her eyelids lowered to hide her dismay.

"Thorfinn is going to come to my party in August," Marigold said in wild-eyed excitement. "I hope that's all right, Aunt Isabel."

Isabel inclined her head in acknowledgement of the arrangement as she sat down on the spread rug but did not venture an opinion.

"Splendid!" Bertie beamed and lifted the whisky bottle in invitation. "A drop of the hard stuff, Thorfinn?"

He refused, which caused some banter between the two men.

Hanna offered lemonade instead but nearly dropped the jug when she heard Rupert calling from the top of the terrace. He was standing there surveying the scene and voicing surprise at seeing them partying when there was a plane to catch.

"Come and join us," Bertie called back. "There's time yet."

Rupert looked at his watch. "The tide's on the turn," he said, reluctantly shuffling down the slope.

"In that case…"

Marigold touched his sleeve. "And, Daddy, Thorfinn is going to stay on for a bit. Perhaps find a job in London."

Bertie chortled and Thorfinn looked towards him with raised eyebrows, questioning his gleeful response, but Bertie just smiled and made an expansive gesture that meant nothing. It was clear to Hanna that his amusement was in admiration of Thorfinn's ingenuity in easing the ache of departure with half promises. No doubt he had done that himself in the past.

"I wouldn't stay too long," Thorfinn assured him.

"You're welcome to stay as long as you like."

Isabel intervened. "Marigold won't be in London after mid-September."

"Don't spoil things, Aunt Isabel. I don't need to go."

Bertie lifted his whisky glass and looked down at Marigold over the rim before taking a sip. "Yes, you do. Your grandpa has gone to a lot of trouble to get a place for you at the art college near him."

Thorfinn turned to her in query. "You didn't tell me that you were gong to study art, Marigold."

"Interior design actually."

"Good for you. You certainly brightened up my hovel with that sculpture you made out of driftwood and grasses."

"You liked it?"

"I told you I did." He sat down beside her and squeezed her hand.

Marigold smiled. "I'd like to do interior design but grandpa lives in California."

"Does he now."

"Would you come with me?" Marigold asked with innocent appeal. "You could easily get a job over there."

Thorfinn chuckled, dismissing the idea.

Hanna could see Rupert opening his mouth to offer his opinion but he changed his mind. She herself was taken aback. Marigold had a beguiling charm but her immaturity and lack of common sense was astonishing. She had no idea what made Thorfinn tick.

"Why not?" Marigold asked with a touch of petulance.

"They seek high-fliers in the States, sweetheart. Not the crash-landed, like me."

Marigold's mouth began to quiver and Bertie said quickly: "There, there, now, darling, no tears," at the same time as Rupert saying, "come on, it's time we were moving."

Isabel and Hanna got to their feet with relief, straightening their clothing and brushing off loose bits of grass. Rupert held the tray for empty glasses and Hanna lifted the rugs, folding them neatly over her arm.

"You'll come to my eighteenth in August," Marigold hiccupped between suppressed sobs, clinging to Thorfinn's hand. "You promise."

"I promise."

"Will you come before that?"

"We'll see," He put his arm around her shoulders. "I'll keep in touch."

"And I'll phone you every single day."

Rupert looked back briefly. "Say your farewells at speed, lovebirds. Time and tide wait for no man."

10

Mrs McFea was on her knees cleaning round the bath when the telephone started to ring, the worst possible place for her to find herself. Her stick was to hand, and she used it to help her to her feet and totter round in the confined space, but it all took time and she became agitated in case the ringing would stop before she got there. Her friends knew that she was seldom away from the house when Callum was at work and she hoped that whoever was on the other end of the phone would not give up.

When she reached the dresser, she leaned on the edge and pulled the phone towards her by the cord. "Yes," she gasped into the half-lifted receiver, expecting the ringing to stop at the crucial moment.

"Sorry, Flo, did I catch you at an awkward time?"

"Hold on." Mrs McFea lowered herself on to a chair and took a few deep breaths to settle the beating of her heart. "That's better, Gemma," she said putting the receiver to her ear. "I was cleaning the bath."

"You should get Callum to do that."

The idea that Callum should do her housework put Mrs McFea back on her mettle. She told Gemma, in no uncertain terms, that she wouldn't ask her man to skivvy after a hard day's work, not while she still had breath in her body.

Gemma ignored the implication. "You're always thinking of others, Flo. Callum's a lucky man."

"Aye, well, what was it you were after, Gemma?"

"I was ringing to invite you to tea this afternoon. At around three thirty, that is."

"Callum can only run me down when he's having his sandwiches."

"I'll get Jill Jimson to pick you up."

Mrs McFea digested that piece of information slowly. "Is it a party you're having?"

"Not exactly a party. I'm just inviting a few friends in to meet Florence Rose, the television star, you know."

Mrs McFea was startled to hear the name introduced into the conversation and it took her a moment to collect her thoughts. "Do you know her then, Gemma?"

"She's staying with me."

"I thought she'd be at the hotel."

"No, she chose to be with me." The boast was made in a tone of barely concealed smugness. "Will you come then, Flo?"

"Does Jill know that she must climb down and help me up the slope?"

"I'll ring and tell her, just to make sure. Around three-thirty then?"

Mrs McFea agreed to be ready by then and they moved on to other topics of conversation – Alec's funeral, Davey's imagination, Cissie's bragging. When they had done the rounds and the phone was once more back on its rest, Mrs McFea sat for a bit taking it all in. She was pleased to be meeting the actress. Callum had aroused her curiosity with his tales, but she was not going to have him bring the lass up to the house and produce her like a goodie on a plate. Being introduced at a tea party was quite different.

Of course the idea that the actress could be her daughter was preposterous … yet it had brought back memories and made her wonder a bit. A howling scrap of a thing with delicate long fingers and a covering of Richie's auburn hair was how she remembered her baby. The nurses had called her Florence Rose but there was no reason to believe that she was called that once she was adopted. At the time of the birth, she'd been thinking less of her baby and more of herself. She was four months gone when she had tracked Richie down and found that he had only married her to get his way. The stories she had had to tell to hide her shame. Looking back now, she doubted if her neighbours believed the reasons she gave to explain Richie's prolonged absence, but she wasn't going to let them know her true circumstance when they could see that she was expecting. Most of her savings had gone on keeping up the pretence that Richie was supporting her and it was a stroke of good fortune that Trowsay House needed a cook when her time was near. The old man's wife had waived the need for an interview or references when she knew who Flo was, but she had expected her to come north as soon as she had worked out her fictional notice.

Mrs McFea pulled herself up and went back to her bath cleaning. Sitting thinking about the past didn't get the work done, as she was prone to say to herself if there was no one around to say it to.

Daphne and Colleen were already seated in the uncomfortable, low-backed armchairs in the front room at The Mains when Jill and Mrs McFea arrived. Gemma's front room was seldom used and it had the faint mustiness of a room where cooking smells had penetrated, lingered, and evaporated, clinging to the walls and soft furnishings. The carpet was heavily patterned, and the dark-blue velvet curtains were bleached to almost white where the sunlight touched them. An electric fire was set into the mantelpiece and brasses of all sizes and shapes were displayed across the top and down the wall on both sides, with substantial brass fire irons lying, unneeded, on the kerb.

There was no sign of the celebrity.

"I don't know what can be keeping Flossie," Gemma apologised, using the actress's pet name with familiarity. "I reminded her before she left this morning." She had claimed intimacy with the TV star and if Florence Rose forgot to come to the tea party, she knew the whispering consequences.

"There, now, Gemma," Colleen said, adjusting the velvet cushion behind her back to make herself more comfortable now that the others had arrived. The room hadn't changed at all since her mother's day and she felt at home. "I'm sure there's a lot for her to do when she's only here for a few days."

"I saw the cameraman passing in his sleeping van yesterday," Jill said, "but the actress wasn't with him."

Gemma put her right.

"It's a personal visit she's making, Jill, just to see Alec's grave and find out more about him and his way of life. That's why she preferred to stay with me rather than at the hotel where she would be gawped at."

Mention of the hotel reminded Colleen of a piece of news that had come her way. "I hear they're going to sell Trowsay House to a family of Arabs."

Jill looked across at her in astonishment and Mrs McFea drew in her breath in outrage.

"No doubt they intend to bring their wives and concubines up with them," Colleen went on, giving a delicious shiver and showing her taste in fiction. "Before you know it, we'll have a harem right here in our midst."

Daphne corrected her: "They want to start a boarding school for Moslem boys."

"It's a disgrace whatever it is," Mrs McFea said, the head of steam erupting. "The old man had enough sorrow in his life without having his home debauched with sexual excess. Aye, and it would be little better to have it overrun with boys who'll vandalise the place as soon as look at it. I wouldn't have credited those Treathams with thinking so little of us here on Trowsay, that they'd sell the house to foreigners to do with as they will."

"Are you sure it's going to be sold?" Jill asked, looking first at Colleen and then at Daphne. "I saw Hanna yesterday and she said nothing about it."

"It's as true as the nose on my face," Colleen said with satisfaction. "It was Lizzie Hope who told me and she should know. The Hope family practically run the place over there."

"Perhaps nothing will come of it," Jill suggested. "Tourists get excited on holiday and dream of living a different life." She went on to tell them about a retired couple from the south who wanted to buy one of their holiday cottages but had lost enthusiasm once they got home.

"Certainly we wouldn't want to lose our hotel."

"We managed fine before, Gemma."

"But it's different now."

They were discussing what Trowsay was like before they had the hotel when they heard the click of the front door being closed. Everyone stopped talking.

"There she is now," Gemma said, brightening up and bustling from the room to welcome her guest back.

The actress could be heard apologising for being late and worrying about her bedraggled state. Unlike the others, Mrs McFea had not seen her on television and so was surprised to find that her voice had a familiar ring. The people hadn't spoken like that in her part of Edinburgh but she knew the flat, precise enunciation well.

Gemma assured her that she was looking lovely. "The Trowsay breeze has brought colour to your cheeks," she added, ushering the star into the front room.

Mrs McFea was the first to be introduced. She took the hand that was offered and looked up into gleaming hazel eyes. Callum was right. The actress was older than she showed in her publicity photo but she was still a good-looking woman with even features and auburn hair.

"Pleased to meet you," she said and their hands parted.

Gemma finished the introductions and went off to make the tea.

"I'm sorry for keeping you all waiting," Flossie apologised, sitting down on the couch beside Mrs McFea. "I hadn't realised the time."

"I believe you were up at the churchyard visiting Alec's grave," Colleen said with a sunny smile.

Flossie blushed, agreeing quickly that she had visited it, adding: "I was also looking at all the stones to see if any of my mother's ancestors were buried there."

"Do you have Trowsay connections then, Mrs Rose?" Jill asked in surprise.

"I'm beginning to doubt it. I'm not sure exactly where my mother came from."

This confession was greeted with amazement.

"She died when I was four."

"But did your father not tell you?"

"Dad knew that she came from one of the islands but he had forgotten which one."

Colleen wanted to know her mother's surname and, on being told, memories were searched.

"It's not a Trowsay name," Jill said.

Daphne thought that a family with that surname had bought a croft out the Eastside back in the early sixties but they had only stayed for two winters.

Colleen was sure that the crofter's wife had not been a Trowsay woman.

"My parents never lived here," Flossie interrupted, "but I thought that Alec might have known my mother when he was a young man. I even wondered about them having a fling and if that was why he had mentioned me in his will."

No one thought that likely but the seed had been sown. Mrs McFea was happy for Alec's carnal sin to be the story that went the rounds. He had not gone on holiday much but he had been south for two years doing national service.

Flossie changed the subject.

"I had an extraordinary experience at the churchyard. There was a woman there who was sitting in the rain, clad in very little. She was shivering with cold and was obviously in deep distress."

"That would be Wilhelmina."

"Oh, you know whom I mean? I wondered if I'd seen a ghost."

"Wilhelmina is no ghost," Daphne said with a smile, and started to tell Flossie about Wilhelmina's tragic history. "Her parents were literally killed in a flash of lightning …"

"It was only her Dad who was struck by the lightning," Colleen interrupted. "Her mother died of pneumonia the following week. In fact it's surprising that Wilhelmina didn't succumb to the pneumonia as well. They'd both stayed out all night in the storm, lying beside the body."

"How dreadful."

"Her mother was my father-in-law's youngest sister. You met him at the causeway the day you arrived. At least he said so."

"I remember him. He told me how to get here."

While they were speaking, Gemma had returned with a trolley, the cups rattling beside the filled teapot and the covered plates on the shelf beneath promising more than an afternoon snack. She interrupted the conversation to offer milk and sugar. Flossie refused both. She was watching her weight, she said. Colleen requested two heaped spoonfuls of sugar, although she had no need of the extra calories or the stimulation. Colleen was a large woman and getting larger. She maintained that she was just big-boned, but a good amount of flesh had stuck to her bones over the years.

"Wilhelmina has strange powers," Daphne said, stirring her tea. "She sees spirits and can communicate with the dead."

"Do you really believe that?"

"She passes on messages, secret things that no one would know outside the immediate family."

"How extraordinary."

"She's a strange girl," Mrs McFea said, lifting her cup and taking a sip. "Always was."

The conversation lapsed. The others were unwilling to admit to a stranger belief in Wilhelmina's spiritual powers.

Flossie turned to Mrs McFea. "I think I met your husband yesterday. I had taken a short cut from here to the hotel and I got bogged down in marshy ground. He came to my rescue."

"Aye, that'll be Callum," Mrs McFea said and the others agreed that Callum was a perfect gentleman.

"I believe we are both called Florence Rose."

Mrs McFea laid her cup on its saucer and took off her glasses, aware of the curious glances and exclamations of surprise.

"I was christened Florence Rose," she said, rubbing the glass against her skirt before putting the cleared lenses back in place.

"But they would be your first names," Jill pointed out.

Flossie told them that they were her first names too. "I dropped my foreign surname when I came out of RADA."

Mrs McFea couldn't focus clearly on the actress because she was sitting too close to her. She shifted her position and looked down the length of her shoulder. There was no doubt about it, the TV star could be the right age and Richie had had that strong hair colouring. She settled back on the sofa, chiding herself for such thoughts. Hers was probably out of a bottle.

"What country did your Dad come from?" Colleen asked, always curious.

Flossie shrugged and showed the palm of her hand in a familiar gesture that delighted the assembled company. "Scotland," she replied with a little laugh, "but he had a Hungarian grandfather."

"And do you have any brothers or sisters?" Gemma asked.

"None. Not even any cousins."

This admission was met with both sympathy and humour. Most people on Trowsay had too many relatives, she was told.

Flossie joined in the laughter. "But that's enough about me," she said, taking another of Gemma's neat sandwiches from the proffered plate. "Let me hear more about you and your life here on Trowsay."

No one wished to be the first to go but there was no mistaking the time when Tavish started clattering around in the kitchen, making his presence known.

Mrs McFea pulled herself forward in her seat and reached for her stick.

"If that's Tavish home, Gemma, Callum will be in from his work and wanting his tea," she said, getting up with Flossie's help. The others agreed that it was time they were on their way too and started collecting together their handbags and discarded scarves or jackets.

At the back door, they shook hands with Flossie, each finding ingratiating parting words. Mrs McFea was the last to bid farewell and she hadn't spoken.

"I believe you don't have a television set, Mrs McFea."

"I'm getting myself a television set," was the determined response. "Callum will see to it for me." She looked up into the face of the woman who might or might not be her daughter and was filled with an overwhelming sadness. She decided there and then that she would have Flossie's publicity photograph framed and she would send her a Christmas card when that time of year came round.

"My mother told me that I was named after the most beautiful city in the world and the most beautiful flower," Flossie said, shaking Mrs McFea's hand..

"Ah, well, that's as may be."

Gemma laughed. "My mother told me that I was named after my star sign, Gemini. My twin sister died at birth and Mum said it was one way of remembering her."

"How sad to lose a twin," Flossie said sympathetically, adding: "I'm Gemini too."

"I'm Pisces," piped up Daphne.

Mrs McFea was wondering what period of the astrological year was covered by Gemini when they started giving their birthdays. As she told Callum later, she could have been knocked down by a feather when she heard the date on Flossie's lips. In fact if she hadn't lent heavily on her stick, she would have fallen right there at Gemma's door.

"Pleased to have met you," was all she was able to say, before taking Jill's arm and hobbling slowly across the farmyard to the car.

Once she was settled in Jill's Volvo, her stick resting on the floor between her legs, tears started to blur her vision. She poked with her fingers behind her glasses to slide them away. She didn't want anything to hinder what she feared would be the last sight she would have of her abandoned daughter.

11

Rupert sat back in his chair, a brandy glass in one hand and a cigar in the other. He looked round the dining room, which was satisfactorily full, and felt content. It was good to be a guest in his own hotel. The food and service were just as he had arranged for them to be and the surroundings were familiar and congenial.

"Isn't that so, Rupert?"

"Sorry, Hanna, what was that?" He put an elbow on the table, holding his cigar away from Duncan who did not smoke.

"I was telling Phil that the French Navy was here during the Napoleonic Wars."

"And the Vikings too, in their time. No doubt raping and pillaging and carrying off the odd maiden or two."

"An island's history is always fascinating," Duncan said, lifting his brandy glass. "Much more so than a stretch of mainland." He glanced sideways at Rupert, waiting for a reaction. Rupert sucked at his cigar once or twice making it glow, and exhaled the smoke away from the table. He didn't rise to the bait and Duncan pressed on: "How did the meeting go, Rupert?"

Rupert knocked the ash from the tip of his cigar. "It went off all right. There was even a contingent from Talhaugh, the tide being favourable."

"So what was the majority view?"

"Hard to say. There were the vociferous few, of course. Professor Fauld was at his most garrulous in opposing and the battleaxe from the co-op backed him at length. The farmers spoke in favour as expected, but it was all predictable stuff until Davey pulled himself up."

"Davey would be against it, bound to be," Phil said, leaning forward in curiosity. "Where would he sit if he didn't have the causeway to guard?"

"Yes, he's against it, but he put forward an interesting reason for opposing," Rupert responded, lifting his brandy glass and taking a sip. "Evidently the variable tides keep professional hitmen on the other side of the water."

Phil sat back, his mirth rising from his solar plexus, to ripple through the fleshy muscles beneath his tightly stretched shirt, wobble his jowls and ooze out of his eyes. Rupert wouldn't have been able to describe a belly laugh before he met Phil.

"So it's contract killers now, is it?" Duncan asked with a smile.

"He's a character is our Davey," Phil said, shifting on to one buttock and extracting a neatly folded handkerchief from his trouser pocket to dab his eyes. "And who on Trowsay is going to fall foul of these gangsters?"

"He was naming no names."

"How disappointing." Duncan swirled the last of his brandy round in his glass. "And the police? Are they still dubious about the accident?"

Rupert pulled a face. "I doubt if they were ever seriously concerned." He lifted his ashtray and ground out the butt of his cigar. "The possibility of its being anything other than an accident stemmed from Davey and they won't see him as a reliable witness."

"What about the mysterious car seen in the area?"

Rupert shrugged. "If it existed at all, it would just contain tourists." He finished his brandy and put his glass on the table. "The conclusion drawn seems to be that it was an accident, pure and simple ... thankfully, I should say. It doesn't do a hotel any favour to have its guests bumped off." He signalled for more drinks but Duncan laid a hand on his arm, shaking his head.

The offer of a quick nightcap back in the sitting room was also refused.

Rupert went off to fetch their coats while the others waited in the hall, Duncan idly turning the pages of a *Country Life* magazine and Phil standing with his back to the fire warming himself.

"I hear that Thorfinn was across here having a few good meals," he said to Hanna, moving aside to let her attend to the fire.

She agreed that he was, poking vigorously and letting the sparks fly.

"Mrs McFea was saying in the shop the other day that he's besotted with that pretty young girl and that her father approves."

"Her father did not object but that does not mean that he approved. He knew that it was just a holiday romance."

She replaced the poker and got up.

"It's more than that. Thorfinn is going to follow the girl down to London."

"Parting promises only. He's not a city man."

"Well, that's what's being said."

"What on earth would he do down there?"

"Get a job."

"I don't believe a word of it."

Phil looked at her thoughtfully. "You're fond of the man, aren't you?"

"Now, Phil, don't embarrass our hostess," Duncan said, closing his magazine and ambling across to the fireside. "We are all fond of Thorfinn."

Phil agreed, adding with a mischievous grin, unaware that Rupert was within earshot: "But some more fond than most."

"Who are you speaking about?" Rupert asked, handing over his anorak.

Phil chortled, unabashed. "Secrets between Hanna and me."

"If I didn't know better, I'd think you'd been making a pass."

Phil put his arm around Hanna's waist. "I have."

"Are you all right, Hanna? You're looking a bit hot and bothered."

"I've just been doing the fire."

Rupert glanced down at the sparking fire and then turned to lay Duncan's Inverness cape across his shoulders.

"How's the work going?" he asked.

Duncan looked up from his buttoning and gave a shrug and a gesture of dismissal. He found it difficult to talk about a painting because he could not explain it himself; it came from within.

Phil had no such reticence. "It's the antithesis of the last one. This time it is a celebration of fire as a cleanser of the land and a renewal of life. The two paintings will hang side by side in the gallery."

"That will be impressive."

"But it's all too much for Duncan. It's taking its toll on his strength."

Hanna took Duncan's arm and sympathised as they walked across the hall and through the vestibule. She knew that his work was very physical and that his canvases were getting bigger as he was getting older.

"A splendid evening, as always," Duncan said when they reached the portico, kissing Hanna's cheek before putting on his wide-brimmed hat. "I will miss our little gatherings."

"Are you going away?"

Phil said quickly: "We're always coming and going," and gave Duncan a warning look.

Hanna watched from the doorway as Rupert walked the two men to their car, rubbing her bare arms for warmth. On rejoining her in front of the hotel, Rupert asked if Duncan and Phil were off on their travels.

"I've not heard any firm date," she said, starting to wave as the car glided past.

"It was all a bit strange there at the end," he mused, watching until the car reached the main road and disappeared from view. "Do you think they know about the sale?"

"Possible sale, Rupert," Hanna corrected him, turning to go inside. "I shouldn't be surprised."

Rupert looked perplexed. "But I've been so careful."

Hanna turned and touched the frown between his brows with her fingertips. "I'm going up. Don't be too long doing the rounds."

They were in bed reading when the telephone rang.

"Who the devil can that be at this hour," Rupert exclaimed in annoyance, dropping his book on the covers and looking at his clock.

Hanna reached over to her bedside table and lifted the receiver anxiously. George Hope was usually very particular about protecting their privacy on their one day off.

"Hi, Hanna."

She listened to the hum of an outside line waiting for the caller to identify himself. When he did so, she gave an exclamation of surprise.

"Ian Gentle," she repeated, "that's a name from the past. How are you Ian?" She had little interest in Ian Gentle's health; she was more interested in seeing Rupert's reaction. He had taken off his glasses, his eyes registering shock. In private the Treathams mockingly called Ian Gentle by his surname because it was inappropriate in their association. He was the UK general manager of a large conglomerate that had taken over the upmarket hotels and leisure centres that had been owned and expanded by Rupert's family over generations. Prior to that happening, the Treathams had wined and dined him generously and Rupert had endured several lengthy rounds of golf, Ian Gentle's enthusiasm for the game being unmatched by his ability. The fact that Rupert had seen these manoeuvres as a softening up process to lure Gentle away from his then employer and on to Rupert's payroll, was doubly galling when the tables were turned. In Rupert's estimation, his stealthy ploy had been legitimate business but Gentle's double-dealing had been underhand.

"I'm fine, Hanna. I've just been watching a programme about your island on television."

"At this time of night?"

"Actually I watched it on Saturday night but I had it on tape and I've been refreshing my memory."

"It's flattering to know that you wanted to record and preserve a programme about us."

"Now, Hanna, sarcasm doesn't suit you. Is Rupert there?"

Hanna turned to Rupert and they exchanged looks of bafflement at receiving this phone call at all, let alone at that time of night.

Rupert took the receiver. "Well, Ian, this is a surprise."

"A nice place you have up there, Rupert."

"Yes, we like it."

"I'm told it is up for sale."

"We were only feeling the market with no firm plans."

"I see it's been on Little & Little's books for nearly a year."

"That was because we were not too concerned about selling," Rupert said smartly, pulling himself up into a sitting position and becoming more alert. "Actually we were surprised when we got a very substantial offer only a few days ago."

"Mmm."

It was clear to Rupert that Gentle didn't believe a word of it and he could not resist elaborating, although he knew that it was not good business to reveal his hand.

"A very rich businessman wants to buy Trowsay House for a boys' boarding school."

"Yes, we were told about him."

"We, Ian?"

"It's like this, Rupert, the Board wants to expand the luxury end of the business …"

"My family's business, you mean."

"Partly, but we're an international company and the rich of the world want to plan their touring holidays in one package, using luxury hotels that are guaranteed to offer the comforts that they enjoy at home, plus traditional country pursuits. Our aim is to have suitable hotels throughout the length and breadth of Britain."

Hanna had her ear close to the receiver and Rupert blanked the mouthpiece. "Sounds as if he's pushing his wares at a conference." They smiled at each other.

"I'm telling you more than I need to about this, Rupert, for old-times' sake."

"Bollocks. I've got something that you want. That's the beginning and end of it."

"Not necessarily." Ian Gentle's voice hardened. "There are plenty of other hoteliers in the north of Scotland who would jump at the chance of selling to us, but we know that your hotel will have been fitted out to the standard we require and will have been well run. Nicely situated too."

"You were always a slimy bastard, Ian, but you won't get round me with flattery."

"I take it then that you're not interested."

But of course Rupert was interested.

"All right, Ian, the fun's over. I suppose you want to come up and have a look around."

"We thought about Wednesday of next week. That is four of us. We'll stay a couple of days."

"I'm in bed just now as any hard-working man is at this time of night. I'll confirm availability tomorrow. What is your number?"

Rupert finished the call in the usual way and gave the handset to Hanna to put back on the rest. "You heard all that?"

"Extraordinary."

Rupert lay back on his pillows. "Our luck is changing, Hanna. Gentle could easily have missed the programme on Trowsay. If he had, we wouldn't have been brought back into his consciousness ... if not conscience."

"But, darling, because he wants to buy doesn't mean that we need to sell. Things are different now that the bridge is in the offing."

"It won't be built for ages. We're looking at three more years at least of problems with visitors every summer and the books barely balancing. Be realistic, Hanna, I'm getting older and I'm stagnating here." Hanna knew that that was the crunch; the difference in their ages was beginning to show. "I've been mulling things over since Mr Ayesh said he was going to make an offer for the place," he went on, laying his book on his bedside table and pulling Hanna down beside him. "We could sell the hotel, dearest, and still keep a base here. Dan Grant wants to buy the Selkie land but he doesn't want the house. I've been up to take a look." Hanna sat up in disbelief. "It would need a lot done to it and I'm not suggesting that we stay there all year round but it could be made into a tolerable holiday house, and if you really wanted to keep working, we could open a restaurant in the barn for the summer visitors. There would be a magnificent view from there if we glassed the wall facing the sea."

"It would be breathtaking," Hanna said softly, still bemused. She dropped back down beside him and rested her cheek in the comfortable place between his neck and his collarbone. "I was so miserable at the thought of leaving for good and I thought you didn't care."

Rupert was amazed that she should think that.

"You know that your happiness is always my first concern," he responded without irony. "But realistically, dearest, it would be madness to think about opening a restaurant until we are joined to the mainland."

Hanna wasn't listening. "If we could buy the Selkie farmhouse and make the barn into a restaurant, it would be the best of all worlds. We could knock down the wall between the kitchen and the bedrooms, and if we blocked off the present front door ..."

Rupert groaned.

"But you mean it, Rupert, don't you?" She looked up at him. "You'd be willing to spend summers here?" He nodded. "And open a restaurant if the road is built?"

"Why not, if it's what you want. But we still haven't sold the hotel yet, remember."

"We will. Everything will be just as it should be. Now let me see ..."

Rupert listened to the determination in Hanna's voice as she decided which rooms she would give Ian Gentle and his board members and the food she would prepare to make them mellow. He wondered if he had been too hasty in revealing his hand; he had only been mulling over the possibility of buying Alec's house and keeping a base on Trowsay.

"I'll pray for the weather to be fine," Hanna finished, nestling in closer to him in contentment. "Trowsay smiles in the sunshine."

"While you're at it, pray for the tides to work in well with the flights," Rupert said wryly, reaching up and switching off the light. "That's the number one priority."

12

Davey sat in his usual place, looking across the stretch of water. There was a young man leaning against the wall on the other side, waiting for the sea to ebb. They eyed each other up, and when it was only the occasional wave that circled the stones and meandered over the causeway, the man reached down and lifted up his rucksack, slinging it on to his shoulder.

Heidi got up and stood stiffly, her tail erect, waiting for her master's reaction.

The backpacker was a sight to behold. Everything about him was anathema to Davey who expected a man to look like a man and not like a walking pincushion. This specimen of manhood wore ragged jeans that were barely decent, and there were metal rings sprouting out of every facial feature, as well as the odd body cavity that should have been decently covered. His head was bald and his face was shaggy. The idea of a man wanting to shave his head and comb his chin was a new one on Davey.

He didn't get up from his boulder or offer a word of greeting.

"A grand evening," the man said, allowing his rucksack to fall at his feet. He looked out to sea as if he had all the time in the world.

"Walked far?"

"Just from Thurso."

"A tidy walk."

"I got a lift or two along the way."

Davey took out his battered tin of tobacco and started to roll himself a cigarette. Heidi relaxed and lay down at his feet. The man was tall and strong with a soft, south-country voice. Davey wondered why he wanted to look so weird.

"Could you point me in the direction of a farm called Brackenlea," he asked, picking up his rucksack.

Davey looked up with more interest. "I could," he said, champing his teeth overtime to keep his smile in check. "You must be Laura's Joe."

The man's face lit up with pleasure. "I see I don't need to introduce myself."

"No, you winna need to do that, but you'll have a bit of explaining to do."

Joe chuckled, a wide grin splitting his facial hair.

That was not a reaction that found favour with Davey.

"It's no laughing matter putting a girl in the family way and leaving her to face the music," he said, beginning to mumble to himself and rolling away at his cigarette, long after it had formed its skinny shape.

Joe said soberly: "Laura dances to her own tune," but Davey did not reply. He put the sagging cigarette in his mouth and struck a match, concentrating on taking his first drag.

Joe picked up his rucksack and started walking on. "See you around," he called.

"You take the left turning at the top," Davey told him, but he didn't return the wave of acknowledgement.

As he smoked his cigarette, Davey thought about Joe. The newspapers often showed men peppered with pieces of metal. They were usually up to no good. Doubtless

Joe was like them, more taken up with his own body than that of the bairn growing inside his woman. He scooped Heidi up and started gently stroking her glossy coat. Yet the man had put in an appearance to take what was given him. Davey could picture Joe travelling all the way up from the south and walking the long road from Thurso to be with Laura. The thought disturbed his memory; but the picture of him coming home to Betsy and being a family man wouldn't stick in his mind. He wasn't good with bairns. Scott and Colleen had had five, and three of them now had family. Only the other week his youngest grandson had brought along his umpteenth great-grandchild for him to hold on his knee. She was the first girl of that generation and was to be called Betsy he was told, which was just as it should be. He had opened the bottle of whisky that had been handed to him and had drunk to the baby's health, but he couldn't see any connection between the small scrap of a thing and himself. It was the same with the other family members who came and went. He got muddled about their relationship to each other and to him. It might have been different if there hadn't been that gap in his time and memory.

Heidi stood up on his lap with a quiver of innate excitement, holding her balance by digging her claws into Davey's tweed-covered thighs. Then she was off, leaping on to the gritty hard sand with a whooph of ferocious delight. Davey watched the rabbit running up the slope, darting hither and thither round tufts of thick grass and heather, with Heidi in distant pursuit. Her short legs made it an uneven competition. Davey wondered if it were the same rabbit that appeared from time to time to taunt Heidi into playing, knowing that it would not be caught.

He spent most of the next morning trying to mend a leak underneath his caravan. There was an old sink out back, nearly obscured by grass and weeds but with a fine piece of copper piping of the right gauge attached. It took him some time to loosen it from its tap (subsequently discarded on the ground), rub it down, clear it with a blow, cut it and bend it to shape. When it was nearly the same as the piece he had taken off, he lit his lantern and crawled back underneath the caravan, but try as he might, he couldn't get a tight seal. He snaked back out and got to his feet, turning the bolt and the washer over in his hand, looking at them more carefully. They had both seen better days. The bolt needed a soaking in Looseall and the washer was thin with a bit of a dent on its underside. He put them in his pocket and crossed the field to Brawtoon to see what he could find there. It was just the right time to visit the farmhouse. Colleen might be on a diet at breakfast time but by midday there was always a full three-course meal on the table and plenty for all-comers.

When he was settled at the table with a plate of soup in front of him, he said: "I see Laura's Joe has turned up."

"He seems a nice enough lad."

Davey couldn't hide his disappointment.

"You've met him, Scott?"

"Aye, Laura had him along at the hotel last night."

"Laura wouldn't miss an opportunity to shock her neighbours," Colleen said finishing her soup and

257

moving her chair closer to Alan. He was sitting with a towelling bib over his chest and a spoon held slackly in his hand. "Did you know that she wasn't at home when her man arrived, Davey? She and Bess were up at Selkie sorting out Alec's things." Colleen took the spoon and started to feed the liquid into Alan's mouth. It opened and shut without complaint as each brimming spoonful came close. "There was only old Agnes Grant there to greet him."

"Is that a fact! Some meeting that would've been." Davey chortled at the thought, describing his first sighting of Joe. He was too late to astound his son and daughter-in-law with Joe's partiality for metal adornment but his meeting at the causeway was still worth the telling.

Colleen finished feeding Alan and got up, taking the broth pot from the stove and emptying the last of the soup into Davey's bowl. She collected the other plates together and took them through to the scullery, talking all the time. "Aye, I hear he's a sight to behold but Gemma says that Mrs Grant took a liking to the man. Flo McFea heard it straight from the horse's mouth."

Davey nearly choked over the last of his soup. The sound and sight of Davey's wheezy laughter raised a memory in Alan's degenerating brain. He opened his mouth to say something, but the thought had gone before it was spoken.

"Now, Davey, you know fine that that's just a saying," Colleen reproached, dishing up the next course. She put a heaped plate of stew and potatoes in front of Scott and lifted away Davey's soup bowl. "The present

258

ructions up at Brackenlea are not over Joe's appearance but over the non-existent marriage plans. Gemma was saying that old Mrs Grant has taken to her room and has announced that she will not come out until the shame on the house has been lifted by the banns being called in the Loch Church."

"Aye, Laura said something to that effect in the bar last night."

Colleen stopped serving to give her husband a look of reproach.

"You never told me that."

"I doubted the truth of it." Scott munched away. "The lass followed it up by saying that the old woman's absence from the kitchen table was the perfect reason for not having the banns called at all."

Davey sat back in astonishment, allowing Colleen to place his plate of stew in front of him. "Laura doesna want the man to marry her?"

"Of course she'll want him to marry her," Colleen said sitting down and starting to cut up Alan's meat. "Laura is always trying to be smart, that's all it'll be."

"Certainly her man didn't laugh when she said it."

"There you are then."

They settled down to eat and enjoy their own thoughts. The Trowsay beef and garden vegetables had been simmering in the pot since early morning and were tender and juicy. As he ate, Davey watched Alan lifting up his fork and settling it in his hand like a shovel. His nostrils were quivering at the smell of the savoury steam rising from his plate. He mashed his potatoes into the gravy and scooped up a few mouthfuls of the succulent meat without Colleen's assistance.

Davey could have told her that Alan had never cared for Scotch broth but he always minded his own business.

Joe stayed at Brackenlea for less than a week and left for the south with Laura.

Davey had been looking forward to meeting him again (just to show that there were no hard feelings) but he missed saying goodbye. That aggravated him. He had only been pottering around in his caravan all morning, bottling some beer and making himself a bit of a meal, waiting for the tide to go out. In fact the water was still swirling over the stones when he came down the cliff path and saw the Grants' car turning at the top. He had quickened his pace, waving and calling, showing that he wanted a word. Heidi had joined in, leaping about and barking, but the car hadn't stopped. He could see Bess at the wheel with Laura beside her. No doubt Joe was in the back. Davey felt aggrieved. He hadn't expected them to be on the move so early.

For most of the afternoon, he just hung around, passing the time of day with anyone who came his way, waiting for Bess to return.

She cut it fine. The tide was already wetting the stones at the edge and splashing on to the causeway before her car came over the brow of the hill opposite. Davey got up to direct her across. It wasn't necessary for him to guide her because she could still see where the road fell away, but if he offered the service, she couldn't drive past him with only a wave.

"Thank you, Davey," she said, rolling down her window, her engine still running.

Davey leaned along the roof of her car and flashed a smile, to indicate that it was a pleasure to have her stop and talk. He had never seen Bess looking so lovely. Her cheeks were pink and her eyes were sparkling. It could mean only one thing.

"You'd be pleased to see Laura's man and give him the once over," he said. "I hear he's nice enough."

Bess agreed and changed the subject by asking Davey how he was keeping.

"Fine, fine. We'll be hearing wedding bells, will we?"

Bess smiled "Perhaps." She gave Davey a wave of farewell and let out the clutch. "They'll soon be back."

Davey sat on his boulder until the tide was well in before he gave up waiting for another car to cross and give him a lift along the road. He got up and rubbed himself a bit to get the circulation moving. His boulder had a natural dent in its surface that fitted him nicely, but it was still hard and cold at the end of the day. He looked at his watch. It was long past his teatime and he could have done with a plate of tatties but he needed a bit of company. He fingered the coins in his pocket. If he went past the hotel, he would have enough for a half-pint, he reckoned, and if Mrs Treatham were about, she would take him through to the kitchen for something to eat before his walk home. He whistled to Heidi and they started up the hill. The hotel prices were steep but by the time he walked the distance, it was likely that Alf would be there or Thorfinn Dukes. They wouldn't leave him standing without a beer in his hand and he could keep his money in his pocket. He didn't expect a drink on the house. He knew that when he appeared with Heidi under his arm, Mr Treatham would just eye him up as if he didn't like what he saw. Davey had told him, with some heat, that he was as good as the next body in himself and his clothes had all come from good homes but it had made no difference.

He reached the top of the hill and stopped to catch his breath. Heidi ran back to make sure that he was all right and then was off again.

It was a grand evening with streaks of cloud moving lazily across the sun and as he walked along the side of the loch, he became absorbed in the changing shapes and colours reflected in the water. He came to a grassy hollow and sat down to contemplate this phenomenon. After a time, he found that he could shatter the beauty of the world as God had created it, by skimming a stone across the loch's surface. Each time he sinned in this way, he would wait for reassurance before hurling another stone. It was a fascinating game, making him ponder on the fragility of nature when man set his hand against it.

The sound of a car got him to his feet. He looked back along the road .to see who was coming. It was the Brawtoon truck with Colleen at the wheel.

Davey lifted Heidi and climbed up.

"Where are you off to, Davey?"

"I thocht I'd take a look in at the hotel."

The noise of the engine made conversation difficult so Davey waited until Colleen had stopped beside Trowsay House before telling her his news about Laura and Joe.

"… aye Bess Grant was full o it," he finished. "A right sparkle she had in her eye."

"She'll be as pleased as punch. Didn't I say the other day that Laura would be getting married."

"I dinna ken aboot that."

"Her man must've come all the way up from the south to speak to Dan."

"Bess said nothing about his speaking to Dan. She's Bess's lass mind."

"Was she talking wedding dates, Davey?"

"Soon is what she said." Davey pushed down the handle of the door to open it and let Heidi jump down. He found the step and started to get out.

"It would have to be soon," Colleen said with a smile. "I'll call for you on my way back."

Davey slammed the door and watched the truck until it disappeared round the bend.

"She winna be telling it as she should," he said to Heidi, shaking his head as he walked up the short drive. "We'll need to be keeping people right."

He reached the front of the hotel and peered through the drawing room window to see who was about. Two fine ladies stopped talking to look at him and he gave them a wave before checking on who was at the bar. Alf and Donnie were there and heard his knock. Donnie beckoned, with a broad welcoming smile and Davey nodded in acknowledgement, before retracing his steps to the front door.

"Donnie Strachan has given us an invite," he said to Heidi, bending down to pick her up. He tucked her under his arm and went into the hotel to earn his drink.

PART III

(May 1995)

The Treathams were in Ireland when they received their invitation to the wedding. Hanna had known that it was coming and was determined to go; she would go alone if Rupert persisted in his opposition.

But Rupert's mood had swung in favour.

"It'll be interesting to see what a mess they've made of it all," he said, his eyes lighting up at the prospect of finding Trowsay House in deterioration.

It was a dreich day when they took off from Dublin airport, spray rising from the rain-splattered runway as the plane gathered speed and accelerated up into the enveloping cloud, plunging and rocking through pockets of uneven pressure as it climbed.

"Poor Slavers," Hanna said to an unresponsive Rupert. She was thinking of Slavers buffeted about in the freight carriage below. He had had to be dragged and pushed into his crate, yelping in protest, although, once in, he was resigned to his fate, twitching his tail in mournful farewell when they got their call to board.

The plane was still climbing through the gloom. Hanna sat with an open book on her lap, listening to the monotonous throb of the engines and watching the vaporous puffs of heated moisture drifting past her window.

"Not much of a day," she said, and Rupert agreed before returning to his newspaper.

There were glimpses of sky as the cloud began to thin and break up, receding and swirling away as the plane flew into sunshine and levelled off in the thin, blue air above the dense bank of clouds. Hanna could look down on a range of snowy white peaks, rising and falling as far as her eye could see; the tips were lit by the sun's rays and the slopes were deepened by shadow, fading into lavender on the distant horizon. It reminded her of the Hallingskarvert Mountains and family skiing holidays in her native Norway.

Rupert's voice broke into her thoughts.

"What are you having?" he asked, and she turned to choose a drink from the trolley and share her thoughts.

The next time she looked out of her window, the clouds below were breaking up and thinning into amorphous, floating wisps. She could see the Irish Sea, shimmering with reflected sunlight, and in the distance, waves were washing over black, rocky islets and splashing against the cliffs of Scotland. She nudged Rupert, leaning back in her seat so that he could see the change in the weather and the land ahead.

"A good omen," she said, squeezing his hand with an excited smile.

Rupert pointed out that the weather was as unpredictable as the future.

She agreed, but added wistfully: "I just feel that everything is going to go well for us now."

In that she was proved wrong.

When they arrived at Glasgow airport, they discovered that Slavers was not in the dog crate they had seen loaded on to their plane. A bewildered, wide-eyed puppy looked out at them through the bars. Rupert was infuriated by the mix-up and went off to throw his weight around while Hanna comforted the puppy, imagining Slavers pining away in the freight shed over in Dublin, his head on his paws and his eyes following the legs of passing strangers in miserable abandonment. (In fact he had flown to Heathrow in the company of a golden retriever bitch and had other things on his mind.)

By the time it was all sorted out, they had missed their connection to Wick and, to crown it all, on reaching Talhaugh a day late, the tide was in and the causeway impassable.

Rupert was uncharacteristically relaxed.

"Unpleasant memories," he said with a smirk.

"We'll miss the service," Hanna wailed. "I was looking forward to it so much." She looked down at the eddying water. "How long do you think it'll be, Rupe."

"An hour, I'd say." He opened his door. "I'll take Slavers for a run while we wait."

Slavers was going mad in the back of the car, recognising the sight, sound and smell of familiar territory. He was turning and twisting, knocking his tail against all the surfaces of his confined space. The tartan rug that Hanna had laid carefully over the back seat to protect the upholstery had been spun into a crumpled ball.

Hanna watched them walking along the cliff edge for a bit and then rolled down her window and breathed deeply, smelling and tasting the salty tang of seaweed and enjoying the feel of a fresh, cool breeze on her face. The weather forecast that morning had been gloomy for the north and she could see that it had been raining, but now the sun shone down on a sparkling clean landscape. She lay back in her seat with her eyes closed, listening to the repetitive sound of the waves breaking against the rocks below, and wished that she was coming home. Even the thought of their rootless existence made her feel weary. She tried to empty her mind and doze off but the wedding ahead and the excitement of meeting old friends kept her awake. She reached for her handbag and took out Phil's last letter. The envelope was coming away at the folds through frequent opening.

The first two pages covered Duncan's latest exhibition in New York. It was to be his last, Phil wrote, but it was his best. He went on to describe the different paintings being exhibited; some she recognised. She skipped down the second page to the start of his news about the wedding.

"... everyone is invited and as far as I can gather there have been no refusals, except us, that is, and our apologies have been made with genuine regret." She turned over. "New perms have been sprouting out of old heads at an alarming rate, and for months the main topic of conversation has been clothes and whether or not to wear a hat. Cissie has had a brisk sale in congratulatory cards, the favourites showing two hearts entwined in everlasting love. The less starry-eyed, however, see the imminent construction of a raised road joining Trowsay to the mainland, as the reason for bringing Rob up to scratch. As Daphne said in the shop yesterday, he can no longer skulk around the fringes of engagement when Trowsay is about to lose its district nurse and he his comforts. I'm devastated that we are still going to be in New York at the time. You must be my eyes and ears." He then went on to describe a new recipe he had tried and the spring planting he had done, ending with the hope that she and Rupert would still be there when they got back.

Hanna wondered about her garden as she folded the letter and put it back in her handbag. She hated to think of it reverting to the wilderness that she and Thorfinn had tamed. The memory of that first spring on the island when she and Thorfinn had got to know each other, brought a dreamy smile to her lips. She still thought of him in the privacy and stillness of the night and fantasised about what might have been, but she was no longer able to feel the magnetism of his personality or the effect it had had on her metabolism, try as she might. Phil seldom mentioned him in his letters and nothing that would evoke Thorfinn's vibrant presence.

She looked round and saw Rupert striding back across the promontory with Slavers running hither and thither round him. The hairs on Slavers' legs and belly were matted with sea-water and she got out to rearrange the rug over the back seat, tucking it in tightly. When she moved away from the door, Slavers jumped up and slumped down, panting noisily over his pink, moist tongue and exuding a fishy whiff of rotting aquatic waste.

"I think I could give it a try now," Rupert said, checking the soles of his shoes before getting in.

Hanna was dubious and reminded him of the fate of Mr Yearts.

"Ah, but unlike the unfortunate Hal, I'm as sober as the proverbial," he said with a guffaw, making himself comfortable behind the wheel.

"We could do with Davey at the other side to direct us."

"Didn't Phil say that the causeway had been resurfaced?"

"He did." Hanna looked at her watch as Rupert started to drive down the slope. "I could make it to the church if we got across now."

She held on to the strap above the door and put her head out of the window to follow the shimmering edge of the road as Rupert started the crossing. The advancing waves nearly touched the hub before falling away and she could feel Rupert's tension as he held the car tightly on course against the pull of the tide. When they bumped up on to the hard-surface of the beach, she exhaled her breath, and they both laughed with relief.

"We're as bad as Sweyn Jimson," Hanna said, flipping down her sunshade to look at her face. She took out her make-up bag and comb. "I'll have to go as I am and change later. Would you hang up my dress when you get to our room, Rupert?"

He said he would.

When they arrived at the open gates of the church, the green was thronging with those who could not be seated inside. Hanna had forgotten that only family and close friends could witness the actual wedding ceremony in the small church, the rest would have to listen to the service outside, relayed through Ted Vale's speaker system. She could see rugs spread out at the lochside and reached over to the back seat for her coat.

There was a flutter of recognition when she stepped out and smoothed down her skirt. She smiled and waved, bending to the open window to remind Rupert again about her dress. He nodded, giving her a parting smile as he put the car into reverse and backed up between the gates at speed. She stepped away quickly, her thin heels sinking into the soft verge.

"Shat!" she exclaimed in vexation, leaning on the gatepost while she tried to wipe away the clods of clinging mud.

"Aye, it's still a piece damp under foot," a voice said from behind her.

She looked up to see Jockie Jay, leaning on his stick. He lifted his trilby in greeting and smiled, the network of lines round his mouth and up through his hollow cheeks to his rheumy eyes creasing and deepening. He had on his church garb, a navy blue suit that hung unevenly on his emaciated frame, a stiff white collar and a naval tie.

"But dinna fash yersel, lass, it's clean enough dirt," he declared. "Come away now." He put an arm across her shoulders to guide her up the path, although who was guiding whom was open to question. Jockie was two years nearer his century and it had taken its toll on his wasted muscles.

Hanna was shaking outstretched hands and kissing offered cheeks when Dan Grant touched her shoulder, saying softly: "A place has been kept for you in church."

It was unlikely that that was so because Donnie and Ria Strachan had to move closer together for her to squeeze into the tiny space left at the end of their pew. She whispered her apologies. Donnie assured her that it was a pleasure to have her with them, patting her knee with a beam of jollity. Hanna knew that he was an innocent flirt but they were so closely packed, she was relieved when his hand resumed its position on his paunch. She put her coat under the seat and looked round, acknowledging smiles from those sitting close by.

Rob Ballater and Alf Strachan were standing together in front of the communion table. Rob had half-turned to see what was happening and he lifted his hand to Hanna in a welcoming salute. He was licked and polished for the occasion, his ginger hair fingered into glistening spikes and his grey suit smartly pressed.

The clapping started outside, heralding the arrival of the bride, and Martha Silver skilfully concluded her medley of tunes to strike the familiar chords. Heads turned and necks strained to catch first glimpses of Ursula as she entered the church on the arm of her father. She glowed with beauty and happiness; her cream chiffon dress floated to her ankles and her matching bridal hat shadowed her eyes. As she approached her groom, Rob turned, his face splitting into a spirited grin.

The marriage service went without a hitch. The hymns were familiar and sung with gusto, the visiting minister was brief in his advice and Alf passed the ring over without mishap. Rob took the gold band and slipped it on to his bride's finger, happily committing himself for life to no-nonsense Ursula McCorquerdale.

Once the official signing had been completed and the newly-weds had walked down the aisle and out into the sunshine (to a reception of flashing cameras and showers of rose petals) Hanna slipped away through the vestry door and took the short cut along the edge of the loch to the hotel. The surface of the narrow path was muddy and overhanging fronds of bracken brushed wetly against her legs, staining her skirt. The path had not been kept in trim and she was glad to reach the steps leading up to the forecourt. She was climbing them two at a time, holding her tight skirt up above her knees, when she was hailed by two elderly women sitting on one of the wooden seats between the terraces, binoculars on their laps. It took a moment for her to recognise Mrs Bartholomew and Mrs Pinkerton.

"Of course, this is your time of year for visiting," she said, going over and greeting them.

Betty Pinkerton held on to her hand. "It is so good to see you," she said, looking up at Hanna with her wide, innocent eyes, heavily fringed with mascara. "Things have not been quite the same since you left."

Hanna made the appropriate appreciative noises.

"And aren't we lucky to be staying when Ursula is getting married," Mrs Bartholomew boomed in her sonorous voice, using Ursula's first name with a gratifying familiarity. "She is such a fine person. Were you here when she took the fly hook out of Arthur's finger?" Hanna thought not and this gave Mrs Bartholomew the opportunity to give her a detailed account of the incident. It was only when Hanna had run out of suitable exclamatory responses, that she felt able to escape and find her room.

Rupert was dressed, except for his bow tie, which she quickly fixed for him. Her dress was lying on the bed, still in its tissue paper. She shook it out and put it on a coat hanger, brushing her hands down its silky, bronze surface to smooth out the creases. It was a sensual dress, knee-length, with a scooped neckline and embroidered in different shades of bronze thread. Her mother had sent it from Norway, with a matching carved comb for her hair.

Rupert left the room while she was in the shower and came back full of beans.

"The manager of the place is not a bad chap," he said, which told her where he'd been. He strode over to the window to see what was happening. "I've offered to help in the bar later."

Hanna sat down at her dressing table and reached for her make-up bag.

"Must you?" she asked, looking up at him dolefully, but he was too taken up with what was going on outside to take notice of her reproach. She could hear the faint sound of the bagpipes as the piper led the procession round from the church to the hotel. "You always desert me."

"What's that?" he asked, turning round to her with a bewildered expression.

She started to cream her face. "Never mind."

"Everything all right, dearest?"

Hanna shrugged in resignation of her abandonment. "Tell me what's going on."

"It's all a bit disorganised. The children are playing round Rob and Ursula, back and forward, touching them for luck. Nearly everyone is taking photos. My heavens, there must be a breeze blowing down the loch because Ursula's dress has taken flight and she's showing most of what she's got."

He stopped talking to watch.

"What's happening now?" Hanna asked, lifting the brush from the eyelid she was highlighting.

"She's let go of Rob's arm and is holding her dress down with one hand and her hat on with the other.

Rob has lifted her and is carrying her up the slope." He beckoned to Hanna "Come and see quickly!"

They stood at the window watching as everyone crowded round, cheering Rob's feat of strength. On reaching the forecourt, he put his bride down carefully and kissed her under the shadow of her hat. She was laughing, in a joyful mood now that she was safely in the shelter of the hotel and the arms of her husband.

While Hanna did her hair, brushing and twining, plaiting and pinning, Rupert leaned over the banisters, puffing a cheroot and watching the guests moving through the hall and along the corridor to the ballroom. When they started to thin out, he returned to their room.

"That's the last of them," he said, stubbing his cheroot out on the open window sill.

Hanna voiced her dismay, quickly inserting the carved comb into her chignon and reaching for her mirror to check the back and assure herself that she had positioned it as she wanted.

"We mustn't arrive after the bride and groom are seated," she said, getting up and slipping into her shoes. "Where's my bag?" Rupert picked it up from the bed and handed it to her, guiding her towards the door. "My earrings!" She returned quickly and lifted them from the dressing table, pushing them through her earlobes and securing them as they crossed the landing and hurried down the staircase. By the time they reached the corridor leading to the ballroom, there was only the bridal party left.

Hanna started to apologise but Ursula interrupted her:

"We've been waiting for you," she said, receiving their embraces and congratulations. "You're sitting next to my father, Hanna."

Hanna was surprised to find herself being introduced to a chubby man in a kilt. She had not realised that she and Rupert would be seated at the top table.

"Rob's sister is ill and his family haven't managed to get over from Canada," Ursula explained, apologising for not asking her beforehand. (Rob was a second-generation Canadian, the grandson of one of the islanders who had emigrated there in the 1930s. His great-uncle had willed him the farm of Shaws.) "I know that you and Dad will hit it off."

Hanna smiled and shook hands.

"Rupert, you are between my uncle," and she introduced him to the minister, "and Miss Silver." When she saw Rupert's horrified expression at the thought of sitting between the two preachers, she said smartly: "An opportunity, Rupert, for you to be reminded of your blessings."

"Don't take any notice of her, old chap," her uncle said as the bridal party formed into pairs to follow the bride and groom down the dining room to an applauding reception. "Once the grace has been said, my professional duty is over. Are you interested in early twentieth century music hall by any chance?"

Ursula's father was a doctor from central Scotland and heavy going. Hanna longed to turn to Dan Grant, who was on her other side, and gossip about island life. He was kept busy retrieving cutlery, food and toys that his young son was throwing overboard from his high chair. She could see Bess at the other end of the table similarly occupied.

"It's a demanding job for you and Bess with two babies to look after," she said in a period of release."

Dan's attention was still focused on his son's impulses. "We manage."

Hanna laid down her knife and fork and took a sip of wine. "Your mother is well, I hope?"

"She's well enough. Just the few aches and pains."

"She would've been delighted to have a grandson, and an extra pair of hands is always a help."

"Aye, she gives Bess a hand when she's in," Dan told her, retrieving a spoon from the floor

Hanna raised her eyebrows in query.

"Mum moved into the cottage a while back."

"I hadn't heard."

"Susie's crying upset her and she could see that the crying would increase twofold after our baby ... our Danny here ... was born."

All Hanna felt able to say in applauding Agnes Grant's departure from the Brackenlea hearthside was: "It always distresses the elderly to hear a baby cry." She wondered what other momentous news Phil had forgotten to tell her. "How is Laura? I don't see her here tonight."

"She's got her finals next week. No, Danny, NO." He had taken his eye off his son for a moment and a piece of meat had been propelled from his spoon on to Cissie Vale's wedding hat. Cissie went on talking to Daphne Glover, unaware of the additional adornment.

"And the perfect Joe. What has happened to him?"

Dan took the spoon from Danny's tight grip and tried to shovel some food into his tightly closed mouth.

"A right fine lad," he said putting the spoon down. "There's hardly a month goes by when he's not up seeing Susie. Helps me a bit on the farm too."

"That's good to hear. So it's all turned out for the best."

Dan picked up his knife and fork and started to cut up his chicken.

"He and Laura are no longer … an item. Aye, that's the word Laura used."

Hanna voiced her regret.

"It's not the way it should be but there's no good talking."

They ate in silence until Hanna's neighbour on the other side reclaimed her attention. She found him an unsettling conversationalist. He had his daughter's eyes and habit (or, rather, she had inherited his eyes and habit) of holding her gaze for a fraction of a second longer than was necessary before replying, as if he was weighing up the possibility that she might not be telling him the truth. She wondered if Rupert was fairing better at the other end of the table. She couldn't see him but at one point she had heard his throaty guffaw and seen Rob lean back in his chair to find out the reason for the hilarity. It seemed that the joke was not worth repeating because it had gone no further. Occasionally she would attract the attention of an old friend or acquaintance, sitting at one of the five long tables radiating out from the dais, and would give a smile and a wave. She could see Davey tucking into his meal near the door and wondered if he had got used to the new caravan that Scott and Tavish had bought for him. He had been staying at Brawtoon with a wheeze in his chest and a bad bout of gastric flu when they had burned down his old one and cleared the site of junk. The replacement had been pulled over rough ground to a more sheltered spot, no more than twenty yards or so farther along the coast, and Patsy had put in climbing plants to soften the surrounding block wall. It had got the islanders' seal of approval but Davey had been raving mad when he was well enough to go home. He was still creating about their intrusion on his privacy when they left Trowsay. During a pause in her conversation with Dr McCorquerdale, she turned to ask Dan about it. He followed her gaze to where Davey was sitting.

"He took a liking to it the day the officials arrived to evict him and found him living in luxury. His word not mine."

"He would've been tickled pink at putting one over on authority."

"Aye, we've never heard the end of it."

Hanna quickly covered her mouth to stifle her hilarity but her laughter still attracted attention. She could see Mrs McFea eyeing her from two tables away, not in disapproval as she would have expected, but with an unusually benign expression. Hanna responded with a mouthed "Hallo" and Mrs McFea raised her hand before pushing fashionable gold-rimmed spectacles up her nose. She had lost weight and the navy blue dress she was wearing had a white lace collar which showed a slither of bare shoulder.

Hanna whispered to Dan: "I see I'm no longer a pariah for desecrating the House."

Dan put down his knife and fork, acknowledging Mrs McFea with a nod. "Aye, she's been in good spirits since she had her knees done."

Hanna hadn't known that her knees could be done. She twiddled the stem of her wine glass, still looking in that direction. "My goodness, is that Florence Rose with her back to us, sitting opposite the McFeas?"

"Aye, she visits regularly," he said, to Hanna's astonishment. "She's bought one of Tavish Martin's old farmhouses and is doing it up."

"Which one?"

"The old croft along past The Mains. The one that belonged to Wilhelmina's folk at one time."

"I remember it."

The sound of plates falling to the floor, one after another, came from the far end of the room and heads turned to see what had happened. After the hush of curiosity had passed, Dr McCorquerdale engaged Hanna in conversation again.

"I believe you are Norwegian, Mrs Treatham."

She said that she was half Norwegian.

"We know your country well, my wife and I."

Hanna smiled and enquired where they had been.

"We have travelled widely." He fingered his neat beard, his eyes glazing over as he relived his holidays in Norway, praising the scenery, the people and their independent state. Hanna was initially pleased that they had found a topic of mutual interest but Dr McCorquerdale was a bore and she did not keep her mind firmly on his rambling stories and complex political comparisons between Scotland and Norway. Her monosyllabic responses were not always apt or suitably encouraging and eventually he decided that his sister-in-law, the minister's wife seated on his other side, would be more attentive.

With both neighbours occupied, Hanna sipped her wine and thought about the croft house that Florence Rose was doing up. She had passed it often on her walks along the coast with Slavers and remembered it as being in a lovely position but in a bad state of repair. Nothing had been done to it since Wilhelmina had gone to live with the Nicols at the joinery, next door to the cemetery.

"How is Wilhelmina?" she asked Dan, looking round and finding her seated at the far end of the room.

"Poor lass, she's not herself these days," Dan said, turning from his plate of roast beef to check on Danny. He was in the cherubic stage between wakefulness and sleep. He was trying to keep his eyelids open but his long lashes were growing heavier and heavier, finally coming to rest on his round, flushed cheeks. Dan took off his messy bib. "She frightened a tourist last summer and they've put her on pills to calm her down."

Wilhelmina turned to look in their direction as if she knew what was being said. Hanna waved but there was no response.

"Does she still spend her days in the churchyard?"

"She's there most days, but the spirits no longer speak to her and she has lost touch with her parents. We don't get messages from the dead either."

"You never believed that, Dan?"

Dan smiled as he pierced a morsel of meat with his fork. "Tell me, Mrs Treatham … Hanna … what have you been doing with yourself these last eighteen months. I had hoped that you would buy Alec's house, you know."

With an inward sigh, Hanna told him about their nomadic existence. She could see that he was not much interested; her experiences were what happened to people away, in places beyond his world.

When she had finished, he said: "It's no life for you always travelling here and there and not having a proper roof over your head. I know that Alec's place needs a bit done to it but it would suit you and your man fine."

"I'm surprised that you haven't sold the farmhouse yet."

"I'm letting it." He turned to look at her. "It's yours for a fair price if you want it."

"We'll see," was all that she felt able to say.

When the speeches were over and glasses had been raised to the health and happiness of the bride and groom, it was time for the tables to be cleared so that the dancing could begin. The wedding guests got up and mingled, wandering out of the ballroom and down the corridor to the cocktail lounge or through the French windows on to the paved terrace.

Rupert left his place and walked along the dais.

"See you," he said, squeezing Hanna's hand in passing.

"Rupert," she called, "stay for a bit."

The spring in his step slackened. He turned back, his smile fading.

"I promised to help out," he said, looking peevish. "I told you about it, remember."

Hanna agreed that he had.

"Anyway I'm no company for you, dearest," he wheedled. "Swapping banalities is not my scene. You'll be much better off without me."

She could see Jean starting to clear their table, pretending not to hear their disagreement.

"All right, off you go and enjoy yourself," she said with a wry smile, turning to greet Jean and enquire how she was.

Jean said she was okay. She was wearing a chef's apron and the change in her was marked. She had put on weight and grown her hair (it was hanging forward as she worked, framing her face) and light touches of make-up had enhanced her translucent skin and the unusual violet of her eyes.

"You're looking very lovely, I must say."

"And you too, Mrs T. You've got a super tan."

"It shows the wrinkles, I'm afraid," Hanna demurred, making a face. "Tell me, how did you get on with your catering course?"

"It was okay." She moved along and started scraping the congealed food from the tray of the high chair and sponging the surface before lifting it to the edge of the dais ready to be taken away. "I'm doing hotel management now."

"Are you …"

She heard Thorfinn Duke's voice and stopped in mid-sentence. He was hailing them from the other end of the dais and she turned to see him wending his way through the pushed-back chairs. She could feel her heart start to pound and a blush suffuse her face.

She turned back to Jean quickly before she betrayed herself. "Are you enjoying it?"

"It's okay; exams next week."

Thorfinn greeted Jean and kissed Hanna on the cheek, laying his arm along her shoulders. She could feel the warmth and strength of his flesh through his thin shirt and the muscles in her throat tightened as she turned to him with a shy smile of welcome.

"Hallo Thorfinn," was all she managed to say.

She was distracted. Her fading memory of his charisma was instantly revived by his presence. He was no longer just an attractive and amusing friend but a predatory male with his roving eye firmly fixed on her.

"Come," he invited, his cupped hand tightening on her arm. "The night is young and the moon is full."

Jean smiled. "I don't think so, Thorfinn. It's still light."

"Ah, Jean, you have no poetry in your soul. A hopeful lover's moon is always full."

He blew her a kiss and guided Hanna towards the steps at the far end of the dais.

"That husband of yours should be shot like a no-good, broken-down old horse," were his first words to her when they were alone.

Hanna looked closely at him for the first time. His cheekbones were sharper and there were light lines on his brow that had not been there before.

"What has he done to annoy you this time, Thorfinn?" she asked with a smile.

The flash of anger in Thorfinn's flecked brown eyes changed to the remembered tenderness.

"He has abandoned the most beautiful woman in the room … barring the bride of course." He drew her close to his side as they passed through the French windows. "However his neglect is my good fortune. I'll have you all to myself."

But Thorfinn had to paw the ground and wait to have Hanna to himself. There was a crowd on the terrace and she was in no hurry. When she stopped to speak, he kept his arm on her shoulder, moving her on when there was a break in the conversation and managing to find the shortest way through the throng with slick manoeuvring. On reaching the forecourt, he gave an ostentatious sigh of relief, and she was chastising him with mock severity for impatience, when she heard a well-remembered voice speaking her name in surprise from the direction of the portico.

"I hadn't expected you to be here, Mrs Treatham. I thought you had left the island when you sold the hotel."

There was no mistaking the elegantly dressed woman. The fine bone structure and the disturbing grey eyes were the same but the streaked, toffee-blonde hair was now cropped in a fashionable mannish style.

"How nice to see you, Mrs Yearts," Hanna said automatically and without inflection. They were empty words. She was shaken by Lily Yearts' presence, which had brought back disturbing memories. "You are looking very well and …" Hanna paused as she tried to find a word to describe the change in her appearance.

"In control?" Mrs Yearts gave a husky laugh of self-mockery. "I no longer see the world through the bottom of a whisky glass, Mrs Treatham. I need to have a sharp eye and a steady hand to succeed in the competitive world of business." She dismissed her acquired sober attributes with a flip of her wrist. "But that is neither here nor there. I was sorry that you were un-well on the day I left the hotel two years ago because I wanted to thank you for your kindness to me after Hal's death."

Hanna inclined her head in acknowledgement but made no verbal response.

"I'm afraid I was drinking more than was good for me at that time," she continued with an uncertain smile of conciliatory explanation. "Ah, there you are, Johnny." A neat man with luxurious black hair and matching moustaches laid a stole across her shoulders. He was dressed in shades of green with a broad cummerbund and an extravagant tie, brightly patterned with the signs of the zodiac. "I don't suppose you remember Johnny Bartini."

"Why, of course, I remember him. How are you, Mr Bartini." Hanna gave the conventional response to cover her surprise. Gone was the reticent, insignificant little man that she remembered, and in its place was this exotic popinjay.

Mr Bartini fluttered in startled amazement. His moustache quivered as he lifted his hand.

"It is delightful to see you again," he said, blinking overtime as he gave Hanna a limp handshake.

"And you, Mr Bartini," Hanna replied, returning the compliment. "If I remember correctly, you were a bird-watcher." She searched her memory. "But didn't you cut your holiday short because you had seen and heard all that Trowsay had to offer."

"There was much to observe and admire on your beautiful island, Mrs Treatham," he cooed, lifting his hands to embrace his surroundings. "But I am not so interested in the delightful birds. It is people I enjoy watching."

"Johnny!" Mrs Yearts exclaimed in displeasure, ticking him off with her finger.

He was crushed by the reprimand, his dark liquid eyes misting over in expectation of a mortal blow. She relented, touching his face with affection. "One watches birds, naughty Johnny, but one snoops on people. It is not something you should confess to doing."

He instantly revived, apologising all round for causing offence.

"We are married, as you have probably gathered," Lily Yearts announced.

Hanna had been surprised to witness their intimacy but had not expected to hear that piece of news. Before she could find the right words in response, Johnny Bartini went into a fulsome explanation of their changed state.

"It was our brief acquaintanceship here at your hotel that led to our romantic attachment," he said, taking hold of his wife's hand to demonstrate the link between them. He elaborated on their courtship, his white smile coming and going where appropriate. "My dear Lillian's sorrow touched me deeply, as you know," he concluded, lifting her hand to his heart to demonstrate where it had touched him, and patting it against his chest to indicate its depth. "Our love grew from those inauspicious beginnings."

Lily Yearts was watching Hanna while her husband was speaking. She gently disengaged her hand, saying: "I'm sure Mrs Treatham has no interest in our affairs, Johnny."

286

He looked at Hanna and saw that that was so.

"You know how these things happen," he whispered, his moustache drooping over his shrinking smile.

Hanna did not know. She could not recall an acquaintanceship being formed between the two of them, brief or otherwise. They had seemed total strangers.

"One is always happy to hear about a hotel romance," she said, forcing a sociable smile. "I am sure Rupert would join me in congratulating you both on your good fortune and wishing you every happiness in the future."

With these words, she took Thorfinn's arm and moved away.

"Johnny Bartini," Thorfinn mused, rolling the name round on his tongue, and savouring the sound. "With a name like that, he must be a gangster travelling incognito, don't you think?"

He put out his hand and helped Hanna down the slope to a seat above the loch.

"Pinch yourself Thorfinn. You're on Trowsay now, not in London. I don't think there would be much work for gangsters here."

"Perhaps he was the inside man at the time of the drowning and Davey was right all along."

"What nonsense!"

"Or he could have come up here to case the joint before demanding protection money from the new owners of Trowsay House," he suggested, taking out a crushed handkerchief and wiping the wooden seat for Hanna.

"I don't think Mr Bartini would put fear and trembling into anyone," she responded evenly, arranging her skirt and finding a suitable place to sit, devoid of dried seagull droppings. "He may have an eye for the main chance but he's a feeble sort of man. The type that is born to please and do as he is told."

"The wife has a steely glint in her eye," Thorfinn drawled, sitting down beside her and leaving a conventionally acceptable space between them. "Who knows what she might demand of him."

"Let's drop it," Hanna said smartly, her voice unusually sharp. "I can't tell you how uninterested I am in them, both husband and wife."

Thorfinn apologised and agreed to cast them from his mind and conversation forthwith. He smiled lazily, the lines round his eyes crinkling and his wide mouth moving and twisting to keep his smile in check. Hanna turned away quickly, feeling the invisible pull of sexual attraction vibrating between them.

"Role reversals do not appeal to me," he said softly, moving closer. "My ideal woman is virtuous and loyal with unconscious sexuality."

Hanna knew that he was referring to her and felt her face getting hot.

"I think your ideal woman comes in all shapes and sizes, Thorfinn," she said to cover her confusion.

He sighed, making the most of his despair. "Cruel, Hanna," he murmured, glancing down at her sideways with his quirky smile.

She lifted her chin, feeling the light breeze from the loch cool her cheeks, and changed the subject.

"Tell me about your life in London, Thorfinn. I see that Marigold has not come with you."

"Marigold is getting married in July. Her husband-to-be has the full approval of her Aunt Isabel. Need I say more?" His gesture was dismissive. Hanna tried to gauge his feelings, but he was looking out over the loch. "We are still good friends, as the saying goes. If she needs an escort because Julian has disappeared for some reason or another, good old Thorfinn is on tap. And, of course, there are always the tears to wipe away when they quarrel. I'm afraid Julian is very dull and self-centred, Hanna, and I doubt if it'll last. But there you are!" He shrugged expansively. "I'm just a bystander now. She's a big girl and must make her own mistakes."

"Will you stay down in London?"

"I only chose to be in London because that was where Marigold wanted to live and it suited me at the time. I had a few contacts in London."

"What do you do now?"

"This and that. I've managed to get an increasing amount of freelance work: A regular slot on radio spinning astrological yarns, and a bit of television, mostly writing and dubbing natural science films that are sent in."

"I keep forgetting that you're a boffin."

He leaned back, chortling with amusement.

"I've never been called that before. Although now I come to think of it, your dear husband once called me something similar. At least the consonants were the same but the vowels were somewhat different."

Hanna looked mystified.

"Never mind, my lovely. Don't tease your brain. And you? How is life treating you?"

She threaded her fingers together and reversed their position.

"Not too kindly I'm afraid. We've not settled."

"How come?"

"We've never really found our niche. Initially Rupert wanted to live in France and possibly buy a vineyard." She looked down at her hands and then turned her head away, not wanting Thorfinn to see her despondent expression. "We stayed out there for most of last year and Rupert worked very hard labouring in the fields and learning the trade but, thankfully, he didn't actually sign on the dotted line because it wasn't for him. Nor for me. I like to be in an English speaking place. We went to South Africa for a month or two in the winter and now we're in Ireland looking for a place like this to do up … and probably sell on." She could not hide the tremble in her voice and Thorfinn put his arm along the back of the bench. She went on: "We made a good profit here by renovating the house and establishing a first-class hotel. That's where our joint strengths lie."

"If that is the way things are," Thorfinn said softly, letting his arm drop to her shoulder, "why don't you buy Alec's house and make the barn into a restaurant. That was your original idea, wasn't it?"

"We thought about that, yes, but it was sensible to go away for a time before committing ourselves."

"I can hear the laird's voice in these words."

"But he was right, you see. If we had gone straight to Selkie after selling up, I would have always felt that he was agreeing to stay because of me. Now it could be different. He's pleased to be back, Thorfinn, I can tell.

It might be he who makes the suggestion to stay and that would be better."

"Ah, the devious wife."

Hanna turned to him with a teasing smile.

"So not the ideal woman."

Thorfinn touched the coil of her thick hair and stroked her cheek with his forefinger.

"Rupert doesn't know how lucky he is having you."

His face was within inches of hers and before she had time to think of the consequences, his lips had brushed gently against her lips.

She gasped. "Thorfinn, we mustn't."

"Must we not?"

His arm tightened as he pulled her close.

She wriggled free and jumped up. He sat where he was. He did not protest or try to persuade her to come back into his arms but he looked so forlorn and hurt that she felt a tenderness for him that went beyond desire. He was a lovely man, good-tempered and kind as well as handsome. She had always known that his light-hearted and amusing speech masked deep emotion and strong beliefs that he kept to himself through a dislike of argument.

She reached out for him and Thorfinn took her hand.

As she pulled him to his feet, he said: "Hanna, my lovely, you must stop sharpening my desire and then blunting my instrument. It could cause permanent damage."

Hanna let out a peel of laughter.

"I very much doubt it," she said, squeezing his hand. "There's the band striking up for the Grand March. Come on!"

They climbed the slope together and Hanna didn't protest when Thorfinn slipped his arm round her waist and kissed her hair. She had never been so close to him and she could feel her heart palpitate and the muscles in her legs weaken with desire. She stumbled on the slippery slope. Thorfinn caught her and held her to him. She lowered her eyes so that he could not see the powerful effect he was having on her, but he lifted her chin and she was forced to look up.

"You're following in the footsteps of the bride, my lovely."

"Silly of me."

"On the contrary."

She knew by the depth of his voice that he was about to kiss her, but they were in full view of the cocktail lounge and Rupert was there. She pushed against his chest with a whispered apology. Thorfinn followed the direction of her glance and understood. He dropped one arm and with an ironic smile, guided her across the gravel to the front door, a hand on the small of her back.

As they crossed the hall, the hilarity coming from the cocktail lounge impinged on Hanna's thoughts. She stopped. For a moment she said nothing and then she looked up at Thorfinn regretfully.

"I'm sorry but I must see if Rupert would like to partner me in the Grand March. It would be expected."

He made a face and let her go.

"I knew it was too good to last."

She went behind the bar to tell Rupert that the Grand March had started. The drawing room was crowded with the noise at a screeching pitch of alcoholic merriment and inflexible self-opinion. Rupert was leaning on the counter with a glass in his hand, talking to a large, florid-faced man whom she did not recognise. He was one of the wedding guests from the south, she learned, as Rupert introduced her with a proprietary arm across her shoulders. She offered her hand to the stranger and smiled quickly before capturing Rupert's attention. Would he like to partner her in the Grand March? He immediately apologised for neglecting her, indicating the crowd standing round the bar with an expressive shrug of explanation. If he noticed the tremor in her voice and the fever in her eyes, he misinterpreted their cause, for he suggested that she should stay there with him and his companion rather than be on her own. Hanna could see that he was happier where he was and accepted the excuse that he could not be spared. She reached up and touched his cheek, giving him the kiss of Judas before returning to the hall.

Thorfinn was leaning against the reception desk with his arms folded, watching the bar door. His face lit up when she came out alone.

She turned to look at Rupert's solid back as he impressed his personality on a stranger and then at Thorfinn's captivating smile and uninhibited pleasure at having her join him.

"Come," Thorfinn invited, putting out his hand.

She knew that it would be wise to step back into the bar and be calmed by Rupert's familiar comfortable presence, but she ached to feel Thorfinn's arms around her again. An irrational madness propelled her forward into an uncertain future.

"My adorable, Hanna, live life at the sharp end," Thorfinn said, spinning her into the alcove at the bottom of the stairs. "It can be fun."

This time she yielded to his embrace. When she broke for breath, he whispered in her ear, "Have I ever told you how much I love you?"

She tilted her head and looked up at him, a mischievous gleam in her eye.

"Frequently. That is the trouble."

He laughed and was taking her in his arms again, when they heard a discreet cough. They turned to see Mr Pinkerton's lugubrious face watching them from between two of the hall pillars. Hanna immediately broke free, guilty and embarrassed at being caught behaving improperly. But instead of hastening to assure Mr Pinkerton that she had been innocently engaged, she just smiled and wished him a good evening, before walking with Thorfinn along the corridor to the ballroom.

The bride and groom had circled the room twice and were walking down the centre in step to the slow march being played by The Livebeats, Trowsay's local band. Martha Silver was in her wheelchair at the piano, her fingers automatically finding the right notes as she watched the proceedings; Tom Nicol had his fiddle under his chin and was keeping time with his foot; Ted Vale sat with his legs apart, his arms wide and his hands moving rhythmically on either side of his accordion; and Stevie Gunn was beating out the rhythm on his massive array of drums.

Ronald and Jill Jimson paused and made way for Hanna and Thorfinn to join the march in front of them. Dan was acting as master of ceremonies and as the couples reached him in front of the dais, he sent one couple to the right and one to the left. The couples joined at the top of the room and came down the centre in fours. With another division to right and left they were eight abreast and the octets had to mark time at the top while Dan divided the lines down.

Pete Gunn had offered Hanna his arm to form their eight, smiling with the shy, uncertain eyes of youth. He was tall and gangly, having sprouted upwards for eighteen years and not yet put on the girth to balance his height. The four on his side included his mother, Alf Strachan and Tara Gunn. Hanna wondered if Madge had taken Alf back or if he now had his eye on her cousin. She could hear Christina Jimson and another schoolgirl giggling behind Pete; Jill Jimson, on Thorfinn's left, began to cluck. In front of Hanna was a smartly dressed woman from the south with Davey clutching tightly to her arm. She looked bemused at being intimately handled by a bouncy, elderly man, with a bulbous nose and a polished head. On Davey's other side was his granddaughter Patsy, her blonde hair loosened from its serviceable knot and falling in a shimmer to below her shoulders. Les was on the outside. He was looking smart in a three-piece suit that had a familiar cut. The church jumble had done its bit for recycling. As Hanna marched time on the spot with the rest of the company, she felt included, happy and safe.

She had her arm linked through Thorfinn's and he tightened his hold, bending over to whisper: "Don't be lulled into a dreary sense of security." It was as though he had read her thoughts.

She went on watching the moving red heels of the woman in front.

"I can't do it," she whispered to herself.

She could feel Thorfinn's sudden stillness beside her and looked up, expecting him to respond to her decision with hurtful reproach or a flippant remark, but he was smiling down at her, his eyes soft with the tenderness of loving understanding.

"I know," he said, clasping her hand and entwining their fingers. "We'll work something out."

They were on the move again, the swirling crowded lines of friends and strangers sweeping down the ballroom in happy turmoil. Pete Gunn let go of Hanna's arm, his quartet swinging away to the right as they swung to the left. Once more round the floor and the Jimsons left them, Ronald warning Hanna, with a wink and a nod in Thorfinn's direction, to watch out.

She said she would, and she knew she should, but as she turned into Thorfinn's arms at the start of their first dance together, she did not think she could.